Fall from Grace

THE FAILED CRUSADE OF THE CHRISTIAN RIGHT

MICHAEL D'ANTONIO

VERNON REGIONAL
JUNIOR COLLEGE LIBRARY

Rutgers University Press
New Brunswick, New Jersey

First published in paperback in the United States of America
by Rutgers University Press, 1992

First published in cloth in the United Kingdom by André Deutsch,
Ltd., London, 1990

First published in cloth in the United States of America by
Farrar, Straus & Giroux, Inc., New York, 1989

First published in Canada by HarperCollins Publishers, Ltd.,
Toronto, 1989

Copyright © 1989, 1990 by Michael D'Antonio
All rights reserved
Manufactured in the United States of America
Designed by Jack Harrison

Library of Congress Cataloging-in-Publication Data

D'Antonio, Michael
    Fall from grace : the failed crusade of the Christian right /
Michael D'Antonio.
        p.   cm.
    Previously published: New York : Farrar, Straus & Giroux,1989
    ISBN 0-8135-1896-2 (pbk.)
    1. United States--Religious life and customs. 2. Fundamentalism.
3. Christianity and politics--History--20th century.   I.   Title.
[BR515.D35 1992]
277.3'0828--dc20   92-9453
                                                             CIP

= III =

FALL FROM GRACE

ACKNOWLEDGMENTS

Several people read the manuscript and offered ideas and criticisms that greatly influenced this book. My editor, David Rieff, was a continual source of insight and support. My colleague Roy Hanson and my agent Philip Spitzer also helped me identify flaws and strengths in early drafts. Professor Timothy Weber at the Conservative Baptist Theological Seminary helped me understand the theology of born-again America. I conducted my research during a one-year fellowship awarded by the Alicia Patterson Foundation, without which this project would have been impossible for me to complete.

M.D'A.

For Toni

CONTENTS

Fall from Grace

Introduction

O N   T H E   N I G H T of September 17, 1986, more than 200,000 right-wing social activists representing all the important groups in conservative Christianity gathered in front of TV screens in hotel ballrooms and auditoriums across America. They came together to watch a closed-circuit broadcast that would mark the culmination of their long political struggle. At 8 p.m., the televisions were illuminated with the smiling image of Rev. Marion G. "Pat" Robertson, the best-known and most successful of America's many TV preachers. Inveighing against "moral decay" and its "flood tide of social problems," Robertson announced he would run for President of the United States. He had already raised millions of dollars for the campaign, and in the days that followed his video rally, he would raise millions more. Soon Robertson would convince the political pundits that he was more than just an able and talented fundraiser. In less than two years he had, in fact, built a remarkably effective national political organization. In the late winter of 1987 he would win a straw poll in Michigan. That spring, in South Carolina, his forces would all but seize control of the state GOP. As Robertson moved from victory to victory, conservative Christianity, already a significant interest group, seemed ready to challenge for control of the Republican Party.

A decade earlier, the idea of a faith-healing television preacher (Robertson had claimed to heal cataracts and ingrown toenails through prayer and had once, in New York, tried to raise a child from the dead) making a serious run for the White House would have seemed ludicrous. Though America had, for generations, been a particularly devout nation, it had grown increasingly secular in the years following World War II. Many people outside the American South and West had come to think of the more rigid strains of conservative Protestant Christianity as fading anachronisms. And if they thought about them at all, they considered the Bible believers to be ignorant, ineffectual Babbitts, doomed to irrelevance and, in all likelihood, to extinction.

In postwar America, such a conclusion was not unwarranted. From the 1950s through the 1970s, every aspect of American life seemed to drive the country further and further from religious orthodoxy. Though it is something of a cliché to say so, America did experience a dramatic social revolution during those decades. Attitudes about everything from sex to childbearing, ethnicity to patriotism, were transformed. Instead of a conservative ethic dictated from the pulpit, morality, for the first time in history, became largely a matter of personal choice. And though conservatives alleged that these changes were forced on the nation by plotting liberals, in fact they were inevitable.

The sweeping changes of the thirty years after the war radically altered the three major aspects of national life: politics, economics, and private affairs. The political turmoil of the time, marked by the assassinations, Vietnam, and Watergate, led to unease and disillusionment. Old institutions no longer commanded the trust and respect of a people who waited, uneasily, for something to replace them. At the same time, Americans struggled to assimilate an equally radical transformation of private life. The old-fashioned assumptions of white-picket-fence America were decimated by a series of cultural developments: suburbanization broke up extended families and stable communities; television homogenized society with universal standards for everything from family life to speech patterns; birth control transformed sexual behavior and suddenly gave women choices about relationships, work, and motherhood. In the post-Pill 1960s, divorce lost its stigma, and the traditional family, with a working father and a stay-at-home mother, began to vanish. Finally, economic change completed the metamorphosis of America. The boom years of the 1960s, which provided the highest standard of living in history, were followed by a series of deep recessions. By the middle of the 1970s

America was no longer the world's unchallenged economic leader but rather a stumbling power threatened by Arab oil sheiks, Japanese technocrats, and Third World sweatshops.

The change that had occurred in America between 1955 and 1975 was enormous and, seemingly, irreversible. That was, at any rate, the conclusion reached by many historians, sociologists, and even theologians. In *The Secular City*, arguably the most influential work of American theology in the 1960s, Harvey Cox declared that traditional religion was about to succumb to the inexorable march of secularization. In such a society "the gods of traditional religion live on as private fetishes or the patrons of congenial groups," wrote Cox, "but play no significant role in the public life of the secular metropolis."

As it turned out, the obituaries written for America's peculiar strands of conservative Christianity were premature. Conservative Christianity—fundamentalism, evangelicalism, and Pentecostalism—was far from dead, and in the 1970s it became clear that a kind of revival, one that was not limited to the Southern Bible belt, was underway. At first this ground swell of religious fervor caught most Americans by surprise, but in retrospect the great revival of the 1970s and 1980s should not have been surprising. After all, how could this enormous postwar social revolution have occurred without engendering feelings of shock and bewilderment in millions of people? America has never been a country where everyday people have felt comfortable thinking in a long-term, historical way. Thus, Americans who had been born in a period when women and blacks were still second-class citizens could be expected to balk at the insistent new realities of the civil rights era and feminism. And though this was less well understood, the same people were confused by the dramatic technological advances of the times and by the changing world economy. For these millions who felt uneasy in the new era, right-wing Christianity, with its promise of unalterable truths and its nostalgia for a simpler past, was bound to be not only attractive but extremely compelling.

Curiously, it was modern technology that permitted the conservative Christian movement to emerge as the great national opposition to the forces of change. Pat Robertson and a number of other evangelists, notably Jerry Falwell, Jimmy Swaggart, Oral Roberts, and Robert Schuller, had begun exploring the uses of television as early as the 1950s. While others talked about the medium's potential, especially as cable systems and satellites made national networking less expensive, the conservative evangelists started using it. Almost intuitively, they seized TV as a pulpit, using it the same way medieval churchmen used their pulpits to dominate community discourse. With the new technologies they could reach more people, more often, at a lower cost. Suddenly the televangelists, as they came to be called, were broadcasting not only in the South but in the Northeast and on the West Coast as well. And their audience was the millions of Americans who felt confused and alienated from their vertiginously changing society.

The TV preachers claimed to explain what had happened to America. In doing so, they obviously ignored a great deal. Guided only by the Bible and their literal interpretation of scripture, they denied (the psychological implications of the word are appropriate here) that the forces that had created the America of the 1970s had any inevitable quality to them. Instead the preachers applied the Bible to what they saw and argued that the confusion and problems of American life, from economic recession to herpes, were the penalty for "turning away from God." Sifting through the events of three decades, they discovered "evidence" that included the Supreme Court decisions banning school prayer and legalizing abortion, the rise in divorce rates, and the challenges to authority posed by the civil rights movement, feminism, and the anti-war protests. According to this "ledger" mentality, these events were national sins, and the troubling realities of the times—the lost war, Watergate, the faltering economy, the disappearance of the traditional family—were God's punishment for those sins.

A good evangelist's sermon follows a predictable pattern. Once they described the sin, and jabbed at the pain felt by the sinner, the TV preachers then held out the promise of redemption. For each individual, redemption was available through a profession of born-again faith. The evangelists taught that by simply declaring oneself "born-again" in Jesus, and accepting a literal view of the Bible, the TV watchers in their homes could look forward to heaven's reward. Some evangelists sweetened the attraction of born-again faith by suggesting that a conversion might also bring a miraculous healing or even a financial windfall. Oral Roberts, who developed this idea most fully, even suggested a formula; viewers could expect ten dollars in found money for every one donated to him. No matter what the specific claim was, from Oral Roberts' promise of riches to Pat Robertson's miracle cures, the emotional and manipulative quality of the appeal was the same. It was no accident that the evangelists reached out to people suffering from illness, poverty, alienation, and loneliness and, in God's name, promised anything that would make viewers give their hearts, souls, and money to the blossoming movement.

The evangelists' prescription for the nation was similar to their soul-saving cure. To be "saved," America had to return to the patriotic style of the Cold War era and to highly conservative domestic policies. That meant, among other things, a renewed ban on abortion, a constitutional amendment to reinstitute school prayer, a military buildup to recapture the nation's strategic dominance, and censorship to outlaw pornography. Through these reforms, the preachers said, a Christian nation would emerge. Christian America, a strain in the national psyche since the Pilgrims, was reconstituted by the evangelists as a kind of religious populism, a vision of a country in which men would be ruled by Bible-based law and reap God's favors, including both unbounded wealth and world dominance.

Both their theology and their right-wing, superpatriotic nationalism led the evangelists to define Americanness in a particular, nostalgic way. In their definitions, true Americans—orthodox Americans, as it were—were remarkably like the conservative, white, Bible-believing, Southern Christians who made up the bulk of their early support. Though, to be sure, over the years the preachers broadened their definition to include anyone who had been shocked by the dizzying change in postwar America and longed for a simple, more stable time.

As their programs grew more polished, and they brought in computer systems to send out letters to their flocks, the evangelists gained new converts and their earnings increased dramatically. Eventually these computer-generated mailings (which could be made to look like personal letters) became just as important a fundraising tool for the evangelists as TV. And even though there were constant rumblings of corruption (the Federal Communications Commission held its first hearings on the finances of televangelists in 1979), the contributions continued flowing, eventually reaching nearly $1 billion a year.

As they preached, begged, and promised, the televangelists were never shy about who was behind their efforts. A transcript from a Robertson broadcast of 1979 is typical. It begins with Robertson's TV sidekick, Ben Kinchlow, reading aloud a letter from a woman pensioner. She had "decided to go all the way, to give God the money she spends for cancer medicine, $120 a month," says Kinchlow. "And three days later—get this—from an entirely unexpected source, she got a check for three thousand dollars!" "Praise God!" Robertson answers. "Let's give God a hand."

These TV preachers, who talked about God as if He lived next door and claimed to hear the voice of Jesus on a regular basis, could seem like caricatures. There was the Baptist minister Jerry Falwell, bombastic and bellowing. There were Jim and Tammy Bakker, who dressed and acted like stars of the Grand Ol' Opry. Tammy was especially grotesque. She had rather noticeably undergone breast enlargement and blubbered through most broadcasts with black lines of mascara running down her cheeks. While Tammy often appeared grotesque, another evangelist, Jimmy Swaggart, expressed grotesque ideas about Jews and Catholics. The saintly Mother Teresa of Calcutta, Swaggart said, was doomed to hell because she wasn't his kind of Christian. But while critics ridiculed them, and the scent of financial and sexual scandal swirled about them, these preachers built empires out of the small donations they received. With his $200 million per year, Robertson developed one of the largest TV networks in the world and founded an accredited university, a legal foundation, and a grass-roots political organization called the Freedom Council. The Bakkers built a conservative Christian amusement park and resort that became the third most popular attraction in America, after Disney World and Disneyland. Oral Roberts built his university in Tulsa, complete with a huge hospital complex and medical school.

Along the way, it seemed, every preacher acquired an enormous array of material possessions. Rolex watches flashed from underneath the cuffs of their expensive suits. They flew in private jets and rode in expensive chauffeured cars. They lived on heavily guarded estates and amassed personal fortunes. But the faithful didn't seem to notice, or mind, that these men and women who posed as simple country preachers were getting rich. In fact, mysteriously, the believers seemed to expect it, perhaps because their leaders were not just the pastors of their church but TV stars as well.

The most impressive achievement of the star evangelists was their effect on Americans' religious affiliations. It should be recalled that conservative Christianity began to flourish at the very moment when the more sedate and rational branches of Protestantism were floundering. In the 1970s the United Presbyterian Church lost 21 percent of its members. The Episcopal Church lost 15 percent. The United Church of Christ and the United Methodists both lost 10 percent. As these moderate and liberal denominations, which recognized the complexities of modern life and resisted biblical simplification, declined, many of their former members defected, sometimes immediately and sometimes after a period of searching, to conservative, born-again Christianity. They filled the thousands of new conservative churches and schools that were founded as the revival spread to every corner of the country and eventually claimed 60 million adherents. The revival became so successful that by 1980, despite the complaints of mainline Protestants and Catholics, the very word "Christian" had come to mean a born-again conservative.

Despite the surge in conservative religious feeling and the rise of the evangelists' media empires, the conservative Christian revival would have remained a fundamentally nonpolitical campaign had Ronald Reagan's strategists not recognized the movement's vast potential for political support. Until the success of televangelism, born-again Christians, while influential in local politics in the South and Midwest, could never have been organized into a coherent national voting bloc. Conservative churches have always been fiercely independent, resisting confederation and the sway of outside authority. The TV preachers, however, had lists of names, and connections with local churches, that made organizing possible. In 1976 Reagan's supporters tried to tap into the conservative Christian network to reach voters. But that was the year that born-again Democrat Jimmy Carter won election, and his candidacy divided the conservative Christian vote. Reagan's emissaries made a more concerted effort to ally with the conservative Christians before the 1980 vote. By then the preachers were better able to deliver votes and Carter had disappointed the conservative Christian community.

For their part, the born-again leaders had concluded that their political agenda meshed perfectly with Reagan's. They felt comfortable with Reagan, in part because he could be seen as an evangelist too, an evangelist for the nostalgic vision of America promoted by Falwell and the others. He not only shared the preachers' orthodox views on Christianity and America, but as a former actor and pitchman, he shared their mastery of the art of television. Reagan clearly believed that America was God's favorite country and promised to restore it to the stature a blessed nation deserves.

The alliance of Reaganism and conservative Christianity was formed in 1979 in a series of meetings between Falwell and Reagan activists. It was confirmed by Reagan himself in a 1980 meeting with Christian Right leaders. "You can't endorse me," he told the group, which included all the major TV preachers, "but I endorse you." It was, in some ways, a nervous match. The evangelists had to overlook Reagan's infrequent church attendance, his divorce, and his fractured family life. But just as the faithful overlooked the evangelists' flashing Rolexes and private jets, Reagan's inconsistencies were forgiven in the interest of the alliance. Reagan's landslide victory would certainly not have happened without the leaders and the foot soldiers of the Christian Right. By the end of 1981 the conservative Christian revival had become the Christian Right crusade, arguably the largest and most powerful and most feared special-interest group in America.

In 1980 and 1984, fueled by the promises he had made to promote their agenda, the Christian Right crusaders mobilized to elect Ronald Reagan. TV inflated the movement, the expectations of the believers, and the seeming power of Robertson, Falwell, and the other leaders. For his part, Reagan appeared frequently with the preachers, gave them a significant role at the GOP conventions, and regularly addressed their rallies. But by 1986, despite two Reagan victories, few of the promises of the Christian Right had been realized. The movement and Reagan had played off each other, and the national media had reported their thundering pronouncements with awe. But while Reagan was winning his landslide victories and using the televangelists in the process, he was in reality paying little more than lip service to the Christian Right agenda. It is significant that even when the Republicans controlled the Senate and Reagan's popularity was at its height, he did not make a strong effort to push legislation through Congress that would have advanced the ideas of the Christian Right. Indeed, he didn't even manage to shut down the Department of Education, one of the more minor demands of the born-again movement. The truth was that the Christian Right had been politically useful for election purposes, but a President who didn't want to go to church was equally unwilling to tackle abortion, school prayer, or any of the other concerns of the Christian Right head-on. In hindsight, Reagan's reluctance could be seen as political brilliance. He obviously understood that the core issues on the Christian Right's moral agenda were politically explosive. A majority of the electorate supported abortion rights, for example. Reagan didn't want to waste his popularity on such fractious causes.

To someone who was aware of the promises the GOP had made to the Christian Right in 1980 and 1984, the realities of 1986 were startling. In 1986 abortion was still legal and school prayer still was not. Homosexuality was not forced back into "the closet" and the continuing rise in the divorce rate and the number of women in the workplace symbolized the further decline of the traditional family. True, the economy was stabilized, but wages never returned to the levels of the late 1960s. Americans had to work harder and longer to maintain their standard of living. And new problems—AIDS, immigration, drugs, international terrorism, and the federal deficit—which defied easy solutions, seemed to arise everywhere. As Reagan's second term began to wind down, the Christian Right started to look for a successor who would, perhaps, more vigorously pursue its agenda and save America from these new dangers.

It was then that Pat Robertson decided to announce his candidacy for President. In a way, he had no choice. The Christian Right crusade had grown into a movement based largely on hysterical enthusiasm and an exaggerated sense of its own power. After all, the preachers had declared, over and over, that God was literally standing behind them, an assertion believed by millions of people. And the media had inflated the reputation of the Christian Right to the point where it seemed unstoppable to both its supporters and its opponents. Robertson could be forgiven for believing as well that his candidacy had a real chance of success.

The inevitable collapse of the Christian Right began shortly after Robertson's announcement and it followed a pattern that was eerily familiar from such works of fiction as *Elmer Gantry* and *The Damnation of Theron Ware* and in real life by the fall of such evangelists as Aimee Semple McPherson and Billy James Hargis. Big-time, moralizing evangelists had always been undone by the sin of greed and sins of the flesh. This time it would be no different. Beginning in early 1987, with almost frightening predictability, scandal swept the movement. First Jim Bakker was discovered to have had an ugly sexual encounter with a church secretary from Long Island named Jessica Hahn. She described the incident as an attack. Subsequently, rumors of homosexual encounters, wife-swapping, and prostitution poured out of Bakker's South Carolina headquarters, followed by convincing evidence that both Jim and Tammy had squandered millions of dollars on everything from pastry to an air-conditioned doghouse. The Bakkers were ruined, losing both their ministry and control of their empire. Their defeat was the stuff of fiction, complete with the denouement of the Bakkers' resort, Heritage USA, being bought by an Orthodox Jewish developer from Toronto while Jessica Hahn had breast-enlarging surgery of her own and earned a fortune posing nude for *Playboy* magazine.

Whereas the Bakkers fell victim to sexual scandal and shady financial dealings, Oral Roberts became a victim of his own audacity when he interrupted a fundraising pitch to announce that God had told him that He might kill him if viewers didn't send $8 million soon. Even formerly credulous Americans were outraged. Roberts went away to fast while awaiting the donations, and the money did come in. But he had finally gone too far. Everyone from mainline church leaders to stand-up comics attacked Roberts' "give or God will kill me" pitch. Roberts' excess unleashed nearly a decade of antagonism that had built up within the opposition to the Christian Right. Opponents had felt restrained from attacking the televangelists because they were loath to be seen as religious bigots. But once the scandals started, the opposition let loose. By the end of 1987 Roberts had become a discredited figure.

Finally, in 1988, Jimmy Swaggart was also implicated in sexual scandal. As the preacher who spent more of his time railing against sexual sin, Swaggart suffered an especially humiliating defeat when it was found he had donned silly disguises for sneaky encounters with New Orleans prostitutes. By the spring of 1988, Jerry Falwell declared that "the credibility crisis is unbelievable." Donations dried up. The evangelists fired hundreds of employees, cut back TV air time, and halted construction of various projects. The crusade was over.

In retrospect Robertson's campaign would be seen as an act of desperation. His failure was not sexual or financial; it was hubris. If Reagan, the most popular President since FDR and one of the most brilliant politicians in modern history, couldn't carry out the conservative Christian agenda, how could anyone have imagined that Robertson had a ghost of a chance? Moreover, under the intensive examination that the national media direct at presidential hopefuls, Robertson's claims about God, country, and his own special connections with Jesus quickly raised more questions than he could answer. In the end, as candidate George Bush's operatives ruthlessly destroyed the Robertson campaign, it became clear that the Christian Right was less a juggernaut than a straw man. The crusade would mark the last gasp for an old idea, not the beginning of a new conservative Christian age. Bush's election ensured the death of the movement, as he returned the nation to the professional politics of Nixon and Ford and abandoned the anomalous populism of Reagan and Falwell.

This book, begun when the Christian Right seemed to be a powerful, cresting social force, became a view of the final days of the crusade as it was experienced by the true believers. They were, for the most part, honest, caring Americans who were genuinely troubled by the turmoil and change that had taken place in their lifetimes. Many had been economically displaced by recession; all had suffered from a sense of emotional displacement as even the oldest structures of intimacy—marriage and family—were radically altered. After all, in the time between World War II and 1980, American society had experienced more rapid change than at any other time in its history. The huge leaps in technology, scientific knowledge, and race relations were indeed unsettling. Searching for something to believe in, the crusaders had latched on to the message of stability and security that came to them on TV. The simple, almost magical ideas promoted by the evangelists were enchanting. And millions of people made enormous spiritual, emotional, and financial commitments to the dream.

Ultimately, any movement built on enchantment and unreason comes face to face with reality. It is always a bitter encounter. Because the Christian Right sedulously resisted critical thinking, because the crusaders spurned most kinds of information, they were bound to be disappointed individually and defeated politically. The closed system they had built could not cope with the challenges that confronted it. For a time, the rigid structure, balanced solely on faith, seemed solid. Eventually it would prove so brittle that when it crumbled it left hardly a trace. This book describes the remarkable edifice built by the Christian Right and its equally astonishing collapse. It is a two-year tour of an American community of trusting, hopeful people who were betrayed by the movement to which they had confided their hopes and fears.

=I=

DISCOVERING CHRISTIAN AMERICA

=1=

We the People

Rev. Gary Moore, the music director, had said that Second Baptist Church of Houston was Texas-huge. When we talked on the phone he had described the health club and the school and the eight-lane bowling alley. In all, the congregation had spent $34 million in cash to build it. "Even by Texas standards, this place is remarkable," he had said. As I followed a winding street called Woodway into Houston's suburban flatlands, I began to understand what he meant. More than two miles away, the top of Second Baptist's dome hovered over the trees and houses, like a flying saucer with a golden antenna. As I got closer, I saw more of the dome and realized that the antenna was a tall gold cross. Rounding a corner, I finally saw the imposing complex of buildings, a brick fortress rising from an ocean of asphalt parking lots. I drove across the lot, past light poles that were marked with names from the Holy Land: Bethlehem, Jerusalem, Galilee. I parked near Jericho and walked through the heat shimmering up from the blacktop and into the center of Christian America.

In 1987 Second Baptist of Houston was the preeminent born-again church in America. In ten years it had grown from 1,000 members to more than 11,000. The new building, completed in 1986, was the largest in the conservative Christian movement. It contained a church seating 8,000 people, a school system for 900 students, the health club and bowling alleys, a TV studio and movie theater, a bookstore, dozens of offices, and even a restaurant. Besides its size, Second Baptist was known for its splashy pageants, all directed by Gary Moore. I went to Houston to see Moore's biggest-ever production, "We the People," a celebration of the 200th anniversary of the Constitution. Moore had hired radio star Paul Harvey to narrate and he was bringing in the Houston Symphony Orchestra. The church and the pageant promised to put all the elements of Christian America on display in one place and at one time.

On the day before the premiere, the lobby of Second Baptist was crowded with a museum-style display of the Constitution. Blown-up copies of the document were tacked on six-foot-high screens lined up across the center of the lobby. On the back wall—a four-story expanse of mirrors—hung an American flag the size of a tennis court. To the left of the flag was the main doorway to the church sanctuary. To the right, a small fountain splashed rhythmically in a grove of potted ficus trees and ferns.

I wandered through the lobby, which was big enough to hold the average church building, and down a long white corridor with gray carpeting. It was about 10 a.m. School was in session, all the office doors were closed, and the hallway was empty. At the end of the hall I found the music department offices and rehearsal studios grouped around a large reception area. Gary Moore, a short, chubby man with sandy brown hair and glasses, came out to greet me. He said he was too busy to escort me around the church. He had the pre-show jitters. "Just wander around, you'll meet people," he said. "Why don't you start upstairs at the Second Helping. Tell people what you're doing. It's OK."

The Second Helping Cafe was a scattering of white plastic tables and chairs on a balcony that overlooked the lobby. I bought a cup of coffee and introduced myself to three middle-aged women, dressed in leotards, who sat at one of the tables. They said they worked out together two mornings a week and their class was about to start. When I explained why I was visiting Second Baptist they were unanimous about what I should do. "You must call John Cavallero," said one of the women in the group. They said he was handsome, rich, and worldly, a suave New Yorker who had come to Houston with the rest of the Yankees during the oil-boom years of the early 1980s. Cavallero's business collapsed, they said, but when he fell, he found Jesus and

Second Baptist Church. There was a hint of sexual excitement in the way they described him, as if he were an exotic male specimen who had not yet been fully tamed. Yes, it was agreed. I must call John Cavallero. One of the women, who said she had attended a singles-only Bible study class with Cavallero, gave me his phone number.

When the women left for their class, I called Cavallero from the pay phone near the cafe. He said he would meet me for lunch in an hour. He gave me directions to the restaurant. "The Lord works in wonderful ways, doesn't He?" he said as he hung up.

Cavallero chose an expensive restaurant in Houston's Galleria, a shopping district of designer boutiques, restaurants, and luxury department stores. Outside the restaurant, uniformed chauffeurs polished a line of limousines. Inside, the Texas rich refreshed themselves. Cavallero, a graying man with a mustache who wore a dark blue Italian silk suit, met me at the door and led me to his table. He fit comfortably in the Queen Anne dining room. He welcomed me to Houston, ordered veal, and told me about his latest business venture, selling a Japanese machine that made high-tech identification cards. The cards can carry millions of bits of information that can be read by computers. Cavallero hoped they would make him richer. "Of course, those IDs could also be the mark of the beast," he said.

Putting down his fork, he leaned over the table. "You know about the mark of the beast, don't you? Before Jesus comes again, everyone is to be marked somehow by the Devil. The Bible says it's the number 666. We think it will be done by credit cards or ID cards and computers. The technology is in place to do it now. That's the prophecy coming true." Cavallero went on to explain the rest of Armageddon prophecy, a part of the Bible that fascinated born-again Americans. According to the prophecy, the "mark of the beast" will be a harbinger of the battle of Armageddon. Armageddon will end all life on earth and usher in a new age under Jesus' rule. In the 1980s the most popular interpretations of the prophecy predicted that the battle would begin in the Middle East, with Israel playing a key role and nuclear weapons supplying the fire and brimstone. Most of America's 60 million born-again Christians believed that the prophecy would soon come true. They also believed they would be lifted into the sky, protected from the battle, and returned to earth when it ended. Then they would live blissfully with Jesus in the new age. Everyone else would burn in hell. "It could happen any time now," Cavallero said. He picked up his fork again and jabbed at his escarole salad.

VERNON REGIONAL
JUNIOR COLLEGE LIBRARY

A year before, John Cavallero thought that Armageddon prophecy and all the rest of born-again Christianity was nonsense. He was too smart, too successful, and too independent to let his life be dominated by a church or the Bible. But by the time we met, conservative Christianity had become the center of his life. He was one of the millions who made up the Great Revival of the 1980s. He was immersed in weekly Bible studies and nervously awaiting his own debut in the church pageant. He was going to sing in the chorus of "We the People." For me, understanding Christian America began with understanding the growth of Second Baptist and the conversion of John Cavallero.

Cavallero was born in New York City, the son of a cobbler, and spent his early years in the city's close-knit Italian community. Back then, when other kids asked, Johnny Cavallero would say, "I'm Italian and I'm Catholic." The Cavalleros eventually moved to the suburbs, where Johnny went to high school. After he graduated he worked in construction and eventually in real estate. He renovated buildings, developed small commercial properties, and bought and sold land. Slowly he realized his expertise wasn't in real estate. It was in selling. He could sell anything.

"I did it all, had every experience you can imagine," he said over lunch. He described a life spent gliding from bar to bar, coasting on the lonely edge of upward mobility. He smiled a bit as he talked about it: LA, New York, Miami, boats, beaches, and drinking. He smiled as if he were describing a wayward old friend, or a footloose brother he secretly admired. At night he traded his smile and some drinks for a good time with casual friends and women he met along the way. During the day he used the same assets to sell advertising, real estate, medical devices, machinery, cars, and more. In Atlanta he helped start up a slick magazine called *The Robb Report*, which began as a kind of classified advertising service for the rich. At first *The Robb Report* simply listed rare, expensive cars: Rolls-Royces, Bentleys, Ferraris, and others. Later it became a marketplace for every kind of luxury item: airplanes, yachts, even real estate. Cavallero left publishing when the Robb organization asked him to put together another magazine, this one to be devoted to soft-core pornography. "That was one of the few things I just couldn't sell," he explained. From Atlanta he moved to Houston and another scheme.

Cavallero's religious transformation began on a muggy Sunday morning in June, in his apartment in a high-rise building in the Galleria. In other parts of town families were getting ready for church, but the upwardly mobile Houstonians of the Galleria sleep in on Sundays. Cotton-mouthed and bleary-eyed, Cavallero rolled out of bed and turned on the background noise that filled his home life. It was too early for the Sunday-morning news and interview programs, so he settled for a fundamentalist preacher on cable. He set the volume low and went back to bed.

At the time Cavallero had no real relationships; no wife, no lover, no children. Even his brother, who was married and had kids back in New York, had become a stranger. It had been years since they had spent more than an evening together. As an adult, Cavallero had dedicated himself to the American dream of independence and success and that didn't leave much time for visits back East. He busied himself with his countless business ventures. He would try to make large sums of money quickly and then he would stop working for several months while he spent it on vacations, fine restaurants, and boats.

Cavallero had come to Houston for his latest scheme: diet supplements. The business was supposed to work like a chain letter, with distributors raking commissions from district managers and a sales force of struggling middle-class people selling powdered protein drinks and other packaged foods to their friends. Cavallero sat near the top of the pyramid, taking in commissions on commissions. It all seemed to work until the company's founder disappeared with thousands of dollars sent by salespeople who couldn't afford the loss. Cavallero locked up the Houston office and fled the ringing phones.

As he lay on his bed, Cavallero raced through the memories of his middle age. He ran a hand through his wavy gray hair and watched the images in his mind. He could count a short marriage, several fortunes, and many good times. But as he added up his life, the good times weren't enough. "I was like so many people who feel like they have nothing to hold on to in their lives. I was lonely, I didn't have any faith. There was nothing but me," he recalled.

Over the din of his memory, Cavallero could hear Rev. Ed Young on TV inviting everyone to Second Baptist Church of Houston. In the vast realm of religion in America, only conservative, born-again Christians have mastered the most important cultural force of the times, TV. In the early 1980s big-time evangelists used it to pump up the Great Revival, converting the masses and raising more than $1 billion a year. The preachers, who all looked prosperous and confident, possessed a down-home kind of charisma. And their programs, slickly produced with music, guest stars, and even commercial messages, were both entertaining and authoritative. All of the major evangelists issued dire warnings that God would soon judge America harshly for its liberal politics and morality. But the country could be saved, they said soothingly, if it turned to Bible-based Christianity and conservative politics. Many viewers tuned in because they were curious. Some, perhaps millions, were captivated by the evangelists' religious message and their utopian vision of traditional, conservative America. While there were few highly educated Eastern liberals among the converts, they did come from every walk of life. And the big television evangelists found that their programs won many viewers, and netted substantial contributions, from New York and Los Angeles as well as Fort Worth and Dubuque. Seeing old-fashioned Bible preaching packaged for the media age, viewers everywhere were persuaded first to consider and then to join the Christian America movement.

While the major evangelists used their programs to try to convert a nation, on the local level Ed Young used TV to try to bring people like John Cavallero, who might be lonely, confused, or depressed, into his church. On that morning when a lonely, confused, and depressed Cavallero tuned in, Young was talking about God's love. "No matter how bad you think things are, no matter how badly you feel about yourself, God loves you" was the message Cavallero recalled. As he heard Young's firm, reassuring voice, Cavallero lifted his head to see the words "Prayer Line" and a telephone number flashing on the bottom of the screen. Cavallero reached for the bedside phone and called.

"Some guy named Bernie answered," Cavallero remembered as the waiters in the Swiss restaurant swirled around him attentively. "I asked if the guy on TV was for real and Bernie said, 'C'mon over to church and see.' He sort of challenged me to consider it. The way I was feeling, I needed something, so I said, 'OK, I'll be there.' " The church was close by, and Cavallero, desperate to feel better about himself, got dressed and drove over.

Cavallero could see the church from several blocks away. He parked in a crowded lot and quietly walked up the steps, through the mirrored lobby, and into the huge round sanctuary. Inside, the vast white space was defined by ornate columns and lit by six-story-high stained-glass windows and skylights. He saw giant stained-glass murals on the sides of the church depicting the Holy City, the Lamb of God, the Tree of Life, and even hell's Lake of Fire. Rev. Ed Young was preaching from a pulpit of white-and-rose marble. Behind him sat a choir of three hundred, a number twice the membership of the average American church.

Standing just inside the door, Cavallero again heard Young's voice. And he saw a sea of well-dressed, happy-looking, middle-class people. The men and boys all wore jackets and ties and the women and girls were all in dresses. Many of them were holding Bibles and following along as Young, hovering above them in the pulpit, quoted scripture. When they were told to sing, the congregation sang loudly. When they were instructed to turn their Bibles to a certain page, the church was filled with the snap and flutter of thousands of pages. John Cavallero had never seen anything like it, not at St. Patrick's Cathedral in New York, not anywhere in his lifetime of travel. Awestruck, he sat down in the aisle seat in the last row.

Although he couldn't know it at the time, John Cavallero was one of dozens of people who were also making their first visits to Second Baptist that day. People came from other churches, to see what made Second Baptist so exciting. Others were drawn by Ed Young's program, or driven by the pain in their lives. The whole born-again movement promised everyone an antidote for the turmoil of life. In the mid-1980s all of Houston was in turmoil and there were many people looking for something to make themselves feel better. The city had been on an economic roller coaster. A decade of furious, noisy growth had made it the fourth-largest city in the country. Early in the 1980s many people had become rich as oil prices skyrocketed and Northern companies rushed South, chasing cheap labor and an upbeat marketplace. Houston became exciting, tense, and modern. The cityscape changed as shiny glass buildings, fed by oil and development money, sprouted from the ground. Washed with light and gleaming with newness, Houston rose as an instant impersonal big city of outsiders.

Then, in 1983, the roar of the bulldozers stopped. Foreign oil producers declared a price war and the bottom fell out of the oil business. In the silence, drilling rigs and stacks of pipe rusted like scrap metal in weedy lots outside the city. Foreclosure notices filled the newspapers. Condominium projects stood empty and prime office space went begging at just a few dollars a foot. One-third of the commercial space in Houston became vacant and nearly one-third of the banks disappeared as they were closed or merged with others. Even Houston's famous heart surgeon, Denton Cooley, went bankrupt. For a while one of the most requested records on local radio stations was a novelty song titled "Who Took the Boom Out of Boomtown?"

When the boom did go out of boomtown, the churches were poised to welcome the thousands who turned to them for shelter and certainty. It is in the tradition of born-again Christianity to offer support and shelter to anyone who declares himself born-again and enters the church. In Houston, the churches had the resources to handle the initial surge of newcomers. Those who came into the churches then donated their time and money to help them grow. Second Baptist, which started the decade with just a few hundred members, reaped the harvest of insecurity to become what in the 1980s was known as a mega-church. Mega-churches grew up across the country in the 1980s, becoming like small Christian city-states. In one of its promotional booklets, published when the new church opened, Second Baptist is described as a city within a city. "In a fast-paced city such as Houston, a person or family needs a subculture, a group of people and a place where they can build a lifestyle. For the Christian, this should be the church," the booklet said.

There were other reasons why Houston became a hotbed of the born-again revival. It was part of the traditional Bible belt, which stretches from Virginia to Texas. Natives were accustomed to turning to the Bible when they were in need. But, more important, Houston had a wealth of isolated, even lonely, newcomers. Those Northerners who had rushed South seeking economic paradise needed comfort when the crash came.

John Cavallero felt both comforted and energized at Second Baptist that first Sunday. The church was a warm, enveloping cocoon that offered the first safety and certainty he had known since he had left his mother and father in New York so long ago. Pastor Young was absolutely certain of the truth of every statement he uttered, and the people in the congregation seemed certain too. Charismatic and handsome, Young taught that the Bible is literally true and that the born-again Second Baptist "family" were God's chosen people, certain to be blessed, as he said, "now and forever. Amen."

On another level, Second Baptist was glittery and exciting. The church complex was a utopian village. Cavallero enjoyed the health club and gym, the café, the movie theater, and the bowling alley. He was welcomed everywhere he went by people who called him "brother" and said they loved him. It was not just a fundamentalist church that John Cavallero entered when he made his first, hesitant visit to Second Baptist. It was a community.

Over the first few weeks that he attended services, Cavallero heard

Pastor Young talk about America's problems in a way that explained his personal crisis too. Decades of rapid social change, in technology, sexuality, civil rights, and economics, had left millions of Americans, Cavallero included, confused about their country and their own lives. Houston was not the only uneasy place in America. People everywhere were worried by the homeless poor on city streets, economic recession, and the specter of AIDS. Ed Young's sermons described the sense of crisis many people felt, and suggested solutions: old-fashioned, conservative Americanism and born-again faith. Those values would work for troubled individuals, cities like Houston, and the nation, preached Young. Believing helped Cavallero start to believe in himself and his country again.

The Catholic Church had once provided a center for Cavallero's thinking, but he had left the church in the 1960s, when the reforms of the Second Vatican Council began. Under Vatican II, Catholicism gently eased away from its authoritarian role, dropping some old rules and bending traditional attitudes. Mainline Protestant churches also underwent liberal reforms. The churches began to demand that the faithful think about their Christianity and make their own moral choices. Those believers who wanted firm direction, who had accepted old church teachings on authority and morality, left in droves. Cavallero was one of those who left.

Beginning in the 1970s, born-again Christianity reached out to the disaffected Catholics and mainline Protestants. With TV preachers and President Jimmy Carter removing some of the old backwoods stigma from born-again religion, conservative Christian groups claimed first a trickle and then a torrent of newcomers. Fallen-away Catholics and Protestants who wanted a more concrete kind of religion began to fill born-again churches. Cavallero's experience was typical. At Second Baptist he found a voice that recovered those old moral lessons. Once again he could be sure that homosexuality and adultery were always evil, that God was on his side, that America was blessed and heaven was reserved for people like him.

Both the message and the messenger captivated John Cavallero. Ed Young was more than a preacher, he was the father figure of the Second Baptist family. Young, who was highly regarded in Southern Baptist circles nationwide, was the consummate pastor of the television era. No one had built a more complete local church empire than Ed Young.

A decade earlier, when Young came to Houston, Second Baptist was second-rate. Housed in a small brick building with a single modest steeple, the church had about 1,000 members and had been losing a few dozen each year. While the boom years had brought prosperity to the rest of the city, Second Baptist Church was stagnating. The church elders met and determined that the congregation had reached a crossroads. Their church could either move into the mainstream of the revival that was being fostered by the TV preachers or become just another quiet local church. Sitting there in the middle of booming Houston, with an exciting born-again revival building all around them, the elders hardly had a choice. They made growth their top objective and set out to find someone with enough charisma, energy, and drive to turn Second Baptist into a mega-church. After months of interviewing prospects, they found Ed Young in Columbia, South Carolina, where he was slowly turning another stalled church around. He declined their proposition at first but when the elders offered him carte blanche to build the church as he saw fit, he was persuaded.

Young arrived ready to use high-pressure marketing techniques, television, and special programs to attract new members. He started small, with a local radio show and Bible study groups. The groups were a kind of marketing tool that offered social contact along with scripture study and entree into Second Baptist membership. He started them for singles, for older people, for business people, for mothers with children, for the divorced, for the disabled, for any special interest he could imagine. Gradually the church grew, and Young plowed the money from the collection plate back into television and radio broadcasts and advertising in the newspapers.

While the Bible study groups, a church school, and other programs helped, the big draw was Young himself. Handsome, athletic, and boyish, Young had wavy brown hair, chiseled features, and a perfect smile. On television he came across as the best of Christian America, clean-cut, intelligent, with a Dale Carnegie smile and an open, expansive manner. More than one woman at Second Baptist told me that Young's good looks kept her coming to church. More than one man told me that Young was the kind of leader they could admire. He would fit in at a corporate board meeting or at one of Houston's exclusive country clubs.

By 1985 the church was overflowing on Sundays as converts and those who had left smaller churches rushed to join Second Baptist. People who were doing well went to Second Baptist because it was an "in" church. People who weren't doing well, as Houston struggled through economic recession, went to Second Baptist because it made them feel successful again. Second Baptist became a status symbol for those seeking balance and stability in shaky times.

After he had successfully built the congregation, Young began to emphasize tithing. The tithing created a cash flow that needed an outlet. More programs were added. The staff ballooned. With new members arriving at a rate of about fifty per week, Young and the cadre of ministers at the church lobbied for a huge new "worship center." They needed a larger church to handle the overflow crowds at Sunday services, more space for offices, and room for the school and other programs to grow. A complex that included entertainment, exercise, worship, and educational facilities would provide church members with a complete born-again Christian "subculture." The building was approved by church members and paid for by special fund drives. The brick-and-stained-glass building put every facility, from health club to movie theater, under one roof. The centerpiece was the towering, domed sanctuary.

A splashy color brochure Young issued at the opening ceremony for the new building outlined the activities planned for "a month of Sundays." During those first thirty Sundays churchgoers were treated to a numbing procession of famous evangelists, popular gospel singers, and "theme" programs. Many of the programs were patriotic. There was a salute to liberty, a special day for public officials, and another one to support the police and fire departments. There was a teachers day and a family day with Dale Rogers, a singles weekend and an "Evening with Pat Boone."

As he built his church, Young was also building his reputation as a conservative in his denomination, the Southern Baptist Convention. With 17 million members, the convention was the biggest and most important born-again church in America. Its recent history has been dominated by a conflict of conservative and moderate forces. A staunch "inerrantist," Young became part of a Texas-based coalition of conservative preachers who took control of high church offices in 1979. The inerrantists insisted that their view of the Bible as factually "inerrant" become Southern Baptist doctrine. Over time Young became an important member of the inerrantist camp, helping to hold the line against moderates who used the convention to argue for more liberal doctrine and policy.

By the end of the 1980s, Young was a fundamentalist conglomerate. His radio show was placed on two different stations every day. His TV show aired weekly in Houston and around the country on a Christian cable network. The Second Baptist bookstore stocked hundreds of tapes of Ed Young sermons and several books he had written. The books and tapes were important because they provided the only sure link between Young and his vast flock. Few of the everyday believers at Second Baptist really knew their pastor. With a congregation the size of a small city, he could hardly know everyone. Even the clerk at the Second Baptist bookstore couldn't direct me to his office. "They don't make that known," she told me. "I don't question why. I guess we don't really need to know that." In a way, Young's aloofness, it seemed, made him even more attractive, more important. It added an air of grandeur to the man. He was like a movie star, a detached symbol rather than a caring, personal friend.

During my visit to Second Baptist, Young preached on favoritism. His underlying theme was reassuring, especially given Houston's economy. Though some Christians may have fancy clothes and others might be poor, God judges them only by their born-again commitment, he said. His only favorites are believers. In the Christian world Young described, everyone at Second Baptist could feel good about himself. He concluded with a long anecdote about a basketball team winning a championship on a last-second shot. Young explained how born-again Christians cannot lose the big game of eternal life. "Ladies and gentlemen," he cried joyously, "church on Sunday morning is always, whether you made the shot or whether you missed the shot, it's like a victorious locker room. We're celebrating that we're judged by the grace that God has given to all who profess Jesus Christ as Savior and as Lord." In the end, the believers of Second Baptist Church could breathe easy because they are born-again.

John Cavallero couldn't recall the sermon he had heard on his first Sunday, but he could remember that all of it, the building, the music, the energy, and the message, had made a deep impression. Ed Young had created a setting, and a message, that worked together to soothe and persuade. He said that despair and loneliness could be blamed on Satan and that America's troubles could be traced to a turn away from God. Both problems could be solved by born-again faith. There inside the opulent church, amidst all the happy people who listened so carefully to their charismatic leader, John Cavallero had found what he would later call "the answer."

Cavallero left Second Baptist that first Sunday with some ambivalence. The people at the church were so clearly convinced they had found God's truth, and there were so many of them, that Cavallero had to wonder if they were right. Still, he was skeptical.

The church was ready, however, to follow through on Cavallero's impulsive first visit and tip the scales toward faith. Cavallero had written in the answers on a visitor's questionnaire. His answers were collected, along with those of other first-timers, and deposited in a computer room on the second floor of the church. There a computer operator transferred his name, address, and telephone number to a computer data base. On the Monday night after his first visit, a church volunteer called to ask Cavallero how he liked the service. Cavallero said he enjoyed it, but he resisted the volunteer's invitation to Bible classes. After a few more weeks, and a few more friendly invitations, he agreed to come back to the church. He eventually enrolled in a study group for older single people. The study group focused on the Bible, but also provided a kind of group therapy. People would read scriptures, discuss problems in their lives, and see what solutions the Bible might offer. The group provided encouragement, friendship, and even love. Members were encouraged to admit their past sins—nothing was too horrible to confess—and were offered forgiveness by the group. Cavallero liked the nurturing support and easy friendships the Bible study offered. No one cared about his past. They only cared that he was born-again. He got hooked.

The study groups, which offer support and reinforcement for new believers, formed the foundation of Second Baptist's recruitment effort. The recruiting process, called discipleship, was supervised by Jackie Bond, a businesslike middle-aged woman I met after I talked with Cavallero. Dressed in a blue skirt and jacket and a red silk shirt, Mrs. Bond looked efficient and purposeful. Upstairs in her quiet paneled office she explained the mechanics of winning and keeping souls. While she talked, several women clicked away on computers in a room nearby.

"Bible study is the key to reinforcing people," Mrs. Bond said in a soft Southern accent that drew the *i* in "Bible" out for several beats. "I'd say sixty-five to seventy-five percent of the people who call we get enrolled in a Biiible study group. That's why we have so many. Pastor Young feels that until people are active in the Biiible, they are not strong Christians."

At Second Baptist, and throughout Christian America, a literal reading of the Bible is the key to life. The Bible is not just inspirational for born-again Christians; it is a legalistic rule book, a specific guide for every situation. Bible believers can find passages that support their views on everything from the appropriate (modest) fashions for women to the virtues of capitalism. Bible lessons on raising children (spare the rod and spoil the child) or on marriage (wives must serve their husbands) are rules to live by in Christian America.

"But we're not just in the Bible business; we're in the people business too," Mrs. Bond said, opening her hand and spreading her fingers in front of her face. "We tell people to come on in, join with us in the Lord, we love you," she said, closing her fist and smiling.

Looking at me, Mrs. Bond suddenly asked, "If you were to die tonight, what would you tell God?"

"I'm not sure," I answered.

"Well, a Christian could tell Him that he is forgiven because Jesus died for our sins and that Christ is in his heart. That's enough."

Jackie Bond credited Christ with everything positive in her life and in her husband's life. He's a traveling executive with Xerox. "He is presented with many temptations out in the world, but Jesus helps him overcome," she said. "In my life He gives me the ability to love people and to forgive people, which I never would do on my own."

Mrs. Bond seemed so painfully aware of the temptations her husband faced on the road that she couldn't help mentioning them, even to a stranger. But she didn't say anything more about it. She didn't say whom she must forgive, or why, without Jesus, she found it so hard to be loving. I had heard similar sentiments expressed by other born-again Christians, who all seemed to have been hardened by life. Their faith gave them a stiffly pleasant exterior that I believed covered anger and pain. While I wondered about what sorrow might live in her, Mrs. Bond raced on to point out that Second Baptist's material success, its 11,000 members, and its big building were evidence of its spiritual purity. God must be behind Second Baptist, or it wouldn't succeed, she insisted. "God is honoring His work and He is honoring His word, which is being preached here."

Sitting in her comfortable office surrounded by expensive furnishings and laden with diamond jewelry, Jackie Bond looked as successful as Second Baptist. Material wealth is a tenet of faith among many conservative Christians who insist that God doesn't want anyone to be poor. "God has His hand on our church," Jackie Bond said confidently. "He is honoring His work, as it's being done here, with all this growth and excitement. It is exciting, isn't it?"

John Cavallero found it all very exciting. In his study group he was

welcomed by about a dozen people who seemed to care genuinely
about him. They weren't condemning of his past. They didn't care
about the collapsed vitamin scheme. They were only interested in his
soul. They told him that if he declared himself "born-again" and
followed the Bible, he would be a new, Christian man, happy on
earth and guaranteed a spot in heaven.

Cavallero went every week and found both a network of friends and
a religion he could believe. After a few months he decided he had
been born again, that he had given control of his life to the supernatural
will of Jesus Christ. Then he was baptized. "I felt, for the first time,
like I was involved in something safe," Cavallero recalled at our lunch.
"The people there are good people, and they already agree on the
basics, so you are not going to go over there and get in some kind of
fight, nobody is going to steal from you or run a scam. It's a community
for me. For the first time in my life I felt I had a community."

There was a sense of relief in John Cavallero's voice as he described
the ease he felt at Second Baptist. He sounded like a person who had
been running for a long time and could finally stop and rest. "In many
ways," he said, "I had spent a lot of time trying to prove myself. With
these people, I don't have to do that. I just have to accept Jesus."

Helped along by aggressive ministers and lay activists, John Cavallero
immersed himself in Second Baptist. New members were routinely
asked to volunteer for highly visible and demanding jobs within the
church. The goal is to have new members become so involved that
they have less time for doubt and fewer distractions to weaken their
emerging, tender faith. So it was not unusual for Cavallero, with just
a few months of study, to be asked to teach Bible classes himself. He
joined the church's huge choir, and he also volunteered to answer the
prayer line, as "Bernie" had, to encourage the curious to join Second
Baptist.

Though still tan and smiling, Cavallero was no longer footloose.
He had found a community, and an identity as a modern born-again
Christian man. Second Baptist was a fundamentalist church, steeped
in a theology that is based on a literal reading of the Bible. About half
of America's 60 million born-again Christians were fundamentalists.
As part of his conversion, Cavallero accepted that every story in the
Bible is literally true, from Armageddon prophecy to Jonah and the
whale. His faith became an insurance policy against his own mortality
and against the dreadful possibility that nuclear war could end the
world. Soon he came to believe that his decisions in life, from his

career to his distant family relationships, were governed supernaturally by Jesus Christ. And he came to rely on the knowledge that he was guaranteed eternal bliss in heaven. "Consider it like a gambler would. If you are a Christian and what we say really is true, you're saved forever," he told me. "If it isn't true, at least I'm living the best life I can with people." Cavallero's gambling analogy did capture his attitude. He believed he had found a "sure thing." The wager required that he suspend his skepticism and seal himself within the Christian subculture. But it guaranteed a payoff. Inside Second Baptist he could feel safe, certain, and secure. He didn't have to think about the choices he made in life. He didn't have to consider more than one way of thinking and acting. And he could at least hope that when he died, he would find a happiness in heaven that made the wager worthwhile.

Second Baptist gave Cavallero a new way of looking at himself. The church also gave him a new way of looking at history and the world around him. Conservative Christianity describes man as tragically flawed and besieged by Satan. History, for the faithful, is the story of disintegration. Everything that has happened since Christ's death points to the ultimate battle between good and evil that the Bible predicts will destroy the earth. Born-again Christians believe that the world wars, communism, fascism, the population explosion, disease, and natural disasters are all part of the process that brings the final battle closer. Everything that threatens traditional values—divorce, contraception, legal abortion, sexual liberation—adds to the evil in the world. But the faithful are rescued no matter what happens. If Armageddon comes, they will be protected by God and survive to live with Christ. Meanwhile, in their daily lives, they can deny responsibility for the problems of life, for troubled relationships and bad behavior, by blaming it on Satan and man's evil derived from human nature. By declaring they are "born-again" they are "saved" from Satan and the jaws of hell.

"Man is basically rotten," Cavallero explained to me without a hint of doubt. "And history is basically the story of things falling apart, getting worse and worse, because man has forsaken God. America doesn't realize that without Christianity we would have anarchy. We would have communism, probably. We've only lasted two hundred years because our country has been graced by God."

Our lunch had lasted until late afternoon. Cavallero said he had to go back to his office for a short time and then to the church for the dress rehearsal of "We the People." He said more than $100,000 had been spent on the show. There would be a forty-piece orchestra in the pit and a cast of hundreds. The nationally famous broadcaster Paul Harvey—revered by orthodox Americans for his conventional wit and wisdom—was hired to narrate. And there would be nearly 8,000 people in the huge hall. Some paid as much as $50 for tickets. "Gary Moore's doing it all," Cavallero said as he left. "He's a genius, don't miss it." I went back to the church, had my chat with Jackie Bond, and went to my hotel to rest.

The next morning, on the day of the premiere of "We the People," I went to the church early and caught up with Gary Moore. At nine o'clock the music office was filled with the sound of ringing phones and Moore was racing from room to room, checking on ticket sales, the status of the star, and the progress of the set builders. As I tagged along, Moore explained that his music ministry was supposed to help put the excitement into Exciting Second. The music ministry provided the entertainment that drew people into the church. Moore said his specialty was patriotic productions that could touch the believers' love of God and country. Every show, he said, must have a conservative Christian theme. "We the People," for example, would show "how the Constitution was helped by the grace of God," he said. A few days earlier Moore had explained it more bluntly to the *Houston Chronicle*. "One of the reasons the Constitution is a success is that it takes into account the total depravity of man," he told the paper.

Moore was well known in Christian music circles. He had been wooed to Houston from First Baptist of Dallas, a church that was the seat of the Texas big-church movement. First Baptist, which occupied several blocks of downtown Dallas, was the largest single born-again church in America. But by the mid-1980s First Baptist had grown stodgy. It had become an establishment church where the idea of calling the congregation "The Fellowship of Excitement" would have been quickly doused. Moore wanted to be part of the Great Revival of the 1980s, so when Ed Young came courting, he left for Houston.

As the morning wore on, Moore moved about the church complex checking details. He made sure the parking lot was cordoned off for the arrival of Paul Harvey's limousine. He checked the script one last time and ran through the technical cues with his staff. He was a whirlwind that flew through the reception area blowing papers off desks and ducking in and out of offices. Secretaries pressed pink telephone message slips into his hand as he passed by. Most were from people who wanted tickets.

"Everything we do, recreation, music, the family life center, has a hook for Jesus in it," Moore told me as he puffed across the carpeted office suite toward the door to the sanctuary. He ignored the phone messages and a secretary's reminder that his star, syndicated radio commentator Paul Harvey, was going to arrive a bit earlier than expected. He wanted to check the set. Light-haired with glasses, Moore wore a sweater and casual pants. He was the image of the easygoing "nice guy." But he became intent when he talked about the Second Baptist view of history, which he would present that night. This was to be a pageant with a purpose, he said.

"Look, the Constitution came out of a Judeo-Christian base we don't have in this country anymore," he explained as we headed back to his office. "The Constitution had its origins in divine law. Nowadays what is good, what is the law, depends on utilitarian standards. What works is OK. So we have abortion, we have drugs, AIDS, all the problems of the world today. Christians know what's wrong. The Bible says that without God we're doomed. And unfortunately, too much of America is without God." Second Baptist, Moore said, "is like a stronghold, one of the last fortresses for people who do have a biblical base. We're trying to show that our people are right to believe they carry on something real. To do that we've looked for the times when the Founding Fathers made a reference to God. We then highlight it in the show."

As noon approached and word came that Paul Harvey had arrived, Moore left me to tend to his star's needs. I wound my way through the hallways back to the great sanctuary hall, where a TV crew was setting the positions of large studio cameras. "We the People" would be taped and aired in full on a local station in Houston. John Megyar, a thin, blond man in his twenties dressed in acid-washed jeans and a white shirt unbuttoned halfway down his chest, was supervising the technical details. He called out instructions to a crew that was installing what looked like a small railroad track along a side aisle. A camera would be placed on a cart that would ride the track. It could move smoothly, following the action of the pageant without jostling the TV picture. It's an expensive technique, the kind of maneuver commonly used for slick commercials or in feature films.

"I like getting things like that to play with," Megyar said, pointing to the track. Megyar was the son of a born-again Christian filmmaker and he grew up around the Christian media industry. He told me that Christian TV, which is mostly talk shows and sermons, limits his professional achievements, but offers other rewards. "I get my jollies, like producing short spots, advertising really, for the church. We did one for this production in an old historic house with the Ben Franklin character. We blasted light in from outside the window. It was very pretty."

Technical "jollies" helped keep John Megyar in Christian TV, but his real motivation, he said, was religious. He wanted to use the media to Christianize America. "I have a kind of calling to be here," he said. " 'We the People' is part of that calling." So was the anti-gambling commercial he was preparing to air before an upcoming referendum that would make horse racing legal in Texas. Second Baptist was against it, for all the biblical reasons. The year before, when Houston was deciding whether to approve an ordinance prohibiting discrimination against homosexuals, Megyar produced a similar ad that helped defeat the proposal. "What I like about Pastor Young is he doesn't wimp away from the truth on issues like that. We believe people choose to be homosexual or not, and to choose it is a sin."

Megyar's job was to get Ed Young's sermon out to the Christian Broadcasting cable TV network and to the ten big broadcast stations airing it each week. In a typical week he might also make commercials for the church and the school or for special projects like "We the People." Second Baptist was a good training ground for anyone interested in television. The church gave him the equipment and the money with which to practice his trade. Megyar said he was using it that way, but he said it in Christian terms. "I think someday I'll move on, to work as a Christian but in Los Angeles or New York in secular TV. I am not called to full-time Christian television. But I am called here for a time."

As the afternoon wore on, performers straggled into the church complex. I looked into a rehearsal studio and saw John Cavallero, in a tuxedo and a stiff white shirt, warming up with others in the chorus. In the sanctuary the TV crews labored over the little railroad track. Young men with tool belts strapped around their waists pounded the last few nails into the scenery. A young woman in jeans and a plaid work shirt pinned red, white, and blue bunting onto a railing in the choir loft.

While the tension was slowly building backstage, a steady stream of people trickled into the church complex for Friday-afternoon activities. On the first floor of the school wing a small group of wheelchair-bound young people held a Bible study class. On the second floor, in the Family Life Complex, two dozen women followed an instructor through a dance-exercise routine in one room while a small group of men pushed and pulled their way through a circuit of weight-training machines nearby. Teenage boys played pool in the open main hall. In the gym several basketball games were underway. Several families ate dinner at the Second Helping, where I met David and Dianne Turner and their children. The Turners had scooped up their children at the Second Baptist school and were having something to eat before attending the pageant.

In their early thirties, the Turners represented the second major group in the Second Baptist community. Not converts, they were longtime believers who had become upwardly mobile and socially aware. They both grew up born-again Christians, but they had not made their faith the center of their lives until they moved to Houston and found Second Baptist.

"We thought we were born-again Christians before we came here," David Turner explained. "I had gone to church all my life and I thought I was born-again, that I was saved. But I came to this church and I saw the power of God's work being done." The Turners became heavily invested, personally, spiritually, and financially, in the church. On any given day they might all be involved in one program or another: exercise, Bible study, recruitment. They said they spent $5,000 a year on church day school for their children and $300 for the Family Life Center membership. They had recently started tithing.

A burly man, comfortable in jeans and a checkered flannel shirt, Turner came to Houston to attend college in the early boom years and stayed. He learned to revere success and achievement. When we met he was starting his own chemical sales business. He was impressed with Pastor Young's accomplishments at Second Baptist. Second Baptist's success, in building facilities, in attracting new members, convinced him it was a holy place. "I could see by their fruits," he said, "they were doing God's work."

Turner's language—"by their fruits"—his business life, and his home life were all shaped by his religion. Though trained in science, he had come to believe that the scientific notions about the origins of mankind and the earth are wrong. He decided to believe instead in the Bible's stories of creation. In his job as a salesman he frequently takes a customer or an oil-field worker aside to talk about Jesus and press a Bible tract into his hand. "I ask God, on an hourly basis, if there is anything more I can do, any way to bring another person to know Jesus," he said.

Turning his attention to my soul, Turner asked for my notebook, pulled a polished-metal pen from his shirt, and drew a cross on a piece of paper. While he drew, the rest of the people at the table were silent. The sound of the fountain, gurgling in the lobby below the balcony, drifted upstairs. Breathing hard as he concentrated, Turner wrote the word "prayer" at the top of the cross. At the bottom he wrote: "the Word." He drew a circle in the center and said, "That's where you've got to be, in the middle of prayer and the Word, right in the middle of the cross with Christ." He wrote a few scripture citations, from John, and asked me to read them later.

The scriptures revealed David Turner's commitment to the Christian America view of life. They joined faith and revealed truth to create a heavenly promise of prosperity. "Apart from Me, you can do nothing," read the first verse. The second was: "If you abide in My word, then you are truly disciples of Mine. You shall know the truth and the truth shall make you free." The last scripture read: "If you abide in Me and My words abide in you, ask whatever you wish, it shall be done for you." Taken together, in the context of Second Baptist's brand of Christianity, those verses boil down to the essence of Christian America: those who believe shall live free and prosper.

Turner viewed his world, from everyday business problems to family life, through the prism of fundamentalist theology. During our talk he explained that he was pushed into self-employment faster than he had planned. He said he had been fired from his previous job, not for a business reason, but because his boss was in spiritual conflict. "He had a problem with the inner peace I had because I was a Christian," he said. "He was going through his own soul searching and my example disturbed him. He'll come around. He'll see the light."

While David Turner talked, his young children, two girls and a boy, wandered about the cafe, trying out different chairs and talking to the people there. "It's really all right here, you can relax," Dianne Turner interjected. "No one here is going to bother the children. This is one place where they'll be safe."

Dianne Turner, a thin woman with long light brown hair and a small gold cross around her neck, said that Second Baptist had replaced neighborhood life for her family. The church had become the "subculture" of the brochure. At home, on a cul-de-sac called Shady Arbor, the Turners were obviously "the Christians in the neighborhood," she said. Foul language and fighting were not allowed in their home and their children were likely to go out for a bike ride wearing "Jesus Is the Rock" T-shirts. Their beliefs, and lifestyle, separated them from their neighbors.

"A lot of people in the neighborhood are just uncomfortable with us," said Dianne. "One little boy threw a pinecone at David because he's a Christian. Another boy yelled at him, 'Satan has more rocks.' Here, we don't have to even think about something like that happening." Second Baptist had become a refuge from the pinecone throwers and the harsher realities of the world.

Turning to prophecy, and every in-depth conversation at Second Baptist seemed to lead to prophecy, the Turners described their faith as protection, even from nuclear Armageddon. And Dianne wondered aloud if AIDS, the deadly, sexually transmitted immune disorder, might be a sign of the end-times prophecy coming true. "AIDS wouldn't be here if we had followed the Bible," she said. "AIDS was initially spread primarily by homosexual men." Many born-again preachers have made heavy use of the gay community's AIDS tragedy, using it to "prove" that God is unhappy with homosexuals and may be punishing a society that is increasingly accepting of homosexuality. Of course, in order to make their point, the preachers have had to ignore AIDS in the heterosexual community, where, many scientists argue, it may have first arisen. The selective use of AIDS facts that I found throughout Christian America was not so much malicious as convenient. Born-again Christians tend to sculpt reality to match their Bible-based view of the way things should be. Facts that don't fit biblical truths are conveniently omitted. So they ignore AIDS in the straight community, just as they ignore homosexuality among born-again clergy. Both are facts that make reality too complex.

"The churches are bursting at the seams. That's another of the signs that are expected, a great revival, before the end," continued David Turner. "Dr. Young has preached that there are no prophecies left to fulfill before it happens. If it happens, I'll be with Jesus. If it doesn't, I have to spend my life serving God and trying to make the world here better for my children. By bringing people to Christ, by bringing the country to Christ, we'll make the world better and hasten the Second Coming."

After finishing their hamburgers, the Turners left to pick up their tickets for "We the People." Then they went home to change into more formal clothes. In the short time between the dinner hour and the opening overture the vast parking lot outside Second Baptist quickly filled with cars. Waves of families and single adults rolled in from the distant lots. They were channeled into the lobby and then through the funnel spout formed by the doorway to the sanctuary. Inside, the orchestra noisily warmed up and Gary Moore watched from the wings as the house filled steadily.

At show time in the church the houselights went down and a single spotlight illuminated Gary Moore in the orchestra pit. He prayerfully introduced the production to a packed house. "I hope you feel the pain and prayer of our forefathers who put the Constitution together," he said, folding his hands in prayer and looking benevolently on the thousands who sat around him. "I hope that when you leave you'll feel strongly about our government and will protect it from enemies, foreign and domestic, so help you God."

As Moore finished, fatherly Ed Young strolled onto the stage above and behind him, trailing another spotlight. He carried a microphone in his hand, letting it rest loosely at his side while the audience applauded warmly, the way nightclub audiences applaud for old stars who make a surprise appearance at a show.

"Our Founding Fathers felt that they were led by God as they were putting together that word," he said, gently cradling the microphone in his hands. He described the show to come as a "vision that comes across in drama and music" created by a "genius," Gary Moore. Finally Young introduced radio star Paul Harvey. "Is there a man in America who is a born-again Christian? A man listened to? A man who is the conscience of America, who loves this land and loves the Lord? This is that man, Paul Harvey!"

Harvey, a fair-haired man with the look of a wrinkly, aging elf, appeared to waves of applause and took his place in a bunting-draped window constructed in the choir loft. As he settled in, the choir of 300 swayed into the hall in an explosion of blue dresses and tuxedos. The orchestra played an overture, and high above, on a long, narrow screen hung from the ceiling, flashed pictures of flags and American eagles and other patriotic symbols.

From his perch in the choir loft, Harvey guided the faithful through a two-hour tour of Christian American history. Through songs, tap dancing, and even slapstick, the show portrayed the drafting of the Constitution, the addition of various amendments, and historical crises. Harvey described the Founding Fathers as "good ol' boys" and the men onstage seemed to fit the description. In Second Baptist's version of the Continental Congress, George Washington sounded like Lyndon Johnson.

At every turn Moore's production bored in on the handful of religious utterances made by the Constitution's framers. "Some historians have been quick to see the hand of God in our history," said Harvey. Much mention was made of Benjamin Franklin's proposal for a prayer to begin each session of the Congress. No one explained that the proposal was voted down. Instead Moore seized on the few references to God he could find in historical documents to show that the American revolutionaries were all God-fearing Christians, just like the members of Second Baptist Church.

As the pageant lumbered along, political events were described as miracles, and threats to America's stability, foreshadowed by Gary Moore's speech, were symbolized by picketing "women's libbers" and "criminals" demanding their rights. But at Second Baptist the faithful could relax. The protesters and libbers looked silly, not threatening. And the audience could bask in big production numbers. The biggest crowd pleaser was called "I'm Just a Flag-Wavin' American."

The first blacks arrived in the pageant's second act, playing slaves who were freed by Abraham Lincoln. While a black woman in chains sang "Sometimes I Feel Like a Motherless Child," a photo of a malnourished black child flashed on the big video screen. When she finished, Abe arrived and ceremoniously lifted off the woman's chains. "Oh, we're free, free! Hallelujah!" cried the woman. "Thank you, Jesus!"

After the slaves were freed, the women's suffrage movement marched onstage. They were quickly granted the vote and were followed by the Women's Christian Temperance Union. Jackie Bond played one of the WCTUers, who demanded Prohibition. The world wars were marked by military music and a call for all the veterans in the audience to stand and take a bow.

Through the show, hard times were marked by pleas for God's help. And the military was always there to save the day. But even in this idealized view, the troubling elements of recent history leaked onto the stage. On the forty-foot-wide video screen high above the stage, Moore's company flashed photographs synchronized with music. Some of the scenes were jarring. There was the famous picture of Saigon's police chief holding a pistol to a suspect's head during a street execution in the last days of the Vietnam War. There were more malnourished black children, campus protests, drug users, and protesters. The most searing image in the final splash of photographs was a giant picture of Christ crucified, against a background of the American flag.

The pageant insisted that the answers to America's problems lie in the Constitution, which, like the born-again version of the Bible, is perceived as an unchangeable literal truth handed down by God. The final sequence of pictures that floated above the stage reflected Gary Moore's view of America under siege. Taken as a whole, the production seemed to say that America was founded as a Christian nation, that the Constitution is sacred, and that somehow the country must recover its Christian soul.

In the end "We the People" was, like Second Baptist Church, Texas-sized, glittery, and exhausting. For Gary Moore, John Megyar, and the other church professionals, it was another milestone in their effort to produce lavish, captivating Christian spectacles. For John Cavallero and dozens of other bit players and singers, the show was a rite of passage. Men and women who had never performed in public got the chance to sing and dance and act. They also got to show their commitment as full members of the Second Baptist "family."

The show affirmed the faith of thousands of recently arrived Yankees, longtime church members, and newly born-again Christians. Its deviations from history didn't matter to them. No matter that many of the Founding Fathers were deists. No matter that for so many those "good old days" revered in the program were filled with racism, illiteracy, poverty, and pain. With its selective view of history, the pageant had captured the essential messages of the Christian Right crusade: that born-again Christians are God's people, America is God's country, and if everyone would just become a conservative Christian, then everything would be all right again.

= 2 =

Family and Faith

"A. All have sinned and come short of the glory of God.
"B. Believe in the Lord Jesus Christ and thou shall be saved.
"C. Children, obey your parents, for this is in the law."

FRANKIE CIOFRONE, a five-year-old with mischievous blue eyes, recited the alphabet as it had been taught to him in his Christian kindergarten. Struggling to remember the verses that went with each letter, he rocked on his heels like a wobbly top. Though obviously anxious, he seemed proud to perform for the adults who had gathered around the family's kitchen table. After finishing the alphabet, he raced straight into the Christian pledge of allegiance. "We pledge allegiance to the Christian flag, and to our Savior, for whom it stands . . ."

"That's wonderful, Frankie," his mother, Amy, interrupted. A tall woman with short black hair and a wide smile, she clapped her hands for a few seconds and then stopped abruptly. "The glory, though, goes to God," she said firmly. "It has to be that way. We know all good things are from God. The bad things come when we listen to our evil nature. So when we have a decision to make, we ask the Lord, 'Is this what You want me to do?' We know when what we do is 'of Jesus' and when it is not." Her husband, Frank, who sat on the other side of the kitchen table holding a cup of coffee, nodded in agreement. Little Frankie, who had been standing quietly, was sent back to the paneled living room to watch a television show called *Highway to Heaven*. It was one of the few programs he was allowed to watch.

The Ciofrones were charismatic Christians. Their faith had little to do with the fundamentalist razzle-dazzle of Houston's Second Baptist. It was more deeply personal. And the church they attended, Smithtown Gospel Tabernacle, was smaller and more typical of the Christian America movement nationwide. Not a gleaming mega-church like Second Baptist, the tabernacle was more a village of faith. The pastors at the church knew every member by name, and they knew their problems and needs. It was more like the kind of church that served the average born-again American family.

In the 1980s, charismatics such as the Ciofrones were the fastest-growing group in conservative Christianity. Fewer than 20 million in 1970, by the mid-1980s their numbers were estimated to be between 30 and 35 million. The charismatics shared all of Christian America's traditional social and political values. They believed the Bible to be literally God's truth and that Americans were a chosen people. And like all born-again Christians, they believed that Jesus guided human affairs. What distinguished charismatics from other conservative Christians was their unshakable faith in dramatic supernatural experiences. While most other born-again Christians thought, for example, that miraculous healings occurred only in Jesus' time, charismatics were certain that they could happen to anyone at any time. Charismatics also believed that the Holy Spirit imbued believers with healing powers and the ability to pray in "tongues." What was meant by "tongues" was a kind of unintelligible, ecstatic prayer, commonly uttered or even shouted by worshippers at charismatic church services. In general, the charismatics believed that Jesus and the Holy Spirit could become actual, physical presences in everyone's life, if only the belief was strong enough.

At the start of the day when we met, Amy Ciofrone sent young Frankie and his older brother off to their private Christian elementary school with a prayer that asked Jesus to guide the bus safely through suburban traffic. Later, at the supermarket, as always, Amy searched the aisles looking for downhearted souls who she felt needed Jesus. Gazing at each one, she silently prayed that they would be born again. In the afternoon, when the girl who delivered the newspaper asked for two weeks' payment, Amy told her to "ask Jesus" if the account was really overdue. And indeed, when the girl looked at her record book she found she had made a mistake. "Praise the Lord," Amy said.

What made Amy Ciofrone different, even from most born-again Christians, was her deeply rooted sense that Jesus Christ was quite specifically in charge of every detail of her life. More than anyone else I met in Christian America, she lived as if Jesus were with her all the time. When she talked to him, she believed that he answered. She saw him in her children's faces, in strangers at the local shopping mall, and in her neighbors' eyes.

It had not always been this way. Amy and her husband, Frank, were both raised in old-fashioned, reserved Catholic immigrant families. They had grown up on Long Island, where, in the 1950s of their childhood, hundreds of thousands of New Yorkers found the suburban good life in subdivisions. The American dream was in full flower. Frank and Amy went to the same high school, where they met and started dating. By the time Frank was drafted, they were going steady. Although he considered it his duty to serve in Vietnam, he instead spent his tour guarding Lyndon Johnson's helicopter at the President's ranch in Texas.

On that first evening I spent with the Ciofrones, while the adults talked, the children, perhaps stimulated by their parents' recollections, went into the basement and opened a box filled with the artifacts of Amy and Frank's early years together. The boys scuttled back and forth like archaeologists who had found the hard evidence of an ancient tribe. Old pictures, a matchbook from their wedding, Frank's discharge papers, even a swizzle stick from their honeymoon, were brought up from the basement. In all the photos Frank wore neat, conservative clothes and his hair was trimmed short. Amy wore little hats and modest dresses. There they were, smiling in front of Frank's first car. There they were again, on the steps of Amy's parents' house. To all appearances, the counterculture of the 1960s never touched them. Frank did his duty in the military and Amy waited for him, living with her parents. She got a secretarial job, walked the six blocks to work in the morning and back home at night, and rarely went out. Frank was discharged at the end of 1968. They were married in 1970. They recalled sentimentally that when they made love on their wedding night, it was the first time for both of them.

As Frank and Amy moved out on their own, they struggled to buy a home and start a family. They held tightly to their conservative ideals about family, politics, and society, but their values were challenged by the people they met at work and in their neighborhood. In their first house they grew close to a couple who lived nearby. Richie was a gym teacher, and Frank, who was interested in sports, fell into an easy friendship with him. Sandra taught English, and though she was from a traditional background herself, she was fast changing under the influence of feminist writers such as Betty Friedan and Germaine Greer.

Amy was intrigued. Her first significant friend as a married woman turned out to be someone who would challenge all of her assumptions. "I loved being married," Amy recalled. "People thought it was unusual, but I loved cleaning the house and cooking. I was submissive in that way. But I remember going to a Tupperware party and I saw it was eleven o'clock and I said, 'I've got to go. I told Frank I'd be home by now.' Well, you can imagine what Sandra said about that. And I said to myself, 'Yeah, why do I need permission from him?' " Under Sandra's influence, Amy began to change.

Sandra gave her books to read. She first suggested romance novels, and Amy grew to like them as much as she liked her afternoon soap operas. As the two women became closer, Amy and Frank were drawn to their friends' very different way of life. Sandra and Richie had a less traditional relationship than the Ciofrones. Sandra shared in earning money and making important decisions. Richie helped with housework and child care. Amy and Frank tried to follow suit. Amy tried to be more assertive. Frank tried to be less domineering. They even experimented with marijuana. But all the while, Amy wondered if Sandra was perhaps a bit too forceful and Frank harbored the feeling that Richie let Sandra push him around in some ways. Still, the four were fast friends, and for the most part, life was good for the Ciofrones.

But there was one serious problem that overshadowed the Ciofrones' marriage. From the beginning, they had tried, without success, to have children. And while Amy was drawn to her friends' rather secular lifestyle, this gnawing problem led her back to the traditional Catholic outlook she had had as a child. She began to pray that she would get pregnant. Every day, she knelt beside her bed, made the sign of the cross, and asked Jesus, Mary, and any saint who might be listening to help her conceive a child. While she prayed for help, Amy was also worried that the diet pills she had been taking since before she was married were preventing her from conceiving. As the years had gone by, the pills had also made it more difficult for her to sleep. She would sit up at night, watching TV and making miniature ceramic figures, a hobby that began to obsess her. While Frank slept, she molded little figures—animals, elves, and Santa Clauses—the subjects depending on the season. She often worked late into the evening, hoping to feel sleepy as she shaped and painted and watched TV. As the late-night TV talk shows ended, Amy searched for some other programs to keep her company. That's when she started watching TV evangelists.

At first the evangelists' programs seemed to her to be like other talk or variety shows, except that the people on them smiled more. She discovered Jim and Tammy Bakker's *PTL Club*. She also enjoyed Pat Robertson's *700 Club*, which used the same format as Johnny Carson, right down to the amiable sidekick and the rehearsed banter. Amy noticed that there were many references to Jesus and God and that most of the guests—football player Rosey Grier or actor Efrem Zimbalist, for example—told stories about becoming born-again Christians. Gradually she figured out that the late-night programs were supposed to introduce her to Bible-based faith. The people seemed sincere and happy. She kept watching.

Her favorite was the PTL show. PTL stood for Praise the Lord and People That Love, and was hosted by the Bakkers. Young, fair-haired, and effervescent, they preached a gospel of modern miracles. Whenever Amy tuned in she could hear a story about miraculous cures or financial rewards brought to born-again Christians. She didn't understand every detail of the Bakkers' religious belief, and certainly she knew it wasn't consistent with Catholicism. But the show was emotional and exciting and she kept watching.

Not long after she began watching the PTL show and thinking about the born-again Christians she saw, Amy discovered she was pregnant. Six long years of waiting were over. After an uneventful pregnancy, filled with excited expectation, her son Paul was born. Amy vowed to thank God for him every day. But over the course of two or three months her attachment to her baby waned. His crying and fitful sleeping pattern unnerved her. Diapers and feeding became an oppressive drudgery. Amy began to feel she had never fully recovered from the delivery. She stopped thanking God for Paul.

Then, when Paul was about four months old, as Amy was preparing for a weekend trip to the beach, something frightening happened. Entering the nursery, she called to him. He didn't move. She moved closer and clapped her hands near his head. He didn't respond. Panicking, Amy ran from the room, convinced her child was deaf. She telephoned friends and relatives, who all assured her that the baby must be fine. They said she was jumping to conclusions. They told her to relax. She sat at the kitchen table and worried. Later, when Frank came home, he too tried to reassure her, but to no avail.

Apparently they didn't consider going for a doctor, and though Amy was still distraught, they went on with their outing. With Amy convinced her son was deaf and Frank waiting to see how the drama would play out, they went to the beach.

As they drove through the countryside, with baby Paul dozing in the back seat, Amy heard a voice say that she had forgotten her promise, that she had come to take Paul for granted. "I, the creator, gave you My most precious creation," the voice told her.

Amy became convinced the voice belonged to Jesus. And certain that, like the people on the *PTL Club*, she could handle anything with Jesus' help, she felt at ease. This all came to her where the Long Island Expressway divides into smaller highways that lead through the island's scenic eastern end. Every time she passes that place she thinks of it as the site of her first miracle.

Once at the beach, the family settled into their rented cottage. They put away their clothes and the groceries they had brought. Baby Paul was laid down for a nap, and the adults moved out onto the porch. As the front door creaked, Amy noticed her baby's head turn with the sound. Weeping, she declared that the deafness had been cured, that his hearing had been miraculously restored.

From that Friday on, Amy believed that her son was once indeed deaf. She came to regard the ordeal as a lesson from God, directed only at her. And while everyone around her argued that the baby had been fine all along, she believed that her son had been cured by a miracle. "I feel that was when He made himself real, and that was when I became a Christian," Amy recalled years later.

Although she had no one to talk to about her miracle, Amy steadfastly believed in it. Her resolve deepened, buttressed in part by the testimony from movie stars and others describing similar experiences on the *PTL Club*. Gradually she decided that she too must try to become a born-again Christian. She began to read the Bible, not in the way she had learned it as a child in a Catholic home, but rather in the way the Bakkers recommended. In stark contrast to traditional Catholic practice, Amy began to consult the Bible every time she needed to make a decision. She started quoting Bible stories to her friends and recommending scriptures that might address their problems.

The Bible became such a force in Amy's life that Sandra was repelled by her friend's obsession. Amy vividly remembers the moment when their friendship ended. She had been caring for Sandra's son while

Sandra taught school. She had told the boy about Jesus and had even read him some Bible stories. When her son came home talking about Jesus, Sandra confronted Amy. "You don't really believe that stuff, do you?" Amy recalled her friend saying. "Yes, I do," answered Amy. Sandra stopped asking Amy to care for her son and the two women stopped talking. When the Ciofrones moved to another, larger house in a different neighborhood, they lost touch with Sandra and Richie entirely.

The new house was, in Amy's eyes, a sign of Jesus' presence in her life. The Ciofrones got it for a low price because the owners were getting a divorce. Someone else might have considered such a bargain simple good fortune, but Amy was convinced that it was divine providence which had seen them through the complex negotiations to buy it. The experience became another landmark in Amy's progression toward charismatic Christianity. It was to set the stage for her ultimate conversion of faith.

Soon after they bought the new house, Amy and Frank went to a cut-rate department store called Sands Salvage. They were looking for supplies to start remodeling when they ran into a man Frank knew from his job as an electrician. Tony was a born-again, charismatic Christian, the first flesh-and-blood true believer Amy had met since she had started watching the *PTL Club*. She was filled with questions. Armed with his Bible, Tony stood with Amy for three hours, answering her questions. While Frank took the two-year-old Paul to McDonald's, Amy remained in the store's housewares department, surrounded by pots and pans and utensils, poring over the Bible with Tony. She asked about faith healing and speaking in tongues, about prophecy and the born-again experience. After each of Amy's questions, Tony turned to a different scripture and offered an answer. When they were through, he looked up from the book and said, "Do you want to give your life to Jesus Christ right here?"

Amy recalled that she then heard a voice in her head, a voice she would later decide belonged to the Holy Spirit. It said, "If you deny Me before men, I will deny you before the Father."

Standing there in Sands Salvage, her head swirling with emotion, Amy declared herself born-again, promising to let Jesus guide her life. Tony hugged her. He then urged her to start attending his church, Smithtown Gospel Tabernacle. She went the next Sunday and was excited to meet others who believed in Jesus the way she did. At Smithtown Gospel Tabernacle she could immerse herself in Bible study. "Jesus told me to stay with that book, and read no others, until I knew it backwards and forwards," she said. "And that's what I did."

It was at Smithtown Gospel Tabernacle, a born-again Christian oasis in the sprawling, anonymous mass of subdivisions and highways that is Long Island, that I first met Amy. Built out of an abandoned elementary school complex, the church is a white maze of classrooms, offices, hallways, and recreation areas. All the hallways eventually lead to the sanctuary, a comfortable, modern church with towering windows and thickly padded pews. The sanctuary is airy, brightly lit, and usually filled with flowers.

The tabernacle offers acceptance, guidance, and support to its 1,500 members, who, in turn, contribute more than $2 million a year to fund its programs. The church is a refuge from the anonymity of suburban living. On Long Island, the place where housing developments were invented after World War II, people move in and out of subdivisions, often without making contact with any of their neighbors. Everyone seems to complain of loneliness. Smithtown Gospel Tabernacle offers a cure: community. The church has several worship services each week, supports a small day school, and sponsors enough programs to keep members involved in courses, recreation, or Bible study every day of the week.

The programs, especially Bible study classes, provide the structure for life in the faith. Often conducted by lay people, the study groups go through scriptures, line by line, mulling over the meaning of Bible stories and lessons. A truly committed Christian could study the Bible almost every night of the week at Smithtown Gospel Tabernacle. There are Bible study groups for men, for women, for children, for marrieds, and for singles. There are Bible-oriented courses on raising children, even a course on the end-of-the-world prophecies and why they may soon come true.

An obsession with the supernatural dominates the theology offered at the tabernacle. Services are filled with music, often the old spirituals of the black church, sung by a large choir and accompanied by an orchestra drawn from the school and the congregation. Pastor Robert Forseth, an older man with white hair and a soft voice, often preaches about applying Christian love to life's challenges and about the need to follow Jesus. Services are punctuated with long periods of "praise," pauses when members of the congregation may pray quietly, sing, or shout their prayers. In those moments the church is filled with the shouts and rhythmic prayers of "Thank you, Jesus, thank you, Jesus," or "Glory to God, glory to God." The music plays and the congregation sways and eventually someone erupts in tongues. Believers consider outbursts of tongues to be proof that the Holy Spirit has descended upon their services.

During a week I spent at Smithtown, a guest preacher was conducting a revival. Even in the age of television evangelists, born-again churches still host traveling preachers who try to invigorate the faithful with revival services. A handful are traditional tent preachers who make the rounds of small rural congregations. Their tents can still be seen on the roadsides of Louisiana and Mississippi. But the modern born-again movement eschews the Elmer Gantry imagery of tent revivals. At Smithtown Gospel Tabernacle, Pastor Forseth tried to take a more intellectual approach to revival. So the church brought in Rev. Richard Mohrman, a gray-haired, professorial man who blends modern classroom-style teaching with a more dignified spiritualism. On a Wednesday night, with the church about half full of curious believers, Mohrman stood before a chalkboard drawing diagrams and writing key Bible citations to reveal the truth about the Holy Spirit and the "gifts." He raced from one scripture to another, pointing out references to first-century Christians who lapsed into indistinguishable languages while deep in prayer. The gibberish is considered to be holy language, brought on by the presence of one special member of the Christian Trinity, the Holy Spirit. Today's born-again Christians believe these "tongues" prove God is in their midst.

The believers who had come to hear Richard Mohrman listened intently, taking notes and reading along in the Bible, because they wanted the gift of tongues themselves. Married couples, young men and women on dates, and singles, who came laden with notebooks and study guides, all sat there soaking up the waves of verse and analysis.

"God supernaturally anoints us with the ability to speak in tongues as evidence that He is real in this world. It is a super"—Mohrman paused to emphasize the point—"a supernatural experience."

On a chalkboard Mohrman then wrote: "(1) an evidence; (2) prayer language; (3) public expression." Tongues, he explained, are evidence of God, praise to Him in a special prayer language, intended to impress the world. But speaking in tongues is not a goal to be pursued, he said. "Seek God, seek the Holy Spirit, and tongues will be a consequence."

When Mohrman finished teaching, he said, "Now, who wants to

pray?" More than half of the people there walked to the altar to stand and pray with their teacher. Morhman moved from one to another, holding a hand or placing his arm around a shoulder. Those who prayed praised Jesus and welcomed him into their lives. But no one would complain if they happened to get the gift of tongues as well. Mohrman prayed and cried out to God to make himself known by the gift of tongues.

"Lord, give her the liberty to praise You, Lord," Mohrman said, placing his hands on the top of one middle-aged woman's head. "You will not be inhibited, you will not hold back." Suddenly, Mohrman erupted in tongues.

"Ahhh, sha, la, la reeeee! We will speak out the praises in us!" he said, returning to English. "Rah, ba, ba, ba. Shah, bah, bah ba."

"Thank you, Jesus," the woman said, her body beginning to sway slowly. "Thank you, Jesus," she said loudly. "Thank you, Jesus, thank you, Jesus. Sha rheee, bah, bah, sham busah. Thank you, Jesus!" she shouted. "Seree, ree, ree, sham busah!"

While Mohrman prayed with the first woman, dozens of other women and men stood silently in the front of the church. Some closed their eyes, deep in prayer. Others looked up to the heavens, waving their arms and praising God out loud. Those who were more experienced helped the others to pray. They would lean close to them, hold their hands, rub their backs, and pray with them. Charismatics sometimes say they want to "pray through," which means they want to pray intently, not stopping until the Holy Spirit comes upon them. Occasionally one of the worshippers would burst out in tongues. "Rahhhh, le, pah loom ah!" said one man. The others would respond, "Praise God!"

Whether a person was able to speak in tongues seemed to depend on how intently he was involved in prayer and how fully he accepted Mohrman's permission to lose control. Those who succeeded were flushed with relief. They wanted to praise God in some way, and the tongues released them from the chore of finding specific words or meanings. They were free to just cry out. And when they were done, they were relaxed and happy in the afterglow of that one moment of unfettered primal experience.

On the morning after the service, I had breakfast with Richard Mohrman. He had told me to pick him up at 8 a.m. at a cheap motel on the commercial strip that leads out of Smithtown. It was a depressing old brick "motor court," more suited to the brief engagements of businessmen and their mistresses. When I met him, Mohrman told me the place was clean, but that one of his neighbors was a young man who had remained in his room all week, staring at the TV. Mohrman said he was worried about that fellow. As we were about to drive off, a silver Lincoln Continental pulled into the parking space beside us. Out of the car came a luggageless middle-aged couple who slipped into the room next to Mohrman's. As we drove out of the parking lot Mohrman told me he was worried about those people too.

Tall, with brown eyes and gray hair, Mohrman was a youthful fifty-nine. He wore an unusual sweater made of alternating patches of blue wool and blue leather. He had been an Assemblies of God preacher for more than twenty years. Assemblies of God is the largest charismatic denomination. Mohrman said he had given up his affiliation because he thought a denominational label would inhibit his work as a traveling evangelist. "Some people don't want to deal with you if you're from a different denomination. They have set ideas and attitudes about you based on that label. I want to be able to reach people anywhere and this way I can," he said.

Over breakfast in a Smithtown diner, Dick, as he insisted on being called, said Americans were hungry for the supernatural, for proof that God exists and cares about them. Everywhere he went, he said, he found people who wanted to believe in God's actual presence. Other denominations—the Catholic Church and the older Protestant sects—had abandoned the spiritual core of their faith. Modern theology had led them into ambiguity. "In most Catholic and Protestant churches God is an abstraction, an idea, not a supernatural presence," Mohrman said. Those churches are less certain about having the one true faith, about the literal truth of the Bible, and about the spirit realm. In charismatic churches, according to Mohrman, "people see, in the tongues or the other gifts, that God is real and present right now, in today's world. They see proof, not ambiguity. But it's not something strange and out of control. When I am praying with someone, I am aware that I am asking God for the experience, say, of tongues, to show His presence. He prompts the syllables that come out of me. I am conscious of what's going on, I am fully rational, but I believe God allows me to have the experience of tongues as evidence for everyone to see."

People needed to believe in a supernatural shepherd, a kind of super father figure, who will help them through life in an ever more con-fusing world, Mohrman said. Interestingly, he defended some of the most extreme aspects of the counterculture of the 1960s. He would be the only born-again preacher I would meet who could find anything good to say about that era. "The hippies and flower children, they saw the fallacy of a lot of the material things that people thought represented life and happiness. They were searching for reality. Today in these churches I meet people, doctors, lawyers, others, who are really searching for the same thing. They aren't happy with the wealth, the success they have. They find the tether they need in Christ."

The praise, the speaking in tongues, and the teaching—in short, the charismatic version of the search for reality—went on day and night at Smithtown Gospel Tabernacle. People hungry for spiritual experiences, hungry for answers to their questions about life and death, streamed into the church. And all this in a region where, a decade before, born-again Christians were found only in tiny, run-down churches in out-of-the-way places. The 1980 census had reported that Long Island was about 50 percent Catholic and 30 percent Jewish. Yet wealthy, active, and growing Smithtown Gospel Tabernacle thrived, its success striking evidence of the inroads made by the conservative Christian movement nationwide. By 1987, born-again, orthodox Americans were no longer the Southern Bible thumpers of caricature. Many were comfortable middle-class Northerners who believed they had found a way to make sense of their lives.

After breakfast with Richard Mohrman, I drove over to the church. In the large whitewashed lobby outside the sanctuary about two dozen women were gathered at four long folding tables. The women, who had come to attend a weekly Bible study called Women in the Word, were dressed modestly. The younger ones wore sweaters and jeans. Many had pulled their hair back into ponytails. The older ones wore conservative dresses. They seemed small, their voices lost in the lobby's expanse of glass and whiteness.

They were Women in the Word, and their leader was Amy Ciofrone. Dressed in a bold gray-and-white sweater and a blue pleated skirt, Amy wore as much makeup as all the other women combined. Her dark hair was cut stylishly short and combed forward, toward high, rouged cheekbones. She stood at the end of the tables and beamed down on her charges. At ten o'clock exactly, she pushed the "play" button on a small tape recorder. She smiled broadly, her eyebrows arching, and she started to sway with the music. Moving nearly in unison, the women at the long tables tilted their heads toward the little machine, struggling to hear the gospel music. When they caught the tinny tune, they closed their eyes. Some swayed. A few murmured, "Thank you, Jesus. Thank you, Jesus." Most joined in with the music.

I want to serve you, Lord.
I want to serve you, Lord.
The greatest thing in all my life
is serving you.

Amy Ciofrone clicked off the tape recorder and started talking. Her voice, unlike the others, filled every corner of the lobby. Animated, even gushing at times, she talked about Jesus Christ as if he were her best friend, her adviser, and her parent. She explained that she trusted Jesus to reveal her subject for each meeting, and was certain he wanted her to talk about how the Holy Spirit guided Christian lives.

"Girls, the Holy Spirit is a person. He's real," she said, "just as the Lord and the Father are real. When I first met Jesus, a lot of people told me, 'Don't praise the Holy Spirit, praise the Lord.' Well, I learned to call on the Holy Spirit to help me when I want to know if something is the Lord's will or not. And it works."

Amy talked for an hour and a half, moving from biblical exegesis and quotations from scripture, to extemporaneous accounts of her family life, to charismatic theology. Everyone had a Bible and followed along with Amy, underlining and highlighting important passages. This Bible study approach, I would learn, was popular with nearly all modern born-again Christians. Bible courses, guidebooks, commentaries, and seminars were considered essential to building the faith. And the seriousness one carried to Bible study was considered a sign of the seriousness of one's faith. Many of the women at Women in the Word came equipped with different-colored markers. They used the colors to match up scriptures that seemed to complement each other. Some of their Bibles were so profusely marked that their pages seemed like paper quilts of yellow, pink, orange, and pale blue.

The language the women used blended American English with the arcane expressions of the Bible and their own religious slang. As she instructed her women's group to seek the spiritual high road, Amy Ciofrone said, "We must die to the flesh, no flesh must be exalted." When she described the wickedness of the world, she said, "I've been in the midst of the pit." In this "Biblese," God "convicts" people of His truth, and all of life is divided into things "of the world" and things "of God." This use of language sets born-again Christians apart from the rest of the world.

"When we become a Christian, it's like we're in a rowboat with a lot of people all rowing in one direction. They are the world," explained Amy. "When we become Christians, we turn around and try to go the other way. But you have to try to turn the boat around in a way that is not rude. The Lord speaks in a small voice. He's never rude. And He's always there for us."

To illustrate the point, she recalled that one of her sons had struggled with his homework the night before. "I said, 'Don't get angry about this. Mommy is always here to help you when you need it.' Well, Jesus is the same way. It's in the Bible. It says that God gives us strength and power." Instructing the group to turn to Acts, Chapter 1, Amy read aloud, "You shall receive the power when the Holy Spirit has come upon you; and you shall be my witnesses . . ." Holding up her Bible, Amy showed where she had crossed out the word "you" each time it appears, penning her name, "Amy," over it. "I believe God is speaking to me when I read this," she explained. "I read this to say, 'Amy shall receive the power.' " She paused for a moment and then added, "I just know God is speaking to me when I read this. Girls, discernment is the greatest gift God can give us. First you have to die to yourself, though. You have to let God's way be your way. The Bible says that when we comfort our flesh the spirit is weakened."

The women all said that God spoke to them as they went about their lives. They said the challenge was to hear what He was saying. When one woman said she had telephoned her sister as a surprise, another explained that "the Lord impressed on you to call." Another woman talked about how her neighbor, who didn't respond to her efforts to bring her to Jesus, is avoiding her now. Any outsider who has ever been hard pressed by a born-again believer would probably assume the neighbor had been put off by the proselytizing. Amy Ciofrone suggested the woman's neighbor withdrew "because the Lord is working on her now." The women in Amy's group could find God at work in every aspect of their daily lives.

Near the end of the study period, Amy captured the essence of her faith: "For me, Jesus is a real living person who is next to me, always. If my husband would let me," she added, "I'd set a place at the table for Jesus every night."

Frank Ciofrone had followed his wife into the charismatic lifestyle. But his journey into faith had been more cautious. For the first few years, while Amy was diving headlong into the world of tongues and everyday miracles, Frank stood to the side, happy with the sense of assurance his wife was developing, but unsure about the spiritual content of her new religious devotion.

Frank Ciofrone is a practical, cautious man. Slightly overweight and balding, he makes one concession to fashion—a neat mustache. He wore glasses and dressed in comfortable work clothes. When we met he was working on a renovation project in the Macy's store at the local shopping mall. He said he was happy with the job because it was near home and the work was steady.

At first, Frank recalled, he didn't understand Amy's new religion. Her stories, like the one about God showing her the shape of His hand so she could sculpt it in miniature, didn't make sense. But he saw that under the influence of charismatic Christianity, Amy no longer flirted with the liberal lifestyle that must have threatened their marriage during the period of their friendship with Sandra and Richie.

"She would do things for me around the house more willingly, like the Bible said, being obedient," Frank recalled, adding, "But it was more than that. She seemed happier."

At first, after Amy was "born again," friends warned Frank that his wife's religious convictions were too extreme. Some suggested he contact an anti-cult organization that would "deprogram" her. But he wasn't sure any deprogramming was needed. Never at ease with the modern model of marriage, Frank found he liked the changes in his wife. "Our relationship started to work more comfortably," he said. In the past, Frank said, Amy was often feisty and argumentative. "As she became a Christian she became much more submissive," Frank remembered. "I liked that."

Concerned about their souls, Amy worked hard to convert the rest of her family. Her parents were most receptive, and they too converted from Catholicism. When they became ill, Frank was impressed by the comfort they derived from born-again Christianity. At the same time, he met a steady stream of born-again Christians who had become Amy's new friends. Gradually, he adopted the faith as his own. He didn't have a strong, dramatic experience like Amy's encounter with Jesus on the Long Island Expressway. But he did come to discern God's hand in everyday events, whether it was finding a new house or getting a plum job. He joined his wife in attending Smithtown Gospel Tabernacle and grew increasingly confident, as the years passed, that born-again, Bible-based Christianity was the only way to heaven.

By the time they reached middle age, Amy's and Frank's views were more or less identical. They both believed in the Bible as the literal word of God, that only born-again Christians would go to heaven, and that American society was hopelessly corrupted by sin. But while they both believed in Jesus' supernatural presence, Frank did not talk about hearing the voice of God, whereas in Amy's life Jesus was so real she could almost hear him breathing over her shoulder. For Frank, faith was a more distant concept, as political as it was theological.

"Look, I'm not as spiritually oriented as other people, and I don't have a scripture I can quote for every situation. But I do wonder: 'Why am I here? Why do I beat my brains out every day at work and struggle through life?' The only answer has to be that there will be another life, in glory, after this one. There's a void in everyone's heart, isn't there? Well, this has filled mine." Recalling an old aphorism about death and taxes, Frank added a twist: "Now I know there are only two things that are certain in life: taxes and salvation."

Frank's faith imposed a kind of order on the world. Before he became a born-again Christian, he had worried about adjusting to a society that seemed to change faster than he could, even in the cloistered environment in which he lived. Events outside his control seemed to shake all the assumptions of his 1950s upbringing. The first real shock came with John F. Kennedy's assassination. He was then sixteen years old. "The Kennedy assassination was upsetting. It made no sense. But what is worse is the way there were never any real answers. The commission they had investigate it never really came up with conclusions. We were just left hanging. That's not right," he said.

The assassinations of the 1960s, followed by Watergate and the economic shocks of the 1970s, left Frank feeling that the world was falling apart. The Vietnam War, which TV spilled into America's living rooms, brought Frank a sense of duty. He was frightened, but his traditional patriotism led him to serve. A quirk of assignments kept him out of the war, though. He watched the last two painful years of Lyndon Johnson's presidency from his post as a guard for the President's helicopter.

After Vietnam, Frank and Amy set out to live the way their parents had. But an uncertain economy and the changing role of women challenged them. Frank and Amy held fast to some very traditional ideas about men and women. She was raised to take care of her husband, to clean the house and cook and raise her children. He was raised to expect that kind of care at home, in exchange for his hard work in the outside world. The Ciofrones were uncomfortable with the idea of women who had full-time careers and men like their friend Richie who refused to lead their families as traditional men. And they resented having to defend Amy's choice to stay at home with their children.

"Women got selfish," Amy interjected as Frank talked about feminism. "They had to get out of the house, they had to try to be just like men. Well, what has it gotten us? Divorce is sky high and children don't feel loved anymore. The most important part of being a mother is to be present, to be there for the children. Most aren't anymore."

As born-again Christians, the Ciofrones had found an outlook, and a community, that supported their struggle to live out the traditional family roles they had been taught by their parents. Conservative Christians place a heavy emphasis on traditional families. Women are encouraged to be "submissive" to their husbands' authority and men are encouraged to care for their wives as they would care for a child. Born-again preachers make the traditional family a holy ideal in their sermons, and TV evangelists routinely blame everything troubling America on the decline of the father-at-work/mother-at-home ideal.

Indeed, this ideal is so important to Christian America that many of the movement's organizations make annual awards to women who exemplify it. Eagle Forum, perhaps the most prominent and most politically powerful of the organizations for Christian women, was quite specific about who could win its Homemaker of the Year Award. According to the organization's rules, the winner must "live in the traditional family lifestyle: husband breadwinner with wife homemaker." She must have one child at home. She must use her husband's last name. And she must not earn more than $500 per year. In 1987 more than half the mothers in America worked outside the home and would thus have failed the Eagle Forum test for Homemaker of the Year. Even among conservative, born-again Christians there were millions of two-worker families. All those women were out of the running too. Economic pressures, divorce, and changing attitudes about women's roles had all pushed the typical American family further from the Eagle Forum's 1950s ideal. But the Ciofrones had made financial compromises—he drove a 1973 Dodge Dart to work—so they could have a "Christian home life," Frank said. Amy could qualify for Homemaker of the Year.

The traditional American family life was the dream the Ciofrones shared with the rest of orthodox America. Finding that life, in a world they believed was filled with evil and deception, was a daily struggle. The sense that Christian Americans are part of a great struggle between good and evil came through clearly at the Sunday-morning seminars the Smithtown church offered parents. I attended a session on the value of Christian education. The lecturer was Joe Attina, the principal of the tabernacle's school, who spoke to an audience of parents in a small auditorium that was part of the school.

Attina stood in front of the stage and spoke into a microphone that was held by a tall chrome-plated stand. A big man with a mustache and thick wavy brown hair, Attina described Christian education the way an Army drill instructor might describe boot camp. "Our children are not just little lambs to be eaten up by the wolves," he said, tugging at the vest of his dark blue suit. "We in the Christian schools prepare our children to deal with the wolves out there in the world. Christian schools can, in that way, be an ally, another weapon, in the fight against the enemy."

A few parents asked polite questions about the school, but it was clear that they really wanted Attina's advice about the everyday problems of child rearing. The parents were frightened about raising kids in the suburbs. "How do you keep a child focused on Jesus when the world is so distracting?" asked one mother. "How do you separate children from friends who are a bad influence?" said another. "You know what it's like on any street, kids and drugs, kids and sex, and my kids live right in the middle of that," said one father.

"Let's start at the beginning," answered Attina. "If a child misbehaves at any level, what is it? It's a sin. Make that clear to your kids. Then realize you have the right to decide what they do with themselves. I have that right with my kids and I exercise it with a vengeance."

One woman said her fifteen-year-old daughter stayed after hours at her job at McDonald's to socialize with other workers. She disapproved, but the girl wouldn't obey. Attina suggested that she force her daughter to choose her friends or her family. "You may have to back your child into a corner, and they may choose to leave home, but you have to be brave. God will eventually honor you for standing up for what is right."

With every answer, Attina made a pitch for Christian education, as if his salary depended on full enrollment. Children spend most of their waking hours at school, he noted. "Would you rather they spend them with people who will deal with them at the Lord's level, or with people who will deal with them at the world's level?" Children educated on the Lord's level are taught that evolution is an erroneous theory that cannot change the fact that God created the earth, and all its creatures, in seven days. They hear prayer at the start of class, and if they are having trouble, their teachers will take them into the hallway to pray. If they misbehave, Mr. Attina has a rod he will use to punish them. All parents who send their children to the school must agree that the rod can be used on their children.

The rod was one of the things that made the tabernacle school different. Guilt was another. "There was an empty bulletin board in the hallway and I asked two teachers to decorate it," Attina explained. "The teachers created an elaborate display, with a picture of a Bible, and the words 'You can be sure your sin will find you out!' It had quite an effect on the students."

Putting their children through the school also had quite an effect on the parents. The Ciofrones spent more than $3,000 a year to send their boys to the Smithtown Christian school. And they adopted the same child-guidance techniques the school uses. They kept a wooden dowel in a drawer and they didn't hesitate to use it. But the most effective child-rearing tool they employed was to harp on the constant presence of an all-seeing God who makes sure, as the bulletin board said, "your sin will find you out." A family legend, told by Amy, showed how well born-again religion can keep children in line.

"My older son, Paul, around the Fourth of July, came to me. He said, 'I have to confess something, Mom. I shot off a firecracker with Hans.'" Hans, who was not a born-again Christian, was Paul's best friend in the neighborhood.

"Anyway," added Amy, "Paul said, 'I know I'll have to stand before Jesus one day and he would want me to tell you about this.'"

"Well, I said to him, 'Didn't you hear the Holy Spirit tell you not to do it?'

"He said, 'Yes, but I did it anyway. I won't do it again, though.'"

Amy told another story, about a birthday party Paul was invited to attend. The party was to include a trip to the movies to see a *Star Wars* film. "It's about good and evil, but it's not God's good that wins, so it's a distortion," noted Amy. She decided that Paul couldn't go, but she relied on Jesus to explain why.

"I said, 'Paul, let me tell you what Jesus told me today about that movie. He said it wasn't a good movie for you to see.'" Amy remembered that she told Paul he could "ask Jesus" to change her mind, if he wanted to. "He said no, though, and he accepted it," said Amy.

Born-again Christian parents must often choose between the seem-ingly innocent ways of the world and the assumptions of their faith. There are some born-again Christians who believe all movies are evil, and that even Mickey Mouse cartoons are satanically inspired. Even more moderate believers can hold that festivities that seem innocuous to most people are intrinsically wrong. Halloween is an especially vexing time, because the whole world seems to participate in what nearly all serious born-again Christians, including the Ciofrones, be-lieve is the blatant worship of evil. When children come to Amy and Frank's door and cry, "Trick or treat," they are given Bible tracts. The Ciofrones tell their own children that dressing up to celebrate an ancient witches' holiday honors the evil spirits who are both real and everywhere.

"There is an enemy, Satan, and he is real and all around us," Amy told me seriously. "He is the one who tempts us to lie and steal and cheat and we must fight him. He is a person and he is real."

As he listened to Amy's stories, Frank winced slightly. He seemed almost to regret the hard lessons he had taught his children about Halloween, movies, and other secular evils. I asked if he thought such lessons were inappropriate for children so young. "No," he answered, "the road to heaven is narrow."

Indeed, the idea of death, followed by judgment and the great reward of heaven, is never far from the minds of most born-again Christians. Their theology stressed the inherent evil in the hearts of men, which was planted back in the garden with Adam and Eve. They believed that the world, already spinning out of control, was doomed to de-struction. They saw the evidence in any daily newspaper or television news program. Even the most random-seeming horrors of modern life can appear, to conservative, born-again Christians, as signs of the pervasive evil of the world. As Frank Ciofrone explained it, a mass murderer, to take an extreme case, is possessed by an evil spirit. Bad things happen, he said, because Satan and his minions are loose in the world and only those who are born-again can escape.

What is true for the individual, in conservative Christian thinking, is true for the world as a whole. The end of mankind is predicted in the foreboding end-times prophecies of the Book of Revelation. His-torically, conservative Christians have been particularly absorbed by apocalyptic prophecies. In the last half of the twentieth century, ever since the atom bomb made life-ending fire and brimstone possible, the prophecies have become an obsession. The battle is supposed to presage the return of Christ, who will reign for 1,000 years. Christians have been anxiously awaiting Christ's return to earth since the crucifixion. The period before his return is called the "pre-millennium." Frank Ciofrone, like most of the members of Smithtown Gospel Tabernacle, believed the horrors on the nightly news proved that Armageddon is coming and he was now living in that pre-millennial age.

To explain pre-millennialism, Smithtown Gospel Tabernacle offered a course on eschatology, the interpretation of the Bible's dire prophecies. The session I attended was held in a classroom at the Christian school, a room decorated with posters and scripture quotations. Across the top of the blackboard was the declaration: "God created the heaven and earth. The rest is up to you." Crammed into the small desks and chairs, the dozen adults who came to the class were very interested in the struggle for the earth and heaven's ultimate role. They were taught by a young lawyer who was a partner in a local firm filled with born-again Christian lawyers. Wearing a vest, tie, and white shirt, Joe Infranco struck a serious tone as he reviewed the competing theories on when and how Satan will rise up to rule the world, and how Jesus will, after the great war of Armageddon, return to reign over all.

Israel's creation in 1948 plays a critical role in nearly all the end-times theories. Certain passages in the Bible seem to refer to the restoration of Israel as a precondition for Christ's return to earth. Most charismatic theologians assert that roughly forty years after Israel's rise, or about 1988, the world will begin to suffer years of economic distress, natural disasters, and wars. Then a ruler will arise who will apparently rescue mankind, only to turn out to be the satanic Antichrist. The Antichrist will begin a massive, earth-destroying battle between good and evil. Christ will come to earth from heaven, end the fighting, and begin, literally, 1,000 years of heaven on earth.

Just what happens to the Christians during the fighting is a matter of great concern to born-again Americans. Some believe they will be lifted into the air in a "rapture" where they will be spared harm. Others say they will endure the battle but be reunited with Jesus. There is great debate among born-again Christians about when the rapture might happen, and some theorists even suggest that the years of suffering, the "tribulation," have already begun. A sizable end-times industry has arisen to support the debate, marketing videotapes, short courses, and study guides to feed Christian obsession with the topic.

Millions of books have been sold by authors who claim to have definitive interpretations of the prophecies.

"The Antichrist is a person," Infranco said as he explained the parts of the theories he considered most credible. "I believe there will be an assassination attempt on this man, who will be a great leader. But Satan will bring him back to life. Remember how upset everyone was when JFK was shot? Well, imagine that that happened, but then suddenly he was found to be alive and well. Wouldn't you think he was a great leader? Wouldn't the world think he was some kind of hero?"

"Wow!" gasped someone in the class.

"Anyway, the way I see it, there's going to be a war or something like that on earth, followed by great panic and fear. Then the world will turn to this authoritarian ruler, this Antichrist, to save it. The world economy will be interlinked as the ruler assumes control of everything. With credit cards and computers there is the capacity to do this. Computers will make that prophecy come true. A lot of it is already coming true."

"Joe, does that mean we're already in the great tribulation?" asked a man in the class.

"No," Infranco answered with a knowing smile. "If we were in the great tribulation, you'd know it."

Frank Ciofrone told me he thought the end-times prophecies must be true. The signs are all there, he said. "Things are much worse in the world than they have ever been." At the time we met, Democratic senator Gary Hart's promising presidential campaign was being dashed by an adultery scandal. The Reagan White House was besieged by the Contragate scandal. "Public officials lie, cheat on their wives, and renege on their promises," Frank said as he reeled off a status report on the state of the world. AIDS scared Frank Ciofrone to death. So did a long list of lesser dangers: murderers, rapists, natural disasters, and tragic accidents. A parade of fear passes in review on the nightly TV news, he said. Even the cartoons on television seemed to have turned evil. "In my day we watched *Sky King* and *Fury*. Today Saturday-morning TV is all destruction and mayhem. We don't let the kids watch that."

While Frank Ciofrone could see that man has made progress on earth—he acknowledged that men live longer, are better educated, and perhaps are more free than at any other time in history—he insisted that modern man had regressed morally. "Technology has brought us a lot of wealth, but morally, it doesn't help," he said. "Look at the space shuttle *Challenger,* how it blew up. That was man thinking he's smarter than God. We saw the ultimate result of that.

"America, which I think God helped create, is supposed to be a moral country, even a Christian country. There's no question about that. But there has been a turning away from God. Taking prayer out of the schools, that was a slap in God's face, for example. But ever since that time America has gone from being a country the world loved to one of the most hated."

Frank had concluded that the end times were at hand. Even leaving aside the decline of America that so troubled him, and the changing morality that so affronted him, Frank Ciofrone found in the nuclear age a host of problems that were, as near as he could discern, unsolvable. Consciousness itself, he seemed to be saying, had been fractured. He felt isolated from those who made decisions and threatened by the shadow of atomic Armageddon. Only through born-again religion could he maintain his sense of having some control over his own life and that of his family. "We get by, we rely on Jesus," he said. "The Bible says that Jesus told Christians to occupy the earth until he comes," added Frank Ciofrone. "That means bringing as many people to the Lord as possible."

The Ciofrones were like millions of Americans who joined the charismatic wing of the Great Revival of the 1980s. Like the fundamentalists at Second Baptist of Houston, they accepted Christian America's political and social agenda. But for them, the revival was, first and foremost, a personal, emotional phenomenon. For the charismatics, faith in a realm of spirits and supernatural forces made the problems of modern life on earth bearable. "The Holy Spirit teaches us that man may be evil and the world may be crazy," said Amy Ciofrone. "But at least we know we are saved."

= 3 =

Jerusalem

TELEVISION had drawn both Amy Ciofrone and John Cavallero into born-again America. It had fueled Second Baptist's transformation into a mega-church and it had formed the frame of reference for Amy Ciofrone's miracle on the Long Island Expressway. Similarly, the televangelists had been the catalysts for millions of conversions and had given new confidence to the born-again community. They were the architects of the entire crusade of the Christian Right. Growing into a billion-dollar-a-year industry by the middle of the decade, the TV ministries introduced millions of people to the basics of born-again faith, set the movement's conservative social agenda, and built the institutions to promote the born-again cause.

By 1987 the big-time evangelists had become larger-than-life figures, crisscrossing the country in private jets, appearing on the covers of *Time* and *Newsweek*, and extending their preaching crusades abroad. Their power seemed to baffle outsiders. To them, the TV preachers were unsophisticated, transparent hucksters. It was not the majority opinion. Shrewd and politically attuned, the preachers tapped the insecurity of the times and the basic religiosity of Middle America, appealing to both with a religiously inspired populism. Beginning gradually in the 1960s, they had built TV networks, colleges, resorts, retirement communities, and far-flung networks of missionaries. By the 1980s the evangelists' headquarters, large complexes of institutional buildings, were scattered across the countryside like medieval castles. Jimmy Swaggart held down the Deep South in Baton Rouge. Jerry Falwell surrounded himself with Liberty Baptist University in Virginia. The Bakkers built a Christian resort in South Carolina. Robert Schuller raised up the Crystal Cathedral in Southern California. The best and the brightest of the born-again community flocked to these complexes, hoping to be trained as modern crusaders who would bring the world to Jesus.

The oldest and most developed of the TV ministries belonged to Oral Roberts, of Tulsa, Oklahoma. Roberts, who had been a tent preacher in the 1940s and 1950s, was a pioneer in the field of modern evangelism. He moved into TV in the 1960s and soon had a national following. He was often compared with Rev. Billy Graham, who was active at the same time, but there was a tremendous difference between the two evangelists. Graham only occasionally preached on television and limited his focus mainly to matters of the soul. Roberts, the first hard-right, born-again crusader of the airwaves, made weekly national broadcasts. And his message included a social critique that called America back to old-fashioned patriotic conservatism. Roberts was also the first to use TV to raise huge sums of cash. Before cable TV brought Swaggart, Falwell, Robertson, and the rest into millions of homes, Roberts had already built an empire with his TV pitches. He was extraordinarily successful in convincing viewers that making a donation to Oral Roberts' ministry was much the same thing as making a donation in a church.

When I arrived in Tulsa, Roberts' fundraising tactics were under attack. The controversy had grown out of Roberts' ominous announcement that the medical school of Oral Roberts University was in dire financial need. He said that God might kill him if he didn't immediately raise $8 million to save the school. Roberts had, over the years, announced other communications from God. Sometimes he said Jesus, hundreds of feet tall, had appeared to him. In other cases he simply reported hearing a voice. This time, it seemed, God had spoken to him. The City of Faith medical school needed $8 million, or else. "I'm asking you to help extend my life," the aging, bespectacled Roberts told his television audience. Tears glistened in his eyes and his voice seemed to choke. "We're at the point where God could call Oral Roberts home." After his announcement he entered the prayer tower that dominates the Oral Roberts University campus to fast and pray for the $8 million.

This was too much, even for many of the people who had previously tolerated Roberts' fantastic visions. The world outside was appalled by Roberts' "give or God will kill me" message. The God who would call Roberts home if he failed to meet his quota seemed quite different from the God whom Roberts always described as "a good God, a loving God." Mainline Protestant and Catholic pastors attacked Roberts from their pulpits, and newspapers editorialized against his tactics. But the arguments didn't move the faithful. They gave, joining the campaign to save Oral Roberts. And remarkably, the last of the $8 million was delivered in a week. Roberts had been lampooned by Johnny Carson on the *Tonight* show and mocked by editorial cartoonists, but life went on as usual at ORU and the City of Faith.

I arrived in Tulsa late on a Saturday afternoon. A clerk at the car-rental agency circled the spot on the map where it said "Oral Roberts University" and told me, "You couldn't miss it if you tried." The Roberts complex was on the southern edge of town, where the city ends and the prairie and the oil wells and the cattle begin. Driving out there, I passed a huge billboard with a picture of a bearded Christ with flowing brown hair and the words: "Come Follow Jesus, The Church of God Prophecy." Just past the Jesus billboard was another sign, which said: "Let's Unite Under God and Save Our Country."

In the distance, looming over subdivisions and shopping strips, was the City of Faith hospital tower, topped by its flashing red light, which was needed to warn off low-flying aircraft. The tower was a wedge-shaped building, sixty stories high, with a façade of gold-colored metal. Next to it were two smaller towers. Together the buildings looked like a huge golden rocket ship straining to blast off. In front of the complex stood a bronze casting of sixty-foot-high hands joined in prayer. Across the street was Oral Roberts University. The spaceship metaphor was impossible to avoid. With its gold and white buildings shaped like cylinders and domes, ORU looked like a parking lot for flying saucers. In the center of the campus was a slender tower. Halfway up was a circular observation deck about forty feet in diameter. Topped by a gaslit flame, the tower looked like a 200-foot needle piercing a saucer.

I parked my car between the tower and the Mabee Center. The center, named for an Oklahoma oilman who had donated the money for the place, was actually two cylindrical buildings. The larger one housed the basketball arena where the ORU Titans played. The smaller one, which everyone called Baby Mabee, was where the Roberts TV shows were produced.

Before traveling to Tulsa I had telephoned Jan Dargatz, one of Roberts' aides, to ask if I would need a special pass to move about the campus.

"Do you have a beard?" she had asked.

"Well, yes, I do. Why?" I had said.

"I just guessed. A lot of journalists seem to have beards. Anyway, we don't allow the people who live and work here to have beards. So security is bound to notice you. Just don't worry about it. I'll tell them you are coming and they'll know it's you. They won't bother you." Dargatz said that about a thousand high school seniors from around the country would be attending a three-day get-acquainted session at the time I was going to be there. "With all the visitors we're expecting, security is ready for some different-looking people," she said.

Dargatz had suggested that my first stop on campus be an after-dinner meeting in the Mabee Center for the visiting high-schoolers. As I walked inside, the auditorium of Baby Mabee was stifling. Hundreds of students packed the bowl-shaped studio, occupying all the steeply banked rows of seats that descended from the entrance. The studio floor, about three stories down from the rim of the bowl, contained several different sets. There was a "living room" setting in the foreground. Behind the living room was a row of tables with telephones. A big map of the United States decorated the right side of the stage. To the left was a grand piano and a small orchestra pit and, on the back wall, a sign that said: "Faith Makes Miracles."

Kneeling in the middle of the floor, lit by a spotlight, was a slightly built black man wearing a shiny black dinner jacket, white pants, a bright white shirt, and a deep red tie. He was curled over a microphone, finishing a song in a hoarse whisper:

> *Fear not, my child,*
> *I'm with you always.*
> *I know how to care*
> *For what belongs to me.*

The students waited for a few beats after he finished before applauding. As the noise spilled down from the banked seats, Carlton Pearson stood up. Perspiring, he smoothed out his shiny black jacket and adjusted the long red handkerchief that was tucked into his breast pocket. Then a smile came to his face.

"Oh yeah. Oh yeah," he said, beginning to grin. "We bad. We baaaad!"

It was stage blackness, just enough to tickle the young white students, but not enough to make them uncomfortable.

"When I came here to school, the university was at its peak," Pearson said as the applause died away. "It was easy to come here. We didn't suffer the severity of the attacks Christians are enduring today. I'm sure you read the magazines and newspapers and you watch the TV. I'm glad you still had the guts to come here and see for yourselves. You didn't write off Oral Roberts because of what the media was saying.

"Let me tell you!" he suddenly shouted. "Anyone who comes here today has to have a lot of guts, a lot of conviction. You came to see this place for yourselves. If you have questions I advise you to look at Acts, chapter 20, verse 22."

He paused, waiting for the students to open their Bibles and find the relevant passage in Acts.

"In it Paul says he felt compelled, by the Holy Spirit—by the Holy Spirit!—to go to Jerusalem. Jerusalem! When I was considering being a student here, I was not compelled by a faculty member, a professor, or my parents and family. I reached an intersection where I was compelled by the Holy Spirit. And this is that same intersection in your lives. Well, if you feel the Holy Spirit is compelling you to come to ORU, that's answer enough for your questions."

Pearson never mentioned the specific criticisms that had been leveled at Oral Roberts. He didn't talk about God's $8 million threat. Instead, he asked the students, in vague terms, to ignore the picture of Roberts presented on the nightly news and listen instead to his message. "Many of you will feel a strong compulsion to go to ORU, to come to Jerusalem," he continued. "But you worry about going here because of what Dan Rather said or what Ted Koppel said." Pearson paused and then began a dramatic, staccato speech:

"Well, let me tell you.

"The Bible says that one day all men will kneel. Every knee will bow before Him."

Pearson paused and smiled.

"Tom Brokaw will bow!

"Ted Koppel will bow!

"Peter Jennings will bow!"

As Pearson went on, shouting louder and faster, the audience began to applaud. Some shouted, "Amen!"

"Dan Rather will bow!"

"Amen! Amen!"

"Castro will bow!

"Gorbachev will bow!

"Cockamamie Khomeini will bow!"

With his last line, the high-schoolers rose in a standing ovation, whipped up like a crowd at a pep rally. From Brokaw to Iran's Ayatollah Khomeini, Pearson had defined Christian America's enemies and declared them vanquished.

"Sometimes you've got to be forceful. As a Christian you have to take a stand," he cried above the applause. He stiffened and grew quiet. Raising the microphone to his lips, he chanted in an even voice:

"I am a tree. I am planted. I will not be move-ed," he said. "Now, repeat after me."

The students joined Pearson's chant.

I am a tree. I am planted. I will not be move-ed.
I am a tree. I am planted. I will not be move-ed.
I am a tree. I am planted. I will not be move-ed.

After the chanting Pearson stretched his arms out to ask for quiet. He waved his hands, as if they were the branches, and the students gradually settled down. Pearson had one last thing to say:

"You know, brother Roberts is going to be seventy this year. He doesn't need anything more in his life. If he goes tomorrow he's leaving behind a world-class university, a medical center, and Lord knows what else.

"But I went to him when he was fasting in the prayer tower and, you know, he looked like he was going to kick the bucket. Well, he told me to sit down with him. But it was like an order. You know, like 'Sit down, son!' And you know what he said? He said, 'A prophet never says please.' Well, I'm not going to either."

The houselights came up. In a normal tone of voice, Pearson told the students to enjoy their weekend, especially the basketball game that was to be played that night. Quietly the students turned and climbed the steep steps out of Baby Mabee and into the adjacent arena. The Titans were already on the court, warming up for a game, and ushers, ORU students dressed in jackets and ties, shepherded the students down a corridor and straight into the gym.

I fell in line with the students and introduced myself to one of them, a tall, blond young man from South Dakota. He was accompanied by an ORU student who was acting as a guide. The Dakotan was an eighteen-year-old named Mark McMillan. McMillan was one of a few of the weekend visitors who were already attending college. He said he was interested in transferring to ORU because his school, Northern State College, "is geared to the needs of the world. I'm out of sync there. Spiritually, culturally, educationally, I think of it as a desert."

McMillan was a recent convert to conservative Christianity and seemed more interested in discussing creationism—"Evolution is a joke," he told me—than in talking about Oral Roberts University. His guide, an ORU junior named Keith Goljan, soon turned the conversation back to the school. Heavily muscled, Goljan wore a fashionable softly spiked, short haircut and a loud sweatshirt featuring a picture of a bighorn sheep and the words: "Tuff Sheep. Baaad to the Bone." The Tuff Sheep turned out to be the name of his dormitory floor's intramural team. He said he was a resident assistant who supervised the third floor of Hughes Hall and volunteered to walk me around the campus. "But tomorrow," he insisted. "Now I want to pay attention to the game."

Before I could leave McMillan and Goljan, the lights dimmed and a spotlight was trained on the locker-room entrance to the gym floor. In the darkness an announcer bellowed, "Here come the Titans." As the team was introduced, Goljan and I made a date to meet. As the announcer said a prayer for the players, Mark McMillan said to me in a whisper, "I'll pray for you too."

The Titans, who lost a sloppy game against North Texas State, were, in fact, more important as an evangelistic tool than as an athletic team. Roberts had hoped to have a nationally recognized team that would attract attention to the school and its Christian mission. He had often explained that God told him to sponsor the team for these reasons. The effort peaked in 1974, when the Titans made it into the NCAA tournament. Since then, however, the team had suffered from coaching changes and morale problems. Many of ORU's players were young blacks recruited from urban areas whose interest in Christianity trailed well behind their desire to become pro players. When they got to ORU they found themselves in an environment dominated by conservative Christian values and very specific rules about dress, travel off campus, dating, and virtually every other aspect of life. To make matters even more difficult, star athletes were all housed in a special dormitory. Because so many of them were black, the dorm became a racial as well as athletic ghetto, isolating the players from the rest of the students. Each season, it seemed, some of the recruits left abruptly. Others muddled through, never playing up to their ability.

At halftime, I struck up a conversation with Jo Ann Smith, a middle-aged Tulsa woman who had come to the game with her brother. While a former Miss America from Mississippi stood at center court and sang gospel songs accompanied by recorded music, Mrs. Smith tried to explain the relationship between ORU and Tulsa.

"I don't support Oral Roberts, but a lot of people do and I'm not about to criticize them," she said. "There are people here who made it quick in oil and gas and they still have old-time religion, so they give to Oral. And there are people like my brother, who's here from out of town, who support him because they believe." Looking down the row of seats where her brother sat engrossed in the halftime show, she added, "The world is so complex. I think believing makes it easier for him."

The next day was Sunday and I returned to the campus, joining a handful of pilgrims who were visiting the prayer tower. Keith Goljan had said he would be at church in the morning, and I wasn't scheduled to meet him until noon. The prayer tower stood on a low, treeless hill just behind the Mabee Center. It was surrounded by fountains and sunken gardens filled with low evergreens. When I saw them, the fountains and their pools were blue concrete basins collecting dried leaves and dirt. Small signs said the water had been turned off to save energy. Concrete walkways led me through the gardens to the prayer-tower entrance, two bronzed-glass doors that looked like golden mirrors.

Inside the base of the tower were a gift shop, an elevator to an observation deck, and the cave-like entrance to a multimedia show about Oral Roberts' life. A few people waited in chairs outside the doorway to the show. I took the elevator up the inside of the needle to the saucer-shaped observation room and took in the panoramic view of the campus. With the other visitors I walked around the outside edge of the saucer, stopping to read small cards which described the view. The middle of the saucer was partitioned by mauve-colored

VERNON REGIONAL
JUNIOR COLLEGE LIBRARY

plastic walls with narrow doors. Behind the doors were prayer rooms reserved for private reflection.

Back downstairs, in the base of the needle, the small gift shop offered postcards and ORU T-shirts and all the books written by Oral and others in the Roberts family. I was in time to take the tour of Oral Roberts' life, so when a young woman in a blue blazer announced the next show, I lined up with the other Sunday-morning visitors. She ushered us into a darkened hallway. We waited a moment and then heard a scraping sound followed by a pneumatic whoosh. A door slowly opened at the end of the short hallway and we all walked forward, into Oral Roberts' life.

The first scene was of a weathered farmhouse on the prairie. It was supposed to be Oral's father's house. Overhead, a woman's voice announced the birth of a baby, Granville Oral Roberts. Then there were the voices of children taunting. "Stutter for us, Oral, come on, stutter," they said.

From there, we followed more whooshing and opening doors through scenes of Oral's bout with tuberculosis, his miraculous recovery, his early days as a preacher, national tent crusades, and TV shows. The doors swung open and shut and we viewers were moved from room to room; six rooms, six minutes per.

The life of Oral Roberts, as it was sketchily outlined in the rooms behind the automatic doors, was in reality a summing up of the course of conservative Christianity in twentieth-century America. After all, Roberts, more than anyone else, had transformed the backwoods, born-again religion of the early part of the century into the 1980s television movement of the Christian Right. He was the role model for Pat Robertson and Jimmy Swaggart and every other TV evangelist who would follow with similar blends of preaching, music, miracle stories, and fundraising pitches; the multimedia show made his connection to those later TV preachers more evident.

Roberts was born in 1918 in an Oklahoma that was still an untamed place, with Old West saloons and plenty of Indians, cowboys, and drifters. His name—Oral—was selected by a relative who just liked the sound of the word. As a small boy, Oral stuttered, but it didn't seem to inhibit him. He was a good student and a gifted athlete. Later in life he would joke that he and his brother Vaden were the most mischievous boys in the county. His father, Ellis, was a poor pastor and evangelist who dragged a portable organ across rural Oklahoma preaching to farmers and small-town families. Authorized and un-authorized biographies of Roberts describe his early life as nearly destitute. On many days his father and mother, Claudius, had trouble feeding their family. But Oral, as he never tired of telling his followers later, dreamed of greatness. In his book *Oral Roberts: An American Life*, historian David Harrell wrote: "As a small overalled boy, his sharp eyes peered out at a world that had passed the Roberts family by; yet in his fertile mind danced dreams of grandeur."

The Oral Roberts religious legend begins in the midst of the Great Depression, when, as a teenager, he was stricken by tuberculosis. He spent long months in bed. Faithful Pentecostals, the Robertses believed that God answered prayer with healing. So when a traveling evangelist came to the nearby town of Ada, they decided to take Oral there in search of a miracle. Riding in a car on the way to the service, young Oral believed he heard the voice of God assure him: "I am going to heal you and you are going to take My healing power to your generation."

On that night, evangelist George Moncey, who was conducting the revival in a hot, crowded tent, prayed for scores who had come to be healed. It was almost midnight when he got to Roberts. He ordered the boy to stand and then prayed for God to heal him. Then he "commanded" the illness to leave Oral's body. "Loose him and let him go free!" cried the preacher. According to the legend, young Oral jumped onto the stage and shouted, "I'm healed! I'm healed!"

Roberts' recovery would still take months, and he would suffer setbacks, but the family were convinced that Oral had been healed that night. And Oral took very seriously what he believed God had told him on the ride to Ada. He followed his father into the ministry and, after a short time pastoring small churches, became a traveling evangelist. A handsome man with dark hair and high cheekbones, Roberts was bright, and passionate—a fiery speaker, preaching to ever-larger crowds. By the end of World War II, Roberts had become a national leader in the Pentecostal movement. By 1948 he was hauling a huge, circus-style tent back and forth across America, pitching it in parking lots and pastures and preaching, eventually, to millions.

As he traveled the country, Roberts built an enormous personal following with a combination of oratory and faith healing. He also melded the thousands of little churches and independent preachers of the Pentecostal faith into a genuinely cohesive movement for the first time. Roberts became the Pentecostals' national spokesman, presenting a forceful, confident image to the outside world while giving the faithful the sense of belonging to something bigger than their local church.

In the 1960s, Roberts saw that attendance at his crusades had peaked and he appears to have grown tired of the grind. He had watched the development of TV with fascination and saw in it a powerful way to bring the tent revivals into people's homes. After consulting with experts in the field, he settled on a style in which his born-again message would be presented in the format of a variety show. Indeed, he recruited many of the same guest stars who were appearing on the Ed Sullivan show—Jimmy Durante, Mahalia Jackson, Johnny Mathis, Jerry Lewis, Johnny Cash, and Pearl Bailey. These early TV shows made born-again belief seem glamorous. Singers drawn from the well-scrubbed ORU student body (the university had been built at the same time), beauty queens, and wholesome stars such as Pat Boone and Dale Evans attracted large audiences for prime-time specials aired over hundreds of stations. The little boy from rural Oklahoma was the first born-again preacher to succeed in presenting conservative Christianity as a modern, prosperous movement, severing it forever from its hillbilly image. "God is a good God," he cried over and over.

At the same time, Roberts was revolutionizing religious fundraising techniques. His television programs and barnstorming tent crusades had enabled him to gather long lists of contributors, whom he referred to as "partners." In the 1960s, Roberts, who had always been fascinated by new technologies, was one of the first to recognize the implications of computers for mass fundraising. He bought IBM computers and used them to store the names and addresses of his supporters nationwide. With this equipment, he sent out millions of letters to his flock, each of which appeared to be a personal communication. Through the letters, Roberts' followers had the impression of being in direct contact with him. He would send out appeals and the partners would answer with money and letters of their own. These letters poured into Roberts' headquarters every day. They were answered by computer operators who selected approved paragraphs designed to address categories of problems—sickness, poverty, marital difficulties, etc. The letters established a flow of money to the ministry. But, perhaps more than anything, they illustrated the loneliness of twentieth-century American life. The partners gave gladly, exchanging five or ten dollars a month for a letter and the feeling that Oral Roberts cared about them.

By 1987, the Oral Roberts ministry was the most advanced born-again organization in the country. Thanks to the partners' contributions, Roberts was able to diversify and to build the $500 million complex that included ORU and the City of Faith. At times his followers sent as much as $2 million a week. Roberts became so highly visible that by the 1980s he was one of the most recognized figures in American life. One poll, in 1980, found that Roberts was recognized by more people than Presidents Jimmy Carter and John F. Kennedy.

The tour of Roberts' life had left me feeling a little disoriented as I walked slowly across the glittering campus to Keith Goljan's dormitory. Keith met me in the doorway of his room. He wore only shorts, displaying his bodybuilder's physique, which was so developed as to be almost top-heavy. He seemed a bit self-conscious and quickly told me that his father, a former Navy doctor who was now on staff at City of Faith hospital, was also a fitness fanatic. He pointed to a canister of protein powder on the dresser in his room and said his mother had given it to him. "She's anorexic, or something," he said. "She thought I'd like to try it. I heard anorexia is some kind of demon, but I don't know if I believe that."

As we sat in his room, Keith described a life dominated by religious faith. In that context, there was nothing outlandish in the idea that his mother's anorexia was caused by a demon. Like many others in the modern born-again movement, he was not from a Protestant fundamentalist background. His father had been raised in a devoutly Catholic family in suburban New York and had attended Mass every day, and even briefly considered becoming a monk. "My dad is a very hard-core person," said Keith. "He's not very emotional at all." He recalled his father's stories about hard physical workouts in bitter-cold weather. He is a man, said Keith, "who is extremely disciplined."

Keith's mother was also raised a Catholic, and when her children came along, she enrolled them in parochial schools. The family's drift into born-again faith began when his mother got involved with a charismatic Catholic group. At the time, the Goljans had settled in Phoenix, Arizona, after Keith's father retired from the Navy. Mrs. Goljan introduced her family to the charismatic Catholic movement, and as her own zeal grew, the whole family converted to charismatic Protestantism. Keith was transferred to a Christian elementary school and declared himself a born-again Christian.

When Keith was a freshman in high school his father signed on as a pathologist at the City of Faith. For the first time Keith found himself in a public school. He was surprised to discover how sheltered his upbringing had been. "I was always small for my size, not real popular, a geek really," he said with a self-deprecating smile. "I didn't know anything about sex or drugs or drinking. People made jokes and they just went over my head." The worst moment of all came in wrestling practice during his first year at the public high school. There, in front of a coed group, a teammate yanked Keith's gym shorts to the floor. He was so humiliated by his own physical weakness that he signed up for the school's weight-lifting program the very next day. Weight lifting transformed him, he told me. It led to the first male friendships in his new school and to a new sense of self-assurance. "I only stayed with people who were weight lifters. That was kind of limiting, I guess. A lot of people aren't weight lifters. In college I've learned to appreciate them, too."

When he graduated from high school, Keith never even considered another university. At ORU he could avoid drinking and drugs ("I always want complete control of myself") and the taunts of antagonistic nonbelievers. He said he was also inspired by Oral Roberts and his family. But more than anything, the atmosphere at ORU—Christian, separatistic, and serious—drew him to the school.

Despite its futuristic veneer, Oral Roberts University was much like a 1930s college. Male and female students were strictly separated, and curfews were enforced for both. There were rules banning sexy posters and profane language, against student protests and petitions. School officials inspected dorm rooms to make sure they were clean and checked to see that men's hair was cut short. Women were required to wear skirts or dresses, and men had to wear ties, to the cafeteria, to classes, and to the library.

These rules were one of the main reasons why parents sent their children to ORU. But more important than the rules was ORU's standing as a separatistic, Christian school with full academic accreditation. Secular colleges and universities frightened some conservative Christian parents, who imagined them, often correctly, as overwhelmingly secular places, where students were exposed to drugs, alcohol, and leftist ideas. But since these parents also wanted their children to get real degrees, diplomas that would be recognized by employers and graduate schools, ORU was attractive. There, students received academic training but escaped the mind-broadening challenge of fellow students who might hold different religious, social, and political ideals. This was exactly what Keith Goljan was looking for when he enrolled at ORU.

After I listened to his short monologue on the virtues of ORU and Christian education, I asked Keith what problems he had. The first thing he said was: "I'm obsessed with sex." Students may be obsessed with sex at ORU, but they are not allowed to do anything about it. Keith said that suited him just fine, except for the tension between desire and control. "Sex should be in marriage because, I think, it should involve a commitment. For that reason, I have never gone to bed with a girl. I've come close, but I never let it get physical."

To bolster his control, Keith said he had thrown out the posters of scantily clad women he once kept secreted in his room and replaced them with pictures of fast cars. He said the threat of pregnancy can also be a strong ally in the struggle for sexual control, especially for someone morally opposed to abortion. A couple who "willfully has sex," he explained, "should have to deal with the consequences of that act. And I'm against abortion. It is morally wrong, except, maybe, in cases of rape."

Physical education, that famous distraction from sex, was heavily emphasized at ORU. Every student had to participate in an exercise program and pass an annual fitness test. But Keith went further, augmenting his involvement in intramural sports with intensive weight lifting. He also took on the responsibilities of serving as a resident assistant. The RAs, as they were called, each supervised a floor of a dormitory, acting as counselor, policeman, friend, and adviser to fellow students.

When we left his room for a walk on campus, Keith steered us straight to the gym. We passed through the main building used for classrooms and stopped to admire the new baseball stadium. Inside the gym, Keith showed me the swimming pool, rows of basketball courts, the weight room, a gymnastics arena, and racquetball courts. In the weight room, he told me that he not only lifted weights himself but tried to get the students on his floor involved as well.

"I've noticed that some of the guys who come here, many of them actually, have a lot of feminine characteristics. Maybe it's because they were raised more by their mothers or are from broken homes. Anyway, when I find some who are too fem, I teach them to talk in a deeper voice or lift weights. I've seen a lot of change in some guys."

As we walked back to his room, past the isolated, ghettolike dorm that housed ORU's star athletes, Keith confessed his one major short-coming. "I'm not completely sold out, spiritually, to Jesus," he said. At ORU, the big men on campus were the ones who had "sold out," committed their entire beings to Christian faith, he explained. Keith said he would deposit me in the room of a friend who "is one of the most sold out on campus. He'll tell you what walking with Jesus is really like."

Keith then went on to explain that there was some smoking and some drinking on campus, but that relatively few students indulged. And the ban on dancing, ORU's concession to the strictest Christian parents, was strictly maintained.

Back at Hughes Hall, Keith took me upstairs to Eric Casto's room. Eric was dressed in gym shorts and a plain T-shirt. Taller and thinner than Keith, he had blond hair and the softly dazed look of someone awakened from a nap.

"This is Michael. He's a writer from New York," said Keith. "I've been showing him around, but he wanted to meet someone who has really sold out."

"OK, I'd love to explain it," said Eric.

"Well, I guess this is it," said Keith, sticking out his hand to shake mine. "Call me if you need any help."

Eric got right to the point. "Look," he said. "The turning point came for me last spring—May, I guess. I was involved in a relationship that was ruining my life. I was desperate. I couldn't stand it anymore."

The problem, it turned out, was that Eric had become sexually involved with a girl. "She was a bit younger than me and, really, neither of us could take it." Tortured by his feelings of guilt, Casto said, he turned to the Bible. Like many born-again Christians, he believed that the Holy Spirit could guide him to meaningful Bible verses that would help solve any problem. The first verse he read that day was from Second Chronicles. "My people, who are called by My name," the verse reads, "humble themselves and pray and seek My face and turn away from their wicked ways . . ."

Eric said he broke off his relationship, immersing himself instead in Bible study and his local church. "I learned the difference between Christians and lukewarm Christians. Jesus was completely sold out for God. Now God's looking for people who are completely sold out too. Those lukewarm people are going to lose in the end. I know it isn't enough to say you are a Christian. You have to live like one."

At ORU, Eric lived in a born-again frenzy. He was, he said, trying to live as he imagined Christ would. He joined a group that attended local rock concerts, proselytizing fans as they went in and out. "I was at a Kiss concert recently," he said proudly. "I saw people doped out, high, girls half naked." Kiss is one of many heavy-metal rock bands whose outlandish performances are filled with allusions to satanism. The band draws a young audience, entranced by fantasies of Devil worship and violence. At the concert, Eric recalled, a young man had approached and taunted him. "He came out with a really rough voice and said, 'I'm going to hell.' Well, he might have been demon-possessed," said Eric. "I told him Jesus loves him."

Eric said that sex was the demon that had almost captured his soul. For others it might be witchcraft, rock and roll, or drugs. "To fight the demons you have to let Jesus into your heart. Then it's a lot easier," he said. At ORU, Eric said, he was able to live secure as a Christian while training to be a minister. He said he wanted to take the gospel overseas as a missionary—work that would, he hoped, be sponsored by Oral Roberts. He defended Roberts' fundraising techniques, arguing that the existence of ORU and the City of Faith proved that God believed in Oral Roberts too. "A lot of people criticize Oral Roberts and ORU. They say the school is weird, isolated. Well, ORU prepares people to go into the world and be Christians at the same time. This place is important to the Christian way of life for that reason."

Eric got up from the desk where he was sitting and put on a shirt and a tie. It was time for dinner. "The Richard Roberts show does introduce a lot of people to ORU," he said as we left the room for the twilight. "You ought to check that out tomorrow."

Richard Roberts Live was broadcast five days a week from the Mabee Center. That program and Oral Roberts' own Sunday show provided the real connection between the ministry and the thousands of donors across the country. People like Eric Casto had grown up watching both shows, and the experience had made them all but a captive audience for ORU and the City of Faith. Indeed, the viewing audience as a whole served both as prospective students for the university and, more lucratively still, as patients for the hospital.

The programs were taped in the same large studio where the high-schoolers had attended Carlton Pearson's sermon the night of the basketball game. When I arrived there the next day, I introduced myself to Andrea Tyner, the assistant to the producer. Though it was only an hour before the 10 a.m. taping, she answered my questions patiently. Andrea said she tried to book guests who might appeal to secular as well as Christian audiences. The program had a talk-show format, and though it was heavy on preachers and Christian singers, conservative businessman Adolph Coors and comedian Jerry Lewis had been two recent guests "and they didn't really talk about Jesus at all, even though Richard tried," she said.

As the red "On Air" light blinked over the door, Tyner led me to the studio, where an audience of about fifty people waited in the front rows of the large auditorium. The guest that day was James Robison, a beefy, middle-aged Southern Baptist evangelist with a traditional fire-and-brimstone style. But before Robison and Richard Roberts bore in on their religious message, the audience was treated to a lineup of singing and reports on life in the City of Faith.

The singers and the large backup band were drawn from the ORU student body. Given the constraints of their material, they were skillful and obviously well trained. Richard Roberts was the ORU music department's star graduate and his father's most dependable child. The Roberts family had been shaken by tragedies—one son had committed suicide and a daughter and son-in-law had been killed in a plane crash. Richard had followed his father's plan for his career. He began as a singer on his father's programs and eventually became an evangelist himself, conducting his own crusades. The fact that he was entrusted with the ministry's most important link with the outside world, the daily television program, testified to his importance in Oral Roberts' organization.

Richard came on and sang a gospel song, then joined his wife, Lindsay, on a sofa in the living-room set and began to read aloud from letters that had come in from around the country. Richard and Lindsay had obviously groomed themselves to look like their audience's mental image of an all-American couple. He is tall, with a firm chin and a stunning pouf of brown hair combed dramatically high and back. He wore an expensive-looking suit and a bright white shirt. She is a slender, brown-haired woman with pale skin and delicate features. She wore a blue suit and high white boots. A lacy collar framed her face. She smiled submissively at her husband while he talked—another manifestation of the ideal notion of marriage that the Robertses wanted to project—dropping her smile only when the TV camera turned away. Flipping through the letters, they alternated reading brief summaries of the messages.

"Here's one from California," said Lindsay. "A lump under the arm healed."

"Here's a three-year-old boy who had ear problems. He can now hear perfectly," echoed Richard.

As they talked, one could hear phones ringing at a phone bank where older women, all volunteers, answered the "prayer line," a telephone number viewers could call to donate money and request a prayer. The number was frequently flashed on the viewers' screens during the broadcast and Richard occasionally reminded viewers to call. In reality, these calls provided an ever-growing supply of new names and addresses for the Roberts organization's computerized list of donating partners. As long as the prayer line kept on humming, the ministry would roll on, inexorable as a chain letter.

The ringing of the telephones added a sense of drama to Richard and Lindsay's review of the day's mail.

Ring, ring.

"From Pinehill, North Carolina, more pain in the head cured."

Ring, ring.

"From Waterbury, Connecticut, a healing of a shoulder."

After they finished reading the letters, Richard introduced a short video report from Africa, where Oral Roberts-sponsored missionaries were opening a clinic. When the tape was over he smiled broadly, looked straight into the camera, and delivered a reminder that was his father's trademark: "I tell you, God is a good God!"

What was most remarkable about *Richard Roberts Live* was that it seemed to have more commercials—invariably fundraising pitches for the Robertses' various ministries—than even the most successful network sitcom. Most of the advertisements were about the City of Faith hospital and were intended to draw the sick to Tulsa. "If you need surgery," said Richard Roberts, "remember, we do surgery every day at the City of Faith—orthopedic surgery, general surgery, even neurosurgery. Holy Spirit-filled doctors are here for you." Another taped message about the City of Faith reminded viewers to make an appointment and confirm their insurance coverage in order to qualify for a free airline ticket to Tulsa.

"Remember," Richard added, "our chief of surgery, who is a cancer specialist, is standing by for you."

The morning's broadcast also included fundraising appeals for ORU student scholarships. Clearly Oral's controversial $8 million threat had not raised enough cash. The medical college, it turned out, was still short about $500 per student. As he asked for donations, Richard reminded viewers that they could use "MasterCard, Visa, American Express, or the Discover Card."

In a way, the pitches were the most exciting parts of the show, and the featured guest, James Robison, was, if anything, an anticlimax. A galumphing, big-fisted preacher with a huge pile of wavy hair, Robison lumbered onto the living-room set and gave a short speech. He only alluded to the credibility crisis Oral Roberts had suffered after his "give or God will kill me" announcement.

"Oral is a Christ-like man, a broken man, a teachable man," said Robison as he sat with Richard Roberts. "Television preachers are suffering, but people who can hear God have to stand together. We as Baptists have heard the word and my wife has been healed, my children have been healed. I've seen miracle after miracle."

Then Robison turned away from Roberts and stared directly into the camera, momentarily upstaging his host. All of a sudden, it was the James Robison show. "Living and giving is a lifestyle. We're being purified and purged right now, but this ministry is so worthy of your support. My son Randy attends school here. If you close up your heart and your finances, everything will suffer."

For the last fifteen minutes of the program, Robison and Roberts stood and prayed together, at first for themselves but then for the people in the audience and for their families. They even prayed for the success of their own ministries. At the very end of the show, Richard closed his eyes, put his hand up near his temple, and swayed a bit. He looked as if he was listening, very intently, to a sound no one else had heard.

"Concerning the cancer in your stomach, I rebuke you, foul cancer," he said loudly. After a pause he added, "The cancer in the stomach, in Jesus' name, I curse you."

Suddenly the orchestra started playing and the audience applauded, on cue. Richard's mysterious telepathic receptions, and his program, were over. He waved goodbye to the crowd, turned, and walked quickly backstage with Robison following behind him. In the auditorium, I fell in line with the rest of the audience, which went out into the hallways of the Mabee Center. There I heard still more Christian music, rock-and-roll chords with lyrics about "the Lord" and "salvation." A guest band was warming up for the mandatory chapel meeting for ORU students, which was held in the basketball arena twice each week. I wandered into the arena to listen.

The band, which was running through a few of its pieces, was a born-again Christian pop band called Truth. I recognized them because I had seen them a year earlier, at the homecoming celebration of Liberty Baptist University in Lynchburg, Virginia. I had gone there to write an article about evangelist Jerry Falwell, whose own born-again empire was every bit the equal of Roberts'. In Virginia I had met Truth's leader, an amiable man named Roger Breland. Truth was a successful troupe, laboring in the middle range of Christian entertainment, below big-name singers such as Amy Grant but well above traveling church choirs. Breland was a former music teacher and preacher from Mobile, Alabama. Each year he and his twenty-one musicians and singers spent more than three hundred days on the road, traveling more than a hundred thousand miles in a private bus.

I found Breland near the entrance to the Mabee Center, where he was arguing with the building's manager over where he could set up tables laden with Truth T-shirts, records, and caps. The manager wanted the display away from the main entrance to the hall. He was worried that if there was an emergency, the tables would block the exit. Breland wanted them where the students could buy easily. Souvenir sales are important for groups that depend on a "love offering" collection to pay their expenses. Eventually Breland won the argument. Reminding Breland that we had met before, I helped him move the folding tables to the better location.

During the service, Truth's music, soft Christian rock, spoke of struggles with sin, the challenge of being a Christian, and love for Jesus. Music and drama were popular courses at ORU and the students appreciated the well-crafted performance. When it was over, Richard Roberts arrived to give a little sermon. It was about basketball. Another game would be played that night, and Richard was calling on the students to turn out and support the team.

"Our athletic department is turning around," he said, "but it didn't get in this mess overnight, so it won't get out of it overnight either. But I for one am going to support the Titans this year. If the city of Tulsa wants to buy a ticket, they can come. But we're going to have this season for our ORU family, and that's enough for me."

After the show and the sermon, eager students surrounded Roger Breland. They wanted auditions. He listened carefully to each one, tilting his head like a judge leaning over the bench to hear a lawyer's private argument. To each one he explained that there were no openings. After dealing with the procession of supplicants, Breland sat in the empty auditorium with me.

"It's always the ones who aren't quite there who want to audition," he said, putting his feet up on the back of the chair in front of him. "You have to seek out the ones with talent. They don't seem to push themselves as hard."

While Breland and I chatted, the members of Truth packed up their instruments, microphones, and speaker system under the watchful eye of Gordon Twist, a New York consultant Breland had recently hired to put some sparkle into the show. With short-cropped hair, a long black leather coat, and black leather pants, Twist was the picture of show-business affectation. The members of the band seemed to hang on his reviews of their performances. He went to each one and told them what they had done well that morning and what they should improve. When the last blue equipment case was snapped shut, Twist came over to meet me and suggested we have lunch at the nearby Grandview Hotel, which was operated by the Oral Roberts organization.

At the Grandview, where the view included ORU and the City of Faith, Breland and Twist relaxed. The pressure of the performance was over and they needed to let off a little steam. Breland howled about a brief hip-wiggling boogie Twist had done onstage during one number.

"The kids loved it. They're so hungry for some life," he said. "Gordon, Gordon," he went on, laughing, "wouldn't it go over big if I used the 'F' word up there onstage here? How much do you think the love offering would be then?"

In their conversation, I felt that Breland and Twist were trying to impress me with their familiarity with big-city, non-Christian ways. They went to great lengths to make clear that their kind of show business was not much different from secular show business. Christian entertainment was music with a religious message, but it was still part of the world of show business, they said, complete with drugs and easy sex and everything else that came with living on the road. In a not so roundabout way, Gordon also made it clear that he struggled with homosexuality.

"You know theater. Well, I'm part of that scene and I'm not embarrassed to talk about what I went through trying to find my place in it. When I talk to gays, I tell them there's no temptation that Jesus can't help you overcome, because I've been there myself. I know."

When Breland left the table for the salad bar, Twist leaned across to tell me his story of stage fever—playing nightclubs in small cities and breaking into the New York theater world. "In New York I tried everything. I mean everything. I wanted to find out who I was." One of the things he discovered was his homosexual tendency. There is no room for homosexuality in Christian America—born-again Christians are uncompromising in their belief that homosexuality is simply evil—and Twist struggled to change. He said he was one of those rare people who found a "cure" for homosexuality in born-again faith. He got involved in Broadway and off-Broadway Christian prayer groups and came to consider his work a religious calling. "My profession is my ministry. By simply being a Christian in show business, I'm ministering to the other artists. There's a lot of pain there, with drugs and sex. I offer an example of something different."

When he rejoined us, Roger Breland elaborated on life on the road. He said the performers earned an average of just $30 a week while they were on tour. Most of the band's dates were at churches and Christian colleges, although amusement parks, especially in the South, would often book them for a "Christian day." The most the band had ever earned for a performance was $7,500, he said. The average was about $2,000.

Breland and Twist seemed suddenly to tire of the conversation. They began to tease me about my work. "How can you stand talking to so many goody-goodies?" Breland laughed. Then a few members of the band dropped by the table to be introduced. Breland noted that two band members were recently married, and he urged them to get some sleep. It was, after all, one of the few days in the year that Truth would have a night off. Several of the members of the group said they might go see singer Debby Boone perform at a local church that night. Others talked about sleeping from early evening until the bus left in the morning.

Before he left for his room in the hotel, Breland asked if I had had any luck obtaining an interview with anyone in the Roberts family. I explained that the Roberts organization had declared the family off limits, in light of the intense media attention that had followed the $8 million plea. "I'll try Richard for you. Let's see."

Breland invited me upstairs to his room, where he cleared some clothes from his bed, sat down, and dialed Richard Roberts' number. After some banter with the secretary he got through.

"Richard, this is Roger Breland. I sure hope you enjoyed our performance today," he said in a honey-sweet drawl.

"Richard, I met a fine fellow here today who's at ORU writing a book about Christians in America and I said I'd call you and ask if he could speak with you. . . . Yes, I know. I know. You're busy. It has been awfully rough lately. . . . No. I wouldn't ask if I didn't think he was straight. . . . No. I understand. Don't give it a second thought. . . . All right. Bye."

Putting down the phone, Breland turned to me and said, "I'm sorry. I guess you heard." He said he was going to take a nap, so he showed me to the door. "Why don't you give Debby Boone a try tonight," he said. "You started the day with Richard and then saw us. You might as well burn yourself out on Christian music all in one day. Maybe I'll see you there."

That night I drove around the outskirts of Tulsa until I found Grace Fellowship, the sprawling modern church where Debby Boone was to appear. Grace Fellowship was the kind of aggressively self-promoting church that could be found in almost every Sunbelt community of any consequence. Tulsa had an abundance of such churches, including Grace Fellowship, Higher Dimensions Evangelistic Center, and Victory Christian Center, to name just three of the larger ones. Each had thousands of members and offered an upbeat atmosphere that was part social club, part religion, and part Dale Carnegie course.

Debby Boone was popular in the Christian subculture, in part because her father, Pat Boone, was a longtime Christian star and in part because she was a crossover entertainer. She had succeeded in the secular world and that impressed the Christian community. Her act for Christian audiences was built around a big finish with the song "You Light Up My Life." It was Boone's one smash secular hit, and Christian audiences loved it. As far as "the world" was concerned, the song was about a great love affair. Born-again Christians shared the secret that the affair was with Jesus.

Grace Fellowship was on the west side of Tulsa, in a sparsely settled area. From the two-lane road it looked like a high school set on a small hill. Inside, a crowd of more than five thousand packed the main hall, a space as big and as plain as an airplane hangar. It was an unbroken expanse of muted gray carpet and softly lit white walls. The only significant decoration in the place was a red-lettered banner reading: "One for Christ, Won for Christ."

I took a folding chair near the door in a section set aside for the disabled. Every other chair in that part of the hall was a wheelchair. There were some adults, but most of the wheelchairs belonged to severely retarded and physically deformed children. Some of the most dramatically disabled kids seemed to be teenagers who were just a few feet tall and had terribly withered limbs. Their parents attended them lovingly and with great dignity. One man lavished attention on a tiny wheelchair-bound girl who made gurgling noises as he touched her head. Her face looked fifteen years old, but her body was the size of a toddler's. When the music started her father took her out of her wheelchair, cradled her in his arms, and rocked with the rhythm.

Boone and her piano-playing warm-up man, Morty, were a cut above Truth and *Richard Roberts Live*. Morty sat at a grand piano and told jokes that depended heavily on the fact that he was a converted Jew. Morty said he followed a peculiar strand of born-again belief, which argued that Jews can accept Christ as their messiah and remain fully Jewish. Such "Hebrew Christians" called Jesus "Yeshua" and observed Jewish customs, including Passover seders. It is a theology that outrages Jews, who consider the whole movement anti-Semitic. Of course, no one at Grace Fellowship objected to Morty's dual religious citizenship. They laughed at his jokes about "Mrs. Dumpleberg," his grade school teacher. And they gave him a standing ovation when he sang, in a Jewish-sounding melody, about becoming a born-again Jew:

> *"I'm a Jew born anew.*
> *Hallelujah to a Jew named Yeshua*
> *From a Jew who never knew ya.*
> *I'm a Jew born anew."*

Morty finished his song and started playing chords. Then Debby appeared onstage, looking like a combination of a choir girl and a show girl. A somewhat immature-looking woman with a tiny upturned nose and wide eyes, she wore a long white silk dress with a white silk jacket and a huge, gleaming smile. She had on gray fringed boots and dangling earrings. Her hair was a glowing blond. The women in the audience gazed at her admiringly. The men just gaped.

Debby sang some gospel standards and in between songs talked about being a mother and about touring with a Christian act. She told the audience about starring in a recent stage production of *The Sound of Music* and then went on to reminisce about what it had been like growing up as Pat Boone's daughter. Over the years many critics had made fun of the Boones, describing them as too perfect, the TV family with the perpetual smiles. Debby tried hard to play on those criticisms to win the audience over. "The world thinks the smiles on our faces aren't real," she said. "I think some people would like to slap the smile off my face. Well, I do smile a lot, but that's because of the Lord."

I didn't stay to hear Debby's finale, "You Light Up My Life." I was tired of Christian entertainment. Twelve hours, beginning with *Richard Roberts Live* and ending with Debby Boone, was more than a nonbeliever could absorb. Even Roger Breland had laughed when I told him my plan for the day. "God bless you. I couldn't stand it," he had said. As I got up to leave, Debby was singing a song about children and faith.

> "Sweet adoration flows from your children,
> Glory and honor and praise are all part
> of our constant devotion."

I stopped at the door as a great wave of singing swelled out of the audience. Rows of born-again Christians swayed back and forth, basking in Debby's childlike message of faith. As I went out the door, I noticed that the man with the gurgling child was rocking her softly and stroking her head. He was singing to her. Walking through the parking lot outside, under the dark Oklahoma sky, I could still hear the singing: "Sweet adoration flows from your children . . ."

The next morning I drove to the City of Faith hospital complex. The hospital administrators with whom I had struggled to get appointments finally had agreed to meet with me briefly and have one of the staff doctors give me a quick tour of the huge facility.

From the vast, windswept parking lots that surrounded them, the three gold-colored towers of the medical center seemed powerful and imposing. In the center was the sixty-story office tower, and flanking it were a twenty-story research building and a thirty-story hospital. It was difficult to imagine that those formidable buildings were mostly empty. But they were. In 1987 just one-third of the space in the complex was occupied. There was no research being conducted in the research tower—no grants or contracts had been won—and the hospital designed for 777 patients had about 125.

The hospital was opened in 1981. Within months, however, it was clear that the project was faltering. The number of patients entering the hospital fell far below even the most conservative expectations. And while Roberts continued to talk bravely about his vision of a great hospital and research complex, the project's administrators called a halt to interior construction and began renting out many of the floors that had been finished. By 1987, no one at the City of Faith talked about serving 777 patients. Tulsa, it had turned out, didn't need a big new hospital. And the far-flung born-again Christians who Roberts believed would fly in for special care didn't come. Like anyone else, sick born-again believers preferred their own doctors and the proximity of family and friends.

I entered the medical complex through a bank of doors just behind the sixty-foot bronze praying hands. My footsteps echoed off the empty lobby's high walls as I searched for the elevators. Once in the elevator and whizzing high into the giant building, I visualized the unfinished floors I passed and thought about the financial burden the hospital had placed on the Roberts ministry. On the fifty-second floor the doors opened onto a space with finished floors and walls and few people. I wandered past a circle of empty offices and eventually found a lone secretary tapping at a typewriter. Soon Dr. Larry Edwards, a tall man in a business suit, arrived to guide me into a small conference room with an impressive view of the landscape below. As dean of the Oral Roberts University School of Medicine, Edwards said, "I train a different kind of doctor."

"When I was at the University of Illinois I wasn't a real fan of Oral Roberts," he began. "But I did sense that secular medicine was overlooking something in man. I'd meet with students and I'd ask them what a man is—just that. They would stumble around. That would amaze me because I knew a human being is a mind, a body, and a spirit. The spirit is the part that helps us relate to ourselves in the universe, to others, and to God. Modern medicine doesn't deal with that."

Frustrated by traditional medicine, Edwards welcomed Oral Roberts' offer. But he admitted that he had worried that when he left Illinois he would leave the medical mainstream. In one sense, he did. The City of Faith had no ongoing scientific research and it was still the object of some skepticism among outsiders. Contacts with other doctors, outside the City of Faith, were infrequent. But Edwards had not completely left the modern medical world, at least technologically.

The City of Faith had the most advanced and expensive equipment available and used every up-to-date technique in treating patients.

"I often speak Christianese, because the people here understand it. But I can say it in secular terms," continued Dr. Edwards. "Historically, medicine came out of religion, whether it was the pre-Christian priests or ancient shamans and medicine men. They dealt mostly with the spiritual because that's all they had. Look at the *Journal of the American Medical Association* from the 1800s and you see God mentioned over and over. Now that we have modern tools, we ignore the spiritual. I think that's a mistake."

The physicians who worked at the City of Faith hospital, the nurses, the medical school students, the orderlies, and the volunteers all emphasized the spiritual aspect of life. They prayed with the hospital's patients and promoted faith in spiritual healing. Everyone was required to follow Oral Roberts' motto: "Expect a miracle."

Certainly an eye for miracles seemed to be the most important prerequisite for doctors and patients at the City of Faith. So when I asked Dr. Edwards to recommend a working doctor for an interview, he chose Don King. King was a forty-one-year-old internist who had graduated with honors from George Washington University, in Washington, D.C. But it was his Christian faith that impressed many at the hospital. King was one of those rare finds whom born-again Christians relish displaying: an atheist intellectual turned born-again believer. King really believed in miracles, Edwards told me enthusiastically.

Don King turned out to be a sturdy-looking man in a white lab coat, with thin, receding black hair. As we sat in Edwards' office, King began describing his work as director of the City of Faith's chemical-dependency unit. His practice seemed to combine psychiatry, internal medicine, and faith healing. His goal, he said, was to prove that the best of complex, modern science could be made still more effective when blended with the tenets of simple faith. From the start he could claim to be a success; after all, many of his patients, born-again Christians who suffered from alcoholism and drug dependency, wouldn't accept medicine offered any other way.

King was eager to establish his bona fides as a scientist. Recognizing that I was from outside the born-again fold, he rightly suspected that I held a skeptical view of born-again Christian medicine. Therefore, he went to great lengths to describe the City of Faith, not as an evangelistic tool to entice unbelievers, but as a vehicle for bringing backward-thinking Christians to twentieth-century medicine.

"One of the most important things we do here is act almost as a place of last resort for Christians who think that taking medical care shows a lack of faith," he said. "Those people will talk to us when they will talk to no one else. They see that we pray with them, that people here are obviously Christians, and they begin to think they can help themselves."

One example King cited involved a young woman, with several children, who arrived with a massive tumor on her thigh. "She had prayed and she came to believe that God told her it would be healed." This message from God, unlike those beamed to Oral Roberts, clearly turned out to be wrong, said King. "When she got here it was an odorous, pussy mass. We told her it was cancer, that it had probably spread throughout her body. We did what we could and then sent her home. Two months later I read her obituary." In another case, involving a child with a similar tumor, the hospital went to court to force her parents to consent to an amputation that saved the girl's life.

"The question I come down to is: Is this person's Christian belief functional? Are they using their belief to do harm rather than good?" In his clinic, where treatment typically involves psychiatric counseling, King routinely applied the "functionality" test to patients' lives. "Take the pastor with a drinking problem. He'll pray three hours a day about it, reading the Bible looking for the answer, and never get better. He's falling into the Bible, using his Christianity as a way to avoid his problems."

King liked to talk about teaching chemically dependent patients to be "functionally Christian." But he said he believed the emphasis had to be on Christianity rather than psychology. "Psychology, when you boil it down, is narcissism," he said. "Anything that is so existential, and excludes God, has to be. What really helps a person, I believe, are the elements of Christianity that include forgiveness—physical, emotional, and spiritual forgiveness. That's what makes you whole, content, adjusted, and balanced." Operating from the Christian idea that everyone was in sin, King's prescription always included God's forgiveness.

King did not move beyond these notions of Christian psychology even when it came to physical illness. He said he believed in spontaneous, miraculous healings, although the only one he had ever attended was his own. He recalled suffering a severe stomach flu and asking for God's help. But instead of simply crying out, King said, "I actually laid hands on myself. The symptoms were lifted. I believe it was a healing."

When we left Dr. Edwards' office, King took me over to the hospital tower. There, on the twenty-sixth floor, a patient named Larry Worthen lay on his bed in a warm room that was flooded with sunlight. When we peeked in his room Worthen was listening carefully to a nutritionist describe how he must change his diet to accommodate his diabetes. Dressed in a white coat, she shimmered in the bright light that came in the window. When she finished talking, she prayed with him. Just past the open door, another nurse, bathed in the glow of a computer terminal, checked charts and looked into the rooms that were clustered around her post.

Pampered and protected in a glimmering hospital tower on the plains, Larry Worthen seemed part of a magical vision of technology. Beeping medical monitors and softly lit computers reminded him he was getting the best high-tech care possible in the nation's only charismatic Christian hospital. He rested comfortably in the holy city-state of Christian America. I realized that for millions of born-again Christians like Larry Worthen, ORU and the giant City of Faith medical center really did comprise a new Jerusalem. The staff, visitors, and patients even called the place Jerusalem. And as Jerusalem, it was orthodox America's most ambitious attempt to institutionalize itself.

Worthen had come to the City of Faith hospital seeking a Christian cure for a painful ulcer on his foot, the kind of complication common in diabetics. His physician at home had said the foot might be amputated. The City of Faith doctors had tried a graft, cutting some skin from Worthen's belly to cover the sore on his foot. One week later, they weren't sure they had saved the foot, but his progress confirmed their decision to try to avoid amputation.

A talkative man in his late forties, Worthen sat shirtless on his bed. His pale skin showed off a pair of tattoos, a dragon and a panther, and a strong physique developed during years working on a General Motors assembly line. He said he lived alone in Dayton, Ohio, and claimed, somewhat incongruously, to be a descendant of George Washington.

"I watched Oral Roberts and I knew about the City of Faith for a long time. God told me to come here once before, and I didn't. That's why my foot got worse. Anyway, one day I told a friend of mine that they were going to cut my foot off. She said, 'You ought to go and call Oral Roberts. He'll help you.' Well, I got on the phone, they confirmed my insurance coverage, and before I knew it I was on a plane here. I never had such service. They just said, 'Go to the airport at such and such a time.' I went, they gave me a ticket, and I got on the plane. When I landed they picked me up at the airport and wham, I was right at the City of Faith. It's a wonder."

Although Larry Worthen's treatment was relatively conventional he insisted that the prayers offered by the staff and the "Christian atmosphere" at the City of Faith had made him recover more quickly. "I feel here that if the doctors can't save you, God can," said Worthen. "God moves the doctors' hands sometimes, if they just let the Lord take over for them. I'm glad I came here, because these people would be more likely to let God work with them. But He is the one really taking care of me."

Like his doctors, Larry Worthen had an eye for miracles. He truly believed that God guided his surgeon's hands. And from there it was just a short leap of faith to the conviction that God had actually done the operation.

As we left Worthen and rode in the elevator down to the lobby, Dr. King said he believed that God performed miracles every day. "If miracles happened in the time of the first Christians, why wouldn't they happen now?" he asked. On the sidewalk just outside the door, he even suggested that my visit may have been an act of God. "This was the first workday I've had open for a year or more, and that's when Dr. Edwards called me to see you. I don't think things like that just happen. I knew it was what God wanted me to do. Thanks for coming."

Above Dr. King, the center tower of the City of Faith rose like a prairie sunflower. I may have seen it as gleaming and mostly hollow, but for Larry Worthen, Dr. King, and the rest of Christian America, that didn't matter. Just as the attacks on Oral Roberts didn't matter. Roberts was their Moses and the City of Faith was the Temple Mount of the American Jerusalem. In their eyes, the huge medical center, the sprawling campus of ORU, the TV shows, and even the Titans, with their losing season and unshakable faith, proved that born-again Christians had arrived. Tulsa would be the base camp from which the Christian Right crusade would go forth to bring about a social reformation.

= II =

THE CRUSADE

= 4 =

Grass-Roots Crusading

O NCE THE INSTITUTIONS of conservative Christian America
had been built, it was probably inevitable that the movement would
look outward. By the early 1980s, millions of America's born-again
Christians had committed themselves to rescuing America from liberalism and converting the nation as a whole to born-again faith. Their
efforts ranged from national political campaigns to regional drives to
force grocery stores to stop selling *Playboy* and *Penthouse*. Perhaps the
most successful of all these grass-roots mobilizations in this decade of
revival was waged by a group of born-again Christians in Alabama who
challenged the authority of the public education system to determine
curriculum. For five years they pressured state education officials and
tied textbook selection committees in knots. History, social studies,
and health books that the Alabama authorities had selected all were
withdrawn under pressure from conservative Christians, who charged
that these texts were "unchristian" and "un-American."

In 1987 the Alabama Christians had sued the Mobile County
schools, charging that the district was using books that undermined
Christianity and promoted an ungodly religion, which they called
"secular humanism." Of course, the born-again crusaders were not
primarily concerned with the Mobile schools. Mobile was a test case,

97

an opportunity to establish a precedent. If it could be shown that there was a creed called secular humanism, and that it was being taught in public schools in violation of the constitutional separation of church and state, then the teaching methods used in virtually every public school would be open to court challenge.

To some extent, of course, what happened in Alabama was anomalous. The state was one of the few places in America where such a campaign could have progressed so successfully, since by the 1980s most Alabamans were proudly born-again Christian and politically conservative. It was also a poor state, where education was little respected and underfunded. In 1987 Alabama ranked forty-ninth out of the fifty states in spending on public schools.

I went to Alabama just a few days after the Christian Right activists had won an important legal victory. W. Brevard Hand, the federal judge hearing the case, had upheld the argument that secular humanism was indeed a religion and that it permeated public education. In a ruling that shocked the educational establishment, he barred the Mobile school district from using forty-four textbooks. Christian Americans cheered the ruling. Teachers' unions and other national school groups decried it as an assault on modern education.

In Birmingham, I had arranged to meet Joan Kendall of Alabama Eagle Forum, one of the activist groups behind the textbook crusade. As I drove from the airport across town to see her, I tuned the car radio to a Christian station where an evangelist named Roy Masters asserted that he knew something every loving parent should know as well. "Beware the intellectuals," he said. "Education is the opposite of enlightenment. The educators are ruining your children. God help America—look at its young."

When I arrived at her home, Mrs. Kendall's husband was perched on a ladder, replacing a board that had rotted on the front of the house. A pleasant-looking man wearing old work clothes, he looked down from the ladder and said, "This is my honey-do day. You know: honey, do this, honey, do that." He climbed down, shook my hand, called his wife, and then told me he was going to the hardware store. As he drove away, Mrs. Kendall opened the screen door, thrust out a bony hand, and shook mine firmly. "I'm Joan Kendall. I hope you'll love being in Birmingham," she said. Slim, carefully groomed, bright-eyed, and energetic, she wore silver earrings, each shaped like a bow, and a pink knit sweater.

Inside the house, which was decorated in an American colonial motif, Mrs. Kendall rather improbably prefaced our conversation by telling me she was a native Alabaman and that her family had lived in the state for generations. I replied by telling her that I was originally from New England. "Oh. We're planning to vacation there this summer," she said. "Now, this might sound sick," she added in a stage whisper, "but I'd really like to see that bridge in Chappaquiddick. You know the one."

As we sat at a pine table in the dining room, Mrs. Kendall explained that she had inherited her political interests from her father, who had been mayor of the suburb of Homewood. He had been known for his direct, hands-on approach. If there was a problem with garbage collection, he would ride one of the trucks. If the police had trouble, he'd be in the patrol car. "He knew how to make a commitment," said Mrs. Kendall. But while she spoke glowingly of her father, she seemed saddened by memories of her mother. "She didn't have any moxie," she said.

Joan Kendall had married at twenty and had her two daughters right away. In 1971, depressed and troubled by the responsibilities of raising her children, she consulted a psychiatrist.

"That didn't help at all, but what did help was a church recommended by my friend's boss," she said. Within a year she had left the Episcopal Church of her childhood to become a born-again Christian. "Becoming born-again, I felt secure about salvation, that I was on the right track," she said. She also grew certain that it was the right track for everyone.

The textbook crusade began in 1982 when Mrs. Kendall's daughter Margaret brought home a science book from school. "I just happened to open it," said Mrs. Kendall. "The book compared the gestation periods of animals, and included human beings, as if they were just another animal. It also said that human babies are the weakest and need the most care." The book's commentary is factual, but Joan Kendall didn't think teenagers needed such facts.

"I think that it denigrates the value of human life. But you know, today I might let something like that go. I've seen much worse since then."

As we talked she delved into files kept in a metal filing cabinet in the dining room. When necessary, she trotted to another room to make photocopies of important papers or sections of books. "I asked for the copier for Christmas," she said, grinning. "It's my 'fur coat.'"

The science book that had the gestation chart was, in Joan Kendall's eyes, just one small example of the flood of "secular humanist" material that was pouring into public schools. Her daughter also brought home a book that described the trial of Copernicus—who had questioned scriptural explanations for the sun's rising and setting—as religious persecution. "That's undermining our religious faith," she pointed out. Another book, from a social studies class, asked students to consider whether lying is acceptable when it is done to achieve an important good. "I found this all very disturbing," she said.

Eventually Mrs. Kendall spoke to her pastor about the books and began to look for information on secular humanism. When she read a born-again polemic called *Child Abuse in the Classroom*, she felt she had discovered the explanation for all those things she hadn't liked in her daughter's schoolbooks. She immediately volunteered to help the Alabama chapter of a born-again Christian women's organization, Eagle Forum, to begin a textbook review project. Eagle Forum and its founder, Phyllis Schlafly, had won Christian America's respect in the 1970s when both were instrumental in the fight against the Equal Rights Amendment. Schlafly had campaigned tirelessly to defeat the ERA. Traveling from statehouse to statehouse, she argued that the amendment would, by legalizing women's rights, destroy the American family. When the ERA was beaten, Schlafly, looking for a new issue, turned her sights on secular humanism, which she perceived as a threat equal to the ERA.

Mrs. Kendall started slowly, collecting complaints from other members of Eagle Forum about history texts that slighted Christianity, about sex education chapters in health books, and about science books that promoted evolutionary theory. She started a newsletter and began pressuring the state textbook committee. Alabama was one of a handful of states in which a single committee chose textbooks to be used statewide. By pressuring the state board, Mrs. Kendall could influence what every Alabama public school student would study. She also made her case with conservative state legislators and started attacking the textbook committee in letters to local newspapers, presenting herself as a concerned, morally upright parent against a monolithic, liberal education establishment.

By 1984 Mrs. Kendall had become influential enough to win appointment to the textbook committee from Governor George Wallace. She was active on the committee, fighting to delete many texts from the lists of approved books and stalling the approval of others. Her particular targets were home economics texts which, over the years, had begun to focus more on sex and family relationships than on cooking and sewing.

Like many conservative activists, when Mrs. Kendall discussed her concerns about changing "family values" she was really talking about sexuality. Disturbed by the ways in which feminism, contraception, abortion, and divorce had disrupted the generations-old balance of power in male-female relationships, she was also confused by the changes that seemed to threaten traditional notions of masculinity and femininity. Joan Kendall firmly believed in the traditional, undivorced family. She also believed that the only good sex is heterosexual sex taking place within the confines of marriage. But as she looked around her, she found a society ever more tolerant of sexual behaviors that were once considered deviant and ever more supportive of nontraditional roles for men and women. It was this tolerance that the public schools seemed to be promoting.

To illustrate her concern about sex education, Mrs. Kendall interrupted our conversation to fetch a book that was, she told me, the worst offender she had come across. Designed for use in senior high school, the book's chapters on sexuality were graphic and nonjudgmental. The authors stressed tolerance for virtually every sexual practice, offering information but little judgment on issues ranging from masturbation to sadism. Indeed, the authors so scrupulously avoided value judgments that neither incest nor exhibitionism was described as deviant, though they did concede that "a few rapists can be classified as psychological deviants."

Mrs. Kendall opened the book, entitled *Health Behaviors*, and showed me scores of pages she had marked in red ink. She seemed particularly incensed by anatomically accurate drawings of reproductive organs. She told me she suspected they would arouse the students sexually. Mrs. Kendall also criticized sections that discouraged antihomosexual bias. Beside a passage stating that the majority of females masturbate she wrote, in red: "Not true." And over a section that explained the "sexual cues" that precede arousal she noted: "Does that free the child from guilt, shame, etc.? Will this text attempt to alleviate good guilt and shame?"

"Here, take a look for yourself," she said, handing me the book. After giving me a moment to flip through the sections she had marked, she asked, "It's not a pretty sight, is it?"

The quiet in the room was then broken by a bang of the screen door. Betty Bostwick, Mrs. Kendall's friend, and another leader of Alabama Eagle Forum, bounded confidently into the dining room. A tall woman with reddish hair, she had a strong jaw and a ruddy complexion. She was even more aggressive about the value of the textbook crusade than Joan Kendall. She announced, as she sat at the dining-room table, that Eagle Forum was involved "in a battle for the minds and souls of our young. It's a battle between those with God and those without God."

Older and more confident, Mrs. Bostwick understood the conservative vision of America in a historical context. She said that conservative Christians had shrunk from social concerns after the Scopes trial of 1925, when Clarence Darrow and the national press convinced the world that Bible-believing Americans were backward, uneducated, and intolerant. The arguments presented in the Scopes trial had marked the end of biblical creationism in American schools. Scopes had also begun a long period of withdrawal and isolation for conservative Christians.

"The orthodox view of how things should be declined," said Betty Bostwick. "By the 1960s we were in the big low. I remember standing up in a Republican committee meeting in 1964 and warning that we were losing our values. We took Marshall County for Goldwater, but no one listened to me." Many of today's conservative Christian activists were Goldwaterites in the 1960s. Their passions were again aroused a decade later by the confluence of the born-again revival and Ronald Reagan's political rise. But among many of them, including Mrs. Bostwick, there was the sense that it was all too little and too late, that no matter what they might do, America was lost. It was a strangely negative view in light of the smashing court victory in Mobile.

"Today," Mrs. Bostwick said, "the worship of evil is rampant in America. Our human nature is sinful and people are responding to that, to this humanism. Many people accept homosexuality, for example. It's disgraceful."

I asked Betty Bostwick to explain why homosexuality was a recurring theme for the Christian Right crusaders.

"Because it's against the Bible and nature, but it's being accepted by so many people. It's on TV, everywhere."

"How do homosexuals get that way?" I asked.

"It's a choice they make. Oh, some may be seduced by older ones. But they could stop it."

"Why don't more people stop it, then?"

"Because it's satanic. Once you start, it's hard to stop."

"Have you ever asked a homosexual person about it?"

"Oh no. I'd love to talk to one, though."

"Do you know any?"

"Well, there are a couple of fellows in our church I suspect." (A wink at Mrs. Kendall.) "But I'd never ask them."

The women laughed. Then Betty Bostwick explained why she's so certain about homosexuality. "It's easy to see when you look at life, at the world, through the scriptures. When you apply the law of the Bible, it's clear."

Anyone who looked at the world through the lens of biblical literalism could also see the humanist threat, added Mrs. Kendall. "I had been seeing the results of secular humanism for years, the decline of morality, problems with drugs and sex. But I couldn't name the cause. I had trouble putting my finger on it. Then when I heard a speaker talk about it at a Bible study group, I recognized it. I could see it was a total philosophy permeating our society. Once you see something is drastically wrong, you have to take action, radical action."

The longer I was with them, the more I became convinced that Joan Kendall and Betty Bostwick were true radicals, using the same tactics that liberals had used in the 1960s. They mounted street-corner protests and filed civil suits. They staged rallies and passed out petitions and pressured the state government, claiming their rights were violated. Along the way they had become powerful people, able to suppress textbooks.

That afternoon I had an appointment to talk with the governor of Alabama, Guy Hunt, who had agreed to discuss Alabama politics, the Mobile case, and the whole question of secular humanism. After our lunch, Betty Bostwick, a great fan of the governor's, led me in her car to Sixth Avenue Baptist Church, where Hunt was appearing. The church had organized a seminar on positive thinking. Hunt was a featured speaker, along with W. Clement Stone, one of America's richest self-made men and a guru of positive-thinking techniques.

Hunt was the only governor in America who was also a Primitive Baptist preacher, one of the smaller of the born-again denominations. He had been elected in 1986, thanks largely to the efforts of the revitalized conservative Christian constituency, including, particularly, Eagle Forum. It was a tremendous accomplishment, since these born-again activists had, in Hunt, elected the first Republican governor Alabama had had since Reconstruction. In return for their help, Hunt had championed their campaign against the state textbook selection process and their suit against the Mobile school district.

As I followed Betty Bostwick to my appointment, the drive led us from Kendall's house in the comfortable Homewood area, through the most depressed parts of Birmingham, to the church. She drove a Cadillac with a "Support the Nicaraguan Freedom Fighters" bumper sticker. When we got to the church she pointed to the parking lot, waved, and drove on.

The church was a plain brick building, big enough to seat about a thousand people. The sanctuary was an airy, whitewashed place with a high ceiling and padded pews. Most of the few hundred people who sat in the pews were black. Most of the people on the altar, including Stone and Hunt, were white. The two men were a curious combination. Stone, an urbane, eccentric, elderly millionaire, was a slightly built man in a well-tailored suit with a huge red handkerchief in the breast pocket. He had a soft, pasty face and slicked-back black hair. Governor Hunt was a tall, craggy-faced man who wore an inexpensive suit and looked as if he would be much more comfortable in overalls. The two men had completely different approaches to their assigned topic as well. Stone spoke of self-motivation and the "human computer." He preached a gospel of capitalist self-interest, stressing that ambitious people must believe in themselves and keep trying.

"Repetition, repetition, repetition," he said in a snippy voice, slapping the back of one hand against the palm of the other. "I'm here to motivate you to action."

Governor Hunt reminisced about a childhood spent picking cotton. He recalled his father, who had lost the use of a hand in a farm accident but still kept working. And he spoke of faith in God, not the faith in self that had been stressed by Mr. Stone. "God is our director," said the governor. "He is the one who gives us strength."

After the two men spoke, a woman in a dress the color of pistachio ice cream sang a song that seemed to wrap the two messages together neatly.

"You can make it, you can make it," she sang, accompanied by recorded music. "God's going to show you just what to do."

Later, in a sitting room beyond the church sanctuary, Governor Hunt sipped a diet Coke and told me that the hard-work-and-trust-in-God spirit he had described in his speech was being undermined by the schools. The parents in Mobile were right, he said. "It's about the moral values of our country. The books downplay the values that made our nation great."

While security men buzzed about and an assistant tugged at his sleeve, the preacher in Guy Hunt warmed to the subject, telling me that Alabamans were, perhaps, more God-fearing than other Americans and that they yearned for a time gone by when God was mentioned regularly in the public schools.

"I don't want to teach religion in school, but a mention of God, a public prayer, a reading of scripture can be all right. Seventy-five percent of the people want prayer back in the schools. And," the governor added, "secular humanism is a real danger. I've been aware of it for some time."

Optimism returned to the governor's voice when he considered a question about America's future. He was not going to be pessimistic, certainly not after giving an inspirational speech. Likening America to ancient Israel, he said, "No nation could reach the heights we have reached, or enjoy the freedom we have, if God didn't bless us." Then he added a quick footnote, explaining why he's optimistic about America's young people. He has found a sign of hope on college campuses. "More and more young girls are not having sex," said the governor.

Suddenly a corps of aides swooped in to bustle the governor off to another appearance. One grabbed the Coke can, another pressed a yellow legal pad into the governor's hand, and a third thanked me for understanding that the governor had to leave. I didn't get the chance to ask how the governor knew about coeds and sex, or why such a trend would be important. He rose and on his way out greeted an older black man who was apparently the former pastor of Sixth Avenue Baptist Church. The governor's photographer, who had taken pictures while we were talking, set the two men in a pose and snapped a photo. While the picture was being taken the old reverend talked, not really to the governor, but to the room.

"Aw, America is wonderful. I grew up afraid of white people, dominated by them really. And look at me now. I'm ninety-four years old, shaking hands with the governor of Alabama." A flash of strobe light and then the governor was gone. A few weeks later, I received copies of the photos in the mail.

The next day, after driving eighty miles south on I-65 to Montgomery, I met a public school teacher and an aggressive young lawyer who had helped turn the battle against humanism in textbooks into an all-out war against public education. Montgomery is a hot little city on the flat plain that is central Alabama. The first capital of the Confederacy, it was also considered the place where the civil rights movement began, with Martin Luther King's bus boycott in 1955.

Not far from King's former church in Montgomery was Cloverdale Middle School, where Douglas Smith was a science teacher. Smith was one of the Christians who filed the suit against the teaching of secular humanism. By chance his name was listed at the top of the complaint, so the case became known as *Smith et al.* v. *Mobile County School District*. As the curious and concerned began to contact him, Doug Smith took naturally to the role of spokesman for the "concerned parents." By the time we met he had become the group's official representative to the outside world.

Cloverdale was a solid brick-and-concrete Depression-era school building. Its old wooden floors sagged in places and the stairs were bowed by the steps of many generations of adolescents rushing to classes. On a Monday afternoon, as students were pouring out of the building, I went inside and found Doug Smith in his classroom, a minimally equipped science lab with rows of small desks facing a teacher's desk and a single lab table. Smith had taped a sign listing class rules on the front of his desk. Among the rules: "No Gum." He had also put up several bright posters. One, an autumn foliage scene, said: "Nature is a name for an effect whose cause is God." It was the kind of poster that could well cause a controversy were it pinned to the wall of a classroom in the North. But in Alabama, where some teachers still began class with a prayer, no one had ever complained about the religious message in Doug Smith's poster.

A quiet man with dark hair and a neatly trimmed mustache, he chatted politely with me about his life and the school. He said he had been educated at Cloverdale in the 1960s, at about the time Montgomery was struggling with integration. The battle had raged over his head, he said. "I don't remember being that much aware of it." By the time we met, half the students at Cloverdale were black and many were bused long distances each morning and afternoon. Smith told me he was sure many of the blacks would be happier attending less integrated neighborhood schools, "if they could be sure the educational quality was as high, which I am sure it wasn't before integration."

Smith said that his father and his brother had both been football stars in high school and that his father had kicked the first field goal ever scored in Auburn University's giant stadium. Doug Smith described himself as "a late bloomer" who, until the lawsuit, had lived in the shadow of the family's football heroes. In a state where football and church represented nearly universal values, Doug Smith had finally found his niche in Christian activism.

"Of course, all of us are born-again Christians. But I guess you could say I'm the most fanatical," he said, chuckling. Smith had been deeply involved in his religion since he was young, and he had grown up listening to preachers complain about the humanist influence in society. When he studied to become a teacher he was certain he would discover that humanism was rampant in the schools. As a working teacher, he came to believe that humanism was at the root of the moral decay affecting America's young. He said he stayed in the public school system to serve as a Christian example, like the students who went to Oral Roberts University because they wanted to be Christian examples in their careers. He believed his very presence as a born-again teacher was a weapon against the forces of humanism.

"America is being duped, and ultimately it's the Devil who is doing it," Smith said as he walked around the classroom lining up desks and chairs. "I'll give you a good example that came up in my class this week. We were waiting to start a test that was being given in every classroom. The kids were talking about a television show, *Moonlighting*. The night before, the leading characters had finally fallen into bed together. The kids thought it was great, romantic, wonderful. But that's not real. First of all, they are talking about two people having a shallow relationship with no commitment. And second, what do these kids think when they find out their wife isn't airbrushed when they get into bed? That's how you end up with AIDS. People searching for this thing based on values that aren't real."

Like the other leaders of the born-again movement, Doug Smith was worried about what liberalism had wrought. In the beginning, before *Moonlighting* and secular humanism, America "was founded with a great spiritual commitment and with Christian values," he said. "America has a unique religious calling. The world cannot survive, as a free world, without America. But nowadays, with kids getting their values from TV, and God out of the picture, we cannot be the country we are called to be."

That afternoon, the tools America used to defend the free world would be on display in an air show at Maxwell Air Force Base in Montgomery. Smith said he never missed the annual open house at the base, and he invited me to go along with him and his daughters. As we left the school, walking down the long, dark hallways, Smith said that his high-profile role in the lawsuit, which his colleagues view as an assault on public education, "has made me a kind of outcast here." He was also a bit of an outcast among scientists, because he rejected the overwhelming evidence for evolution, in favor of the Bible's stories of creation. "Let's just say I'm not one of the teachers who mix a lot in the lounge," he said.

We had to pick up Smith's daughters at his home, so I followed him there. He drove slowly, leading me in an old Chevy station wagon that was spotted with rust and plastered with "Robertson 88" bumper stickers. We crossed Montgomery, weaving past old houses with wrap-around porches and making long slow turns through new neighborhoods of small ranch houses. Smith's home was nestled among tall trees. It seemed a safe, secure place to raise children.

As Doug Smith drove his car into his driveway, his daughters flew out the front door to greet him. Two little girls with big eyes and clear faces, they shouted, "Hi, Daddy," and piled into the back seat. Smith and I sat in front, separated by a small pile of books. The books were from a Christian home-school program, which Smith supervised for a small network of parents who educated their children at home rather than allow them to be influenced by the values of public school teachers and texts. His daughters were in the program. They did their schoolwork for a few hours each morning with their mother, he explained, using texts published by a conservative Christian publisher and taking periodic exams to prove to state officials that they were learning at grade level.

At the height of the born-again revival of the 1980s, thousands of conservative Christian families had turned to home schooling. Each state monitored the programs in a different way. Some states prohibited it; others allowed it with minimal regulation. In Alabama, officials permitted home schooling as long as the periodic tests were given and the work was supervised, on some level, by a certified teacher.

As he drove to Maxwell Air Force Base, Doug Smith tried to explain in more detail "the unspoken conspiracy" that was gnawing at America. His daughters—Molly, seven, and Sarah, five—sat quietly holding little plastic umbrellas. Sarah had a little blue plastic pocketbook which she kept by her side.

"Secular humanism is an evil and it's everywhere, even in the schools. I've seen it," Smith said in a tone that was both knowing and urgent. "Take evolution, or the origins of the earth. I've been exposed to a lot of theory interpreted through the biblical creation viewpoint and I know there are a lot of holes in evolutionary theory." Creation science, developed by born-again Christians, reinforces the idea that God created the earth in biblical fashion. It is based almost entirely on the argument that because evolution cannot be proved beyond a shadow of a doubt, it is not sound science.

"Still, I'm forced to present these explanations about creation and the earth's formation and its age even though I know there are serious problems with them," he complained. "I think that's manipulating science to teach kids ideas that take God out of the picture." Looking in the rearview mirror at his two girls, who were quietly watching Montgomery pass by, Smith added, "If my children were in school they would be getting all this material that tears down our Christian beliefs about creation and God. Those are competing religious ideas, not proven fact. It violates the Constitution's separation of church and state."

Smith's argument relied on a creative twist of logic to make almost any idea a religious idea. It had been the central concept that the lawyers for the conservative Christians had used in the Mobile case. According to this argument, profanity in literature, evolution, sex education, and other subjects were all religious issues. And conservative Christians demanded that their children be protected from them in the same way that non-Christians were protected from school prayer. "I don't understand the legal details of the argument completely. For that you'll have to see the lawyers," Smith said as he steered the big station wagon past a guard post and through the entrance to Maxwell Air Force Base.

At the air base, Smith parked his car and walked through a crowd of thousands, stopping occasionally to greet students and former students. He was certainly no outcast at the air show. We had arrived in time for the precision-flying team called the Thunderbirds, who were the highlight of the show. As we looked for a spot to lay down a blanket, the Thunderbirds were preparing for takeoff. Within moments the Thunderbird jets screamed and whined, tracing white streams in a cloverleaf pattern against the clear blue sky. They climbed, twisting and crossing. The people watched, heads back, mouths open. They seemed like hungry nestlings feeding on the glory of it all.

"Did you feel that in your stomach?" Smith asked as two jets screamed past just a few feet from the ground. "You know, I look at this and I feel proud about America. But I realize we can't do it all with technology. Look at the *Challenger* space shuttle. It blew up in our faces. Technology has become our God. But my brother is in the hospital and the doctors can't even find his kidney stone. I think God is bringing us to our knees, with *Challenger* and AIDS and everything else. When the bottom falls out, when things start getting tough, people will return to God."

As her father talked, five-year-old Sarah Smith, weary of craning her neck to peer past the adults, rummaged through her plastic purse. She pulled out three lollipops and a little orange book.

"Look, Daddy," she said, holding the book aloft and flopping it from side to side.

"Oh, good, Sarah," said her father, looking down for a moment. "You've brought your New Testament."

Sarah's interruption seemed to bring Doug Smith back to a more mundane reality. He explained that his goal was to provide a more sheltered life for his children, a life where they could feel comfortable carrying and reading the New Testament everywhere. The lawsuit was part of this crusade, as was his decision to keep his children out of the public schools. Although he left open the possibility, he said he would probably never allow them to have anything to do with the system in which he continued to teach.

"The most important thing for children, as far as academics is concerned, is how secure they feel as people," he said. "You get that at home, not among the wolves in the world. In school the kids learn it's a rough place out there. Christians are a minority who are threatened out there in the world. I'm not in a hurry to expose my children to that."

As the air show ended, we picked our way through the crowd and back to the car. More young people called out to Doug Smith, and he greeted each in turn, recalling the names of them all, even those he hadn't seen in years. We got in the car and drove past the saluting guard at the main gate and across town to the state capitol area to meet Thomas Parker, one of the lawyers who represented the parents who filed the Mobile suit. Smith said that he had gotten involved in the suit after hearing Parker describe the case at his church. It was then, he said, that he realized that by joining the lawsuit, and testifying, he could take his one-man fight against humanism one step further.

Behind the state capitol, a squat, domed building with dusty white walls, were streets lined with antebellum houses that were now mostly lawyers' and lobbyists' offices. Inside one particularly well-restored green clapboard house I met Thomas Parker. He was in the front room, kneeling on the floor shuffling through stacks of papers. The place looked as if someone had ransacked it, emptying files on the floor and randomly opening lawbooks and leaving them on tables and chairs. The other side had appealed the textbook ruling and the deadline for his written arguments was fast approaching. A small, young-looking man with short hair and a neatly clipped mustache, Parker jumped up from the wreckage and said, "Believe it or not, this is a system. This is how I work. I really get involved."

Thomas Parker and his partner, Thomas Katouc, had started in general practice in Montgomery, handling mostly matters involving the state of Alabama. Within a few years, they had built a solid reputation representing clients before commissions, boards, and state agencies. Parker became known for his toughness. His opponents said he had a bullying courtroom style that was effective, if abrasive. Katouc was more cerebral and more aloof.

The firm got involved in the Mobile case at the request of the original plaintiffs' lawyer in Mobile. Katouc had gained some notoriety a few years before when he lobbied the state legislature on behalf of an initiative that briefly instituted an official state school prayer. The prayer, written by the governor's son, was later struck down in the courts. But the Mobile lawyer recalled Katouc's involvement. Before long, Parker and Katouc came to be the lead lawyers on the case. They enlisted more parents from around the state to participate and eventually the suit filed by a few individuals became a class-action case. Parker and Katouc got financial aid and help in their legal research from the National Legal Foundation, which had been started by TV preacher Pat Robertson. The case had received extensive coverage on Robertson's TV show and Parker and Katouc became two of the most prominent "Christian lawyers" in the country.

The Mobile case was one of the rare instances in which lawyers from a little-known specialty, which they called "Christian law," gained some public attention. Christian law had been formulated in the 1980s by a handful of small institutes and legal-aid societies founded to research and fund cases affecting the born-again movement. Christian lawyers fought cases involving the separation of church and state and religious freedom. They opposed state regulation of church facilities and what they saw as the secular humanist infiltration of public institutions.

Parker did not have time to talk that afternoon, but suggested we discuss the case over dinner at a Chinese restaurant. Walking me outside, he praised Doug Smith as "part of the core of our case." Smith took me back to his house—his daughters slept in the back seat as we drove—and we parted. Before I left, Smith told me that though he admired Parker and Katouc and prayed often about the case, he still expected to lose. "The Bible says that's the way the world is going to go, against us until the end," he said. "The world is probably just too far gone now for us to do anything but make a point. I hope we've done that."

That night, Parker and his wife, a tall, auburn-haired woman named Dorothy, met me at a Chinese restaurant on a busy intersection in suburban Montgomery. "D'Antonio, that's Italian," she said as we met. "But you don't sound Italian. Isn't that interesting." She said she thought there was a TV anchorman in town named D'Antonio. "Or maybe it's D'Amico. Anyway," she added, "you ought to call him up. You have a lot in common."

As we ate the somewhat bland Chinese food, the Parkers, speaking almost as if they were one person, told me the story of Tom's growing up, his education, and his conversion to zealous born-again faith. The way they talked was curious, as if only Tom's experience mattered; Dorothy's life was mentioned only when it related to Tom's.

"I was raised in the Southern Baptist Church, but it didn't take," he said. "Then in college, at Dartmouth, I slowly became aware of the relativism I had taken on in the way I looked at the world. I didn't really have any ability to determine what was right and what was wrong. I wasn't able to argue, intellectually, against the things I knew, deep down, were wrong."

One of the things he came to think of as wrong was homosexuality. Two of his childhood friends were gay. At Dartmouth, he had had little difficulty accepting his friends and their sexual orientation. But when he left New Hampshire and came back home to Alabama, he met Dorothy, who was a schoolteacher, fell in love, and followed her into born-again religion. With the new certainty of religious orthodoxy, his tolerance of his friends vanished. He decided that he should have condemned their homosexuality all along, that he had been wrong to overlook "such sinfulness" in the name of friendship.

Prodded by Dorothy, Parker came to believe that the relativistic way of thinking that he had come to accept at Dartmouth was the same secular humanism that Dorothy insisted was threatening the public schools in which she was teaching. "I saw I was following a view of morality that is ultimately destructive to our legal system and democracy," he said, setting down his chopsticks. "Humanism is subjective, personal, relative, and situational. It has no objective values and that's what's wrong with it. Take shoplifting. That's an example used in some class discussions. You'll always see someone rationalizing it, suggesting there may be good reasons. Well, the humanists will never just say that it's wrong."

At the time, the nation's newspapers were full of stories about Marine embassy guards who were charged with selling secrets to female Russian spies in exchange for sex. Many of the Christians I had met in Alabama had mentioned the stories. It was an unnerving, horrifying notion, they said—U.S. Marines, symbols of patriotic strength, succumbing to sex and then serving communism. The stories confirmed for Christians the evils of sex and their belief that the world will inexorably fall apart until Armageddon and the Second Coming.

"That's what happens," Parker said, "when education fails to teach moral absolutes. We've lost home ec in the public schools to the feminist movement, and look at the problems our young girls have today." Dorothy wrapped her arm around Tom's back and hugged him when he said that.

The born-again conservatives saw their effort to save America from humanism as a duty, like the Marines' duty to guard the embassy. In the Mobile case, Parker saw his lawsuit as a counterattack against secular humanism. He and his allies developed a legal argument that followed three steps. First they set out to prove there was indeed a religion called secular humanism. Then they attempted to show that secular humanist beliefs were being disseminated in the classroom. Finally they argued that the dissemination of secular humanist ideas, and the omission of elements of Christianity, undermined the religious beliefs of born-again Christians and violated the separation of church and state.

"What people don't understand is that this is actually a liberal case, a civil rights case," explained Parker as he finished his scallops in hot garlic sauce. "The schools have been very subtly undermining religion, the beliefs of Christians. Their kids were being taught something in Sunday school and having their religious beliefs undermined the very next day in school. That violates their civil rights as a minority. They needed protection."

While Tom Parker labored over the points of law in the case, the star witnesses in the trial, who were featured in *Time* magazine and on network news programs, were the members of the Whorton family of Mobile. Presented as a kind of Christian "every-family," the Whortons had taken the stand to explain how their children had suffered when they transferred from a private church school to the local public school. According to the news reports, little Ben Whorton had been tormented by the non-Christian values presented by teachers who shrugged off his attempts to apply the Bible to his lessons. He often cried before leaving for school in the morning and eventually landed in a psychiatrist's office. On the courthouse steps the Whortons continued to make their case before the microphones and cameras of the national media. "I just believe the Christian values we were taught at home should be in our school, and all religions, not just one: humanism," Ben had said.

When Judge W. Brevard Hand ruled for the Christian complainants, the Whortons became instant heroes for the conservative Christian community. They were hailed as simple, God-fearing Americans armed with only their faith who had wounded the dragon of secular humanism. Mrs. Whorton had given countless interviews, so when I called, she told me she was weary of them. But she said she would, out of a sense of Christian duty, go over the case one more time. She warned me, however, that we would have to talk on the run. She would have her sons to care for, and then there would be dinner to prepare. "Of course you'll eat with us," she said.

I drove down to Mobile on the morning after I had dinner with the Parkers. The hundred and fifty miles of straight highway were broken only by a scattering of interchanges, with gas stations and truck stops and the occasional motel. The center of Alabama is sparsely settled, with stands of southern pine alternating with pastures and cattle range. For a short stretch, right between Mobile and Montgomery, the only clear signals on the car radio were from local gospel stations that broadcast taped messages from far-flung preachers. *The Watchman*, a program from the Southwest Radio Church of Oklahoma City, told me about missionaries spreading Christianity in Israel. "Israel is very important," the announcer said. "Our Lord is going to return to Israel." *The Watchman* was followed by a program about "having authority over your thoughts." As far as I could tell, the announcer and his guest were telling listeners that stray thoughts could be sinful. "Evil forces have skillfully conditioned us to believe we are not responsible for our thoughts," one man said. "That's right," said the other. "But it's a lie to believe you can't control your thoughts, like lustful thoughts. God requires that we control them, that we cut them off."

I tuned out the radio preachers as I approached Mobile. Another band of thunderstorms crossed the southern part of the state in the early afternoon as I drove into the city. Mrs. Whorton was just leaving her house, umbrella in hand, as I drove up. She waited on the small porch of the ranch house, which was surrounded by tall trees. "You must be Michael," she said. "I've got to get the boys at school, so c'mon, let's talk as we go."

She got behind the wheel of a silver van, turned the key, and pressed a spotless white Nike sneaker down on the gas pedal. We backed out of the driveway, wound our way out of the development, and headed down the long, straight country road that led to the Christian academy where her two sons waited for their after-school instructions. Judy Whorton was a thin, athletic-looking woman with short, carefully trimmed light brown hair. She wore mirrored sunglasses, small gold earrings, a white shirt, and jeans. She reminded me of a young Joan Kendall.

Inside the van, Judy Whorton talked about the need for "concrete actions" to stem the tide of "godless humanism" sweeping society. "America lost its way in the 1960s and early '70s," she said. "We became permissive, hyper about sex, and irresponsible." We talked about the Iran-Contra scandal, which was unraveling during televised Senate hearings, and Whorton said, "It's a sign of the times."

As we approached the school, Judy Whorton said, "It is possible to fight the trend." Her court case was an example. And she said she brought the same determination to her family life. Her values had not been shifted by the winds of liberalism that had swept the country. She was raising her boys to be moral, patriotic, and responsible. "I'll give you three concrete examples of that," she said.

On sex.

"Sex is God in this country. If you haven't slept with fifty people this week you're weird. That's why we have the problems we have. And the textbooks just reinforce this attitude. They say to the kids, 'Do what you think is best.' We don't do that in our family."

On America.

"The state is teaching the kids there simply is no God, or that God is irrelevant. It's discrimination against those who believe there is God. What's going to happen? We could end up just like Russia, where the state is God and you lose your freedom. That's what the lawsuit was about."

On the algebra test.

"Ben hasn't been doing as well as he should. His father said he has to get an 82 or he has to leave football practice early today."

At the school, Mrs. Whorton pulled the van into the long line of parents' cars waiting to take children home. The yard was awash in uniformed children. The girls wore plaid jumpers and white shirts. The boys wore white shirts and navy blue pants. Soon Andy and Ben emerged from the swirling sea of plaid and white. Except for nearly a full foot difference in height, the boys were very much alike. They had short light brown hair, slight bodies, and long, angular limbs. Andy settled into the back seat of the van to review his homework, an assignment on the Civil War battle of the *Monitor* and the *Merrimac*. Older and taller, Ben, head down, stood beside the van and announced the algebra verdict: 77. Judy Whorton took off her mirrored sunglasses.

"Well, you know what this means. You'll have to tell the coach why you can't stay late. We'll be here at six o'clock."

"Yes, ma'am."

Andy was silent in the back seat as we drove back to the Whortons' house. "He's had enough of the media," Judy explained. She began to tell the story of her family's assault on secular humanism. In the winter of 1984 the church-sponsored school Andy and Ben had attended closed for lack of funds. With some skepticism the Whortons decided to try the public school. Judy and her husband, Robert, had both attended public school growing up, back when scriptures were read every morning and the Ten Commandments were posted on the wall. In their hometowns, as in most of Alabama in the 1950s and 1960s, the women who taught public school on weekdays taught Bible school on Sundays to the same children. And for the most part, no one complained if, once in a while, the Bible drifted into the public school lessons.

"I always thought it was kind of nice," she said. "We said prayers and sometimes read the Bible. It didn't hurt anyone. But those days are gone." The Whortons knew things had changed, but they wanted to try to use the school they paid their taxes to support.

In the autumn of the Whortons' year of public school, Ben, an eighth-grader, "slowly began to change." As she eased the van into the driveway beside her small brick-and-wood house, she remarked, "He wasn't smiling and happy. I knew there was something seriously wrong. He was tired. He wasn't eating well. He'd walk out of the door in the morning and then come back inside bawling, saying, 'I can't go. I can't go.' "

Inside the house, in a living room neatly filled with overstuffed furniture covered with plaid fabric, Mrs. Whorton settled down with a glass of iced tea. Andy retired to his room to study the battle of the *Merrimac* and the *Monitor*. On the coffee table was a copy of a Christian book called *The American Covenant: The Untold Story*. The book focused on the devout Pilgrims and interpreted the pre-Revolutionary history of the United States as a Christian progress.

"When Ben started having trouble, we took a look at the kids' books. Take the history books. We found what we thought was a distortion, an absence of facts about the role of religion in this country." An apt example, she said, was Ben's history book, which omitted religious references in its presentation of the Mayflower Compact and didn't mention just whom the Pilgrims intended to thank with their first Thanksgiving celebration. The Whortons also found that English classes used some stories and books that showed parents in a negative light. And a creative writing assignment that asked students to write a menu for a "Cannibal Banquet" (eyeball stew, blood soup) brought them to the school principal to complain. "I remember the teacher sort of laughing about it," she said. "Slowly," she said in a knowing voice, "I began to see a pattern to all this."

Just then Mr. Whorton arrived home with son Ben, who was holding a bag of ice to his elbow. "The guy who hit me was bigger," he said gamely. "But I'll get him tomorrow. I'll jump on his chest or something." Ben retreated to the kitchen. Judy said her older son was unlikely to want to join the conversation. He too was suffering from media shock, she said.

Mr. Whorton was tall, with gold-rimmed glasses and short light brown hair combed to the side. He wore a short-sleeved, button-down plaid shirt and tan pants. He sat on the sofa and immediately began outlining the religious and political convictions that had led his family into federal court. He said he believed the United States had a special relationship with God, that it was a new promised land. And the proof was the country's wealth and worldly success. "America is special in God's eyes. Just look at how it has been blessed," said Bob Whorton. "And we've been used by God as a force for good. If this nation were to fall, it would be a tremendous blow to evangelism."

Dinner was a macaroni-and-hamburger casserole with a salad of lettuce and tomato. The Whortons asked me about my background and about my family. Judy said, since my children were very young, "You haven't had to experience the real problems of public schools." The phone on the kitchen wall rang during the meal and Judy got up to answer it. She cupped her hand over the mouthpiece, talked very quietly for a moment, and then hung up. When she came back to the table she explained that until recently she had been active in an anti-abortion group called Save-A-Life. Save-A-Life offered counseling and support for people who would forgo abortion and have an unplanned child. The Whortons had even given temporary care to eight different infants whose mothers were giving them up for adoption.

"That was a post-abortion trauma case they were calling me about," said Judy. "I don't take new ones, but that was someone we had dealt with before and I was the only person she said she would see. She's really feeling guilty about what she did," she said. "You know, it just shows how far we've gone away from when we were growing up. We never would have had that kind of problem back then."

The Whorton boys listened and ate without saying a word and then, with permission, left the table. Though shy, they didn't seem very traumatized by their encounters with reporters; indeed, they were curious enough about me to wander from their rooms to the kitchen and back all through the evening. Eventually Andy brought out his drawing of the *Merrimac* and the *Monitor* and showed it off.

After dinner we sat in the living room and talked about the 1950s and 1960s, when the Whortons were young. They had both grown up in small towns in northern Alabama. They said their parents were conservative "yellow-dog Democrats" who voted for Goldwater in 1964.

"God blessed America back then, the way He blessed Israel, because we were obedient," said Mr. Whorton. He said he regretted not serving in Vietnam. He had tried to sign up for the Marines but poor vision had kept him out. In college he had been taught about evolution and geological estimates of the earth's age. All the material conflicted with the Bible lessons he learned as a boy. "That was my first real exposure to humanism," he said. "But I resisted it. I learned the information but remembered there had to be some design, something behind creation.

"The problems of the nation—abortion, the schools—can all be traced to humanism," Bob Whorton said as I was about to leave. "Our basic values, even the Ten Commandments, have been thrown out.

The values of the community aren't controlling things anymore; the courts and the government are. That is what is wrong. In our case, though, we were able to use the courts to start to turn things around. Thank God for Judge Hand, even if he is likely to be overturned."

With Bob Whorton's pessimism, so reminiscent of Doug Smith and Betty Bostwick, still in my mind, I said good night to the Whortons. I had another appointment that evening, with Ishmael Jaffree, the man who had actually started the Mobile textbook controversy. Jaffree had been eager to tell me his side of the story, and we had agreed to meet at a seafood restaurant on the Mobile waterfront. Jaffree was director of the Mobile Legal Aid office, a nonprofit agency serving the poor of Mobile County. It turned out that the textbook case grew out of a suit he had originally brought when a teacher asked his children to pray with her in a public school. Jaffree sued, and a group of born-again Christians rose up to oppose him. Among them were the Whortons, who said that humanism, not Christian prayer, was the real problem in the schools. Jaffree eventually won his case, but the judge then asked the 624 Christian parents to come back and litigate other issues raised in the trial. Namely, that secular humanist religion was rampant in the schools.

"It was the damnedest thing I've ever seen a judge do, though I can't say it was out of character for Judge Hand," Jaffree told me over what turned out to be my second dinner that evening. Jaffree was a black man who had moved South from Cleveland. He said he delighted in confronting what he called "the system." As a boy he had listened to the sermons in church and then one day just stood up and asked out loud, "But what if there is no God?" As a lawyer he had practiced a kind of guerrilla law, giving up high fees from private practice to handle a never-ending stream of tenant disputes, job-discrimination cases, and divorces for clients unable to pay. Though he put on coat and tie for court appearances, he usually worked in sport shirts and pants, the kind of clothes worn by most of his poor clients. "Ishmael means 'the outcast,' " he said.

The first trial of the Jaffree case "was done in very personal terms," said Jaffree. "They were slamming me in the newspapers and sending me Bible tracts. I wasn't on a soapbox telling people God isn't real. I could care less whether He is or not. I just wanted it to be clear that those kinds of beliefs are all relative and they shouldn't be advanced in the school."

In 1983, Judge Hand ruled against Jaffree, and in a footnote warned that if he was overturned, he would reopen the case, rearrange the parties, and try the born-again parents' claim that humanist religion had infected the schools. In 1984 he was overturned. The court of appeals barred Alabama teachers from praying in their classrooms. Hand then called on the born-again parents to come back to his courtroom and settle the humanist issue. "A judge has the power to do that if he sees something that should be tried, but it hardly ever happens," Jaffree told me.

In the end, Judge Hand was able to use Jaffree's case against school prayer to write a decision that declared secular humanism an anti-Christian religion that was being taught in the schools in violation of Christian citizens' right to separation of church and state. "To me that looks like a very activist thing for a conservative judge to do," Jaffree said. "I'd like you to ask him how he justifies it."

I did have an appointment with Brevard Hand the next morning, though the judge, a Nixon appointee, had turned down all requests for media interviews. He agreed to talk with me on the condition that his comments not be made public until after the U.S. District Court of Appeals in Atlanta had reviewed his ruling.

The next day was surprisingly cool for a Gulf Coast summer. A moist breeze off the harbor shrouded the waterfront in fog. Downtown Mobile, emptied out by commercial flight to the suburbs, still shows the influence of its French founders. Like the grand old houses of New Orleans, Mobile's old pastel-colored homes with their ornate ironwork recall the city's French beginnings. The federal courthouse was a plain building a few blocks from the city's center, Bienville Park. I arrived a few minutes early, so I took a walk in the small park, which was a green square about the size of a city block, shaded by very tall trees and carpeted in bluegrass. In one corner was an eight-foot-high stone cross, a memorial to the city's founder, a French naval officer from Montreal. The inscription read: "Jean Baptiste Le Moyne Sieur de Bienville of Montreal, Governor of Louisiana and founder of first capital, Mobile, 1711. With the genius to create an empire, and the courage to maintain it. Patient amid faction and successful even in defeat, he brought settlement, the prosperity of true civilization and the happiness of real Christianity."

At five minutes before eight I walked through the metal detectors in the courthouse lobby and took a slow elevator up to the second floor. I found the frosted-glass door of the judge's office, and a middle-aged man who seemed to be a clerk asked me to sit in a small anteroom. Soon Judge Hand, a courtly, soft-spoken, white-haired man in shirt sleeves, opened the door to his inner office and welcomed me. We stood and chatted a bit about Mobile and its charm. He said that he missed the old Mobile. The city had doubled in size, to more than 200,000 people, in just one generation. As a boy, the son of a lawyer, young Hand had found good hunting and fishing within an easy walk of his home. Now there were shopping centers and houses in place of the woods, fields, and unspoiled streams.

Judge Hand sat behind the big desk that was in the middle of the room and the tone of our meeting changed. A book titled *Christian Visions: Man and Mind* was on the desk. A photo of the sun, super-imposed on the shape of a cross, looked down on him from behind his right shoulder. "Now, about this case. The Supreme Court has said that the states cannot advance the tenets of faith," he said. "But that is what they were doing in the school. I became convinced that those parts of the books addressed by the witnesses amounted to a faith system."

The two-week trial had been dominated by the struggle to determine if secular humanism was a religion and whether it had been unjustly foisted on the schoolchildren of Mobile. The defendants presented witnesses who said that it could not be a religion because it had no sacred beliefs and no sacred objects. It was, testified philosophy professor Paul Kurtz, a human-centered view of the world that encompassed all of man's progress. The born-again plaintiffs argued that if humanist ideas threatened religious beliefs, then they must, by definition, have a religious quality. And since schools presented the progressive ideas Kurtz described, they must be teaching humanism.

Judge Hand had agreed. In his ruling he determined that virtually all of life and learning could be seen as religious. It's a line of thinking which, if carried further, would make it all but impossible to write textbooks that treated religion neutrally. "That problem is not mine," said the judge. The courts should never have tried to take religion out of the schoolhouse in the first place, he said. But as long as they did, he wanted everything religious removed. Humanist ideas, which the judge considers religious ideas, must be barred along with Christian prayers.

"I am greatly concerned over the viability of the republic," he said, in explaining why he took such a radical stand. "I worry about people's perception of what freedom really is, of what their responsibility to their country really is. I guess it all ties in with morality, love of country, a willingness to sacrifice for its best interests."

Somehow the country had changed for the worse, Judge Hand said. He traced it to the era when school prayer was banned, when Vietnam and then Watergate shook America's sense of itself. But the blame rested, not with the government officials who conducted an unpopular war, or the politicians who broke the law, but with the media that introduced these messy problems to the public consciousness. "Why do people have less respect for their leaders? I guess it's the mass misinformation," he said. "Vietnam was probably lost because of the media." And President Reagan's Iran controversy was another example, he said. Egged on by the press, congressional investigators and federal prosecutors had embarked on a wrongheaded mission. Although administration officials lied about their activities, and despite evidence of profiteering and lawbreaking, Judge Hand labeled public criticism of the affair "lint-picking."

There had been no "lint-picking" directed at the powerful people of Judge Hand's youth. There was an orderliness to life then. Everyone, it seemed, was a born-again Christian, so no one objected to Bible verses being read in the classroom. Granted there was racial discrimination, rampant sexism, and a kind of rural poverty few other regions of the country suffered. Still, people knew where they stood then, and Judge Hand returned nostalgically to that time to describe the way public schools ought to be run.

"I cannot tell you exactly what I was taught in public schools, but there was no great emphasis one way or another on religion," said the judge. "I found an old high school book of mine a while back. It was 1980. We were cleaning out my parents' house after they had died. That book discussed evolution and creation as the Bible tells it. They were presented as two theories."

As Judge Hand talked about his old science book I realized he was describing the central issue of the Scopes trial. Like Southerners who have yet to accept the results of the Civil War, he was suggesting that the outcome of Scopes was wrong, that the battle between science and scripture should be fought again. So far, Judge Hand said, "the federal courts haven't had the stamina to address this problem, to recognize that it is what is destroying the very fiber of the republic. I'm a lone voice, crying in the wilderness," Judge Hand said. "But you've got to start somewhere. I have."

= 5 =

Christian Politics

At 7 A.M. Rev. Ray Moore, born-again political engineer, was already wedged into a sunshine-yellow plastic booth at Tasty World, the coffee shop next to the airport Day's Inn in Columbia, South Carolina. He was dressed in a maroon sport shirt with "South Carolina" written across the breast and had placed a stack of papers three inches high on the table in front of him. Outside, the sun was turning the morning hot. Small puddles of water, left by the night's rain, were slowly disappearing from the parking lot. Families who had spent the night in the motel were loading suitcases into their cars.

Ray Moore was in the center of a political gutter scrap. A few weeks earlier he had engineered a blitz of local Republican Party caucuses, carrying many precincts and winning the majority of the delegates to the state convention. At the convention, the party regulars fought him to a draw in a bitter struggle, during which they likened his born-again Christian activists to Nazis. The born-again Christians had answered by calling their opponents racists. "It's been quite a fight," Moore said as he made room for me on the plastic bench. "Now I got to figure out what comes next."

In the summer of 1987, in South Carolina born-again politics was at its apogee. For nearly a decade conservative Christians had been muscling their way into the political process. Outsiders watched with wonder as TV preachers and local pastors learned to be effective political organizers. The Christian activists created committees and lobbying groups, conducted voter registration drives, and issued "moral report cards" on the candidates. Those candidates who opposed abortion, supported high levels of defense spending, and backed school prayer got high grades. Those who didn't were subject to attack. As the 1980s progressed, the born-again voting bloc became a powerful force, especially within the Republican Party. In turn, candidates began to pay attention to them, wooing them with promises of a return to "traditional values." But until 1987 few of them had ever really satisfied the Bible-believing voters. It was not until TV preacher Pat Robertson decided to run for the Republican nomination for President that born-again America had a candidate of its own.

On the hot summer morning when we met, Moore was working on two problems. He wanted to make some calls to bolster his network of campaign workers. Many had been shaken by the rough turn the campaign had taken. He also needed to find a place to live. Robertson's national campaign officials had finally taken his advice. They were making South Carolina the place where Robertson would try to win his first major primary victory. Moore had told them the state was "wired" with a network of Robertson loyalists. With six months of work, he figured, he could almost guarantee Robertson would win the state in 1988. Moore was happy about staying in South Carolina full-time. "I can finally move out of the motel," he said.

Few people had been more intimately involved with the rise of born-again politics than Ray Moore. An ordained preacher, Moore left full-time ministry and entered local politics in 1980 when he helped Dan Quayle, a conservative Republican from Indiana, ride the Reagan landslide into the U.S. Senate. In 1982 he worked on another successful campaign for born-again Republican congressman Mark Siljander of Michigan. After the 1982 campaign he became the Southern coordinator for Pat Robertson's Freedom Council, a lobbying organization that focused on issues such as school prayer and abortion. In 1986 the Freedom Council was converted to Americans for Robertson, an exploratory committee to test Robertson's strength as a presidential candidate.

"What the politicians have yet to realize is that there are millions of people out there for whom the Bible is the thing. It is the authority that orders their lives," explained Moore as he sipped his coffee. "There is a lot in the Bible about Christians and politics, and mostly it says that we should be involved, that man should have dominion over the world and that means political dominion. That had been lost in the Christian community since Scopes, when the idea of 'separatism,' separating Christians from the evils of the world, became so popular. Rather than adjust to the way the world is, the preachers said, we must withdraw from it.

"Separatism took hold, especially among conservative Christians in the South, until Goldwater came along. Goldwater touched a nerve with Southern Christian conservatives and they came out for him, and they didn't see that they were all that tainted by the experience," said Moore. Moore paused to ask the waitress, "Ma'am, another cup of coffee, if you would, please." When she brought the coffee to him he looked up and said, very slowly, "I thank you, kindly."

Moore went on to say that after Goldwater's loss in 1964, Southern born-again conservatives shifted their support to Alabama governor George Wallace, who campaigned as a third-party candidate in 1968 and 1972. But it was not until 1976, and Democrat Jimmy Carter, that a Southern born-again candidate actually won the presidency. "I believe people thought they had elected a conservative Christian in Carter, but they soon found out they hadn't, and there was a lot of anger about that," Moore said.

I had found a deep sense of anger and disappointment about Carter's presidency wherever I had gone in Christian America. I had heard countless complaints that the born-again President was weak, ineffective, and far too liberal. In fact, Carter was, in a way, a victim of a reality conservative Christians denied. Born-again America thought it had voted for one of its own. Instead it got a President whose face grew sad and lined as inflation and oil prices soared and dozens of Americans were held hostage by religious extremists in Iran. The born-again voters, who believed America to be blessed by God, never forgave Carter for the pain the nation suffered at the end of the 1970s.

"After Carter, people like Jerry Falwell started to speak out for Christians," Ray Moore explained. Rev. Falwell endorsed Republican Ronald Reagan and, with other Christian Right activists, was instrumental in getting Reagan elected in 1980 and reelected in 1984. Though not a churchgoer, Reagan gave voice to orthodox Americanism. He called on God in virtually every speech, and his agenda mirrored the conservative Christian agenda. He was against abortion, supported school prayer, and was stridently anti-communist. But, more important, his presidency seemed to promise a return to 1950s America, a return to restrained morality, economic certainty, and American supremacy. Christian Americans were entranced.

"People loved Reagan but he wasn't able to do much about abortion or school prayer and now, in 1987, you have to look beyond him," said Moore. By 1987 born-again Christians had little to show for their long-standing support of the conservative wing of the GOP. "We gave and gave and gave and didn't get much in return. So along comes someone like Pat Robertson and people start to think: 'Why not? Why not one of our own?' "

Moore's candidate, Robertson, was a smooth, handsome man, the son of a former U.S. senator from Virginia, who had become one of the nation's most watched television personalities. In the mid-1980s his 700 *Club*, a born-again Christian talk show, was viewed by millions every day. The show was chatty and warm, without a trace of fire and brimstone in the presentation. Robertson preached that believers, especially those who "give to God" by sending him money, would be rewarded on earth and in heaven. In a typical year, as many as 500,000 people contributed to God through Pat Robertson. Their contributions built an international operation that included a small college, the country's fifth-largest cable TV network, a publishing house, a legal foundation, and a presidential campaign.

Robertson was a born-again American blue blood, with strong credentials from the world of politics and the world of conservative Christianity. He was from an old Southern family, and his official résumé went to great lengths to describe a "heritage" that included a vague connection to Winston Churchill and direct kinship with two Presidents and a signer of the Declaration of Independence. His father, Willis Robertson, had served in the Senate for twenty years. A conservative Democrat, the elder Robertson had been part of the Dixiecrat bloc that had resisted integration right up to the Civil Rights Act of 1964. As a boy, Pat Robertson had listened to his father's stump speeches and visited his offices on Capitol Hill. As a young man, he had been better known for drinking and poker than for piety. At Washington and Lee University and Yale Law School, he had a reputation for being both a sharp student and someone who could carouse all night and still be alert for class.

It wasn't until after he had graduated from Yale that Robertson, in part at his mother's urging, first began to consider seriously, then accept wholeheartedly, the teachings of born-again Christianity. When he did, however, he committed himself fully, entering a seminary in New York and quickly immersing himself in the mysteries of tongues, faith healing, and prophecy. As a seminarian, Robertson was part of a small prayer group that held lengthy Bible studies and prayer services. During those meetings people spoke in tongues and claimed to be healed. Robertson became convinced that a supernatural power guided his life. That power drew him back to Virginia, where he bought a foundering TV station for just a few thousand dollars. Starting slowly, he made that first station profitable and built a successful Christian TV network, which by 1987 had more than 15 million regular viewers, most of them receiving programs via cable systems. By the mid-1980s Robertson came to believe the power was calling him to the presidency.

When he announced his candidacy, Pat Robertson had a twenty-year-old national organization of TV supporters to draw upon. Those same people who had called his prayer line and contributed to the Christian Broadcasting Network became his campaign volunteers. And they threw themselves into the task as if they were divinely inspired.

"Pat Robertson is not a candidate, he's a prophet of God," one Robertson canvasser had told me as he passed out literature in downtown Columbia. A thin man with an angular face, Leo Mullins was employed as a boiler-room engineer at a state hospital, which he described as "an institution for people whose minds are messed up by the Devil." Mullins said he would not work for any politician but Pat Robertson. "God has given Pat Robertson the wisdom and anointed him to lead America," he said, adjusting his baseball cap. "That's why I'm spending my vacation doing this."

When he arrived in South Carolina, as Robertson campaign coordinator, Ray Moore brought a notebook filled with the names and addresses of people such as Leo Mullins. Lists of names and addresses sustain modern political campaigns. With the lists candidates can bypass the press and go directly to their supporters, by mail, with appeals for votes and money. The Robertson organization collected many of the names for its list on a single day in 1986. Campaign officials arranged a telethon, bringing thousands of conservative Christians to ballrooms and auditoriums across the country. They watched Robertson announce, by satellite TV transmission, that he was forming a committee to explore a run for the presidency. If enough people signed petitions and donated money, said Robertson, he would run for President. The assembled believers signed attendance and pledge cards that were quickly compiled into a list of more than 200,000 potential donors and activists.

Armed with those names, Moore didn't have to pry campaign workers away from commitments to other candidates or causes. The people he turned to were already accustomed to donating time and money to the Robertson religious and social agenda. "We're going to end up with a list of 80,000 to 100,000 names in South Carolina alone," Moore told me gleefully. "Vice President Bush can't get that. He can't get thousands of people coming out of the churches to speak for him to their friends and neighbors. Robertson can."

South Carolina, where a majority of people claim to be born-again Christians, was the ideal place for a Robertson push. The state had a history of conservative Christian activism and strong born-again institutions, the most prominent of which was Bob Jones University, a four-year unaccredited college in the western part of the state. Bob Jones U. had produced a wide network of educated, established conservative Christians in virtually every business and profession. The state also had strong born-again churches, many of which were independent of denominations. This was important because pastors in such churches were more likely to get involved in politics since they didn't have to answer to denominational authorities who might disapprove of their political activism on behalf of someone like Robertson, who was outside the mainstream. The state also had a small number of prominent politicians who identified themselves as Christian candidates. One, Henry Jordan, had even run for the U.S. Senate in the previous election.

When Moore arrived in South Carolina, he quickly invited a handful of prominent activists to lunch at a Columbia restaurant called the Lizard's Thicket. The group consisted of a born-again lawyer from Charleston who was active in GOP politics, a Columbia-based activist named Wayne Mitchell, a few pastors from around the state, and, most important, a statehouse lobbyist and lawyer named Orin Briggs.

Over lunch, the group talked about the 1987 South Carolina caucuses, which would choose delegates to the state convention. In South Carolina, as in just about every other place, caucuses were usually poorly attended. In many precincts meetings failed to draw enough participants even to fill the delegate seats. Moore and his allies perceived that, simply by showing up, Robertson supporters could dominate the caucuses and, later, the state convention itself. They outlined a plan that would surprise the opposition. Relying on churches and established Christian activists, they would teach hundreds of political novices the mechanics of taking over these local party caucuses. If everything went according to plan, the Robertson forces would overwhelm meetings from Charleston on the coast to Anderson in the hills.

Orin Briggs was a key player in the strategy because he had the connections that could make the plan work. Briggs had spent a decade developing the state's born-again Christian power base. He had begun as an aide to U.S. Senator Strom Thurmond and then had gone into business on his own, as a lawyer and political consultant. He had written a booklet that showed, step by step, how born-again Christians could affect the political process. He spent nearly a decade traveling from church to church, lecturing on what he called "the Christian duty of politics" and distributing thousands of his booklets. By 1987 he knew precisely the preachers who would help organize the Robertson push and the politicians who could be coaxed onto the bandwagon.

Tall, with sandy blond hair and glasses, Briggs was hardly a high-pressure political arm-twister. He grew up in a neighborhood of row upon row of little brick houses built by Pacific Mills, the textile company that employed his mother. She had worked in the textile mill all the years that Briggs and his brother were growing up, a detail that was very important to him, and he obviously remained grateful to her for her sacrifice. Briggs's father was a full-time National Guardsman.

After breakfast with Ray Moore, I met Briggs at his office, a large Victorian-era house that had been turned into a professional building. It had started to rain as I walked up the sidewalk. A crew of black workers who were painting the front of Briggs's building scrambled to put away their drop cloths and buckets. Briggs met me at the door, led me back to his office for an umbrella, and then back outside. We spent much of the remainder of the day touring Columbia in his car.

Downtown Columbia was dominated by tall bank buildings and a crowded shopping district. Just outside the center of the city stretched shady neighborhoods of rambling, graceful houses. There were only a handful of antebellum homes left; one, Briggs pointed out, was near his office. "General Sherman," he noted, "burned the rest on his way to Atlanta."

If people in the South still bear the animus of the Civil War, and according to Briggs many do, then South Carolinians must suffer it the most. South Carolina was the state most dependent on slave labor and it was the first to secede from the Union. Although after the Civil War, South Carolina politics was, for a brief period, dominated by its black majority, whites quickly organized to disenfranchise them. Festering racism remained a part of state politics as late as 1970, when supporters of a gubernatorial candidate opposed to desegregation overturned three busloads of black schoolchildren. The incident embarrassed the state, and since then South Carolina has progressed, at least on the surface. Sometime in the 1970s, Briggs said, public racism finally became socially unacceptable and politically disastrous.

"The shift happened in the early 1970s. I was changing at the same time too. I had gone to Washington to work for Senator Thurmond. Other Christians may isolate themselves from cities, fearing their evils, but I learned something very important there. That was where I really learned that people are just people and that racism is just plain wrong."

Washington, and Senator Thurmond in particular, played important roles in Briggs's life. Thurmond had been a major force for two generations of South Carolina politics. He was governor from 1947 to 1951 and senator from 1956 on. He stood for segregation and against civil rights well into the 1960s, enjoying easy reelection as a reward. He was so popular he could even switch from the Democratic Party to the GOP, as he did in 1964, and still roll to easy victories. In 1987, at age eighty-three, Thurmond was contemplating running for reelection when his term expires in 1990.

Briggs went to work as a junior legislative aide in Thurmond's Washington office in 1967. "Back then," Briggs said, laughing, "we still had a first-name file so we could address letters personally. You can't do that now. Everything has gotten much more complex." It was from Thurmond that Briggs learned about political organizing. Thurmond also imbued Briggs with his own conservative values, those of an archconservative Baptist who had spent his life wrestling the world, and winning. Briggs came to believe he could do the same.

Briggs returned to South Carolina in 1976 after a few years in a low-level job in the Nixon administration. In Columbia, he established Christian Action, a local organization that promoted the involvement of conservative Christians in politics. In 1979 Christian Action published Briggs's *Political Handbook for Christians* and sponsored his speaking tours around the state. The booklet begins with a reference to politicians who "were placed in their position of leadership by God." For examples Briggs drew on the Bible stories of Joseph in Egypt and

Daniel in Babylon. From modern times he selected North Carolina's reactionary U.S. Senator Jesse Helms. Briggs's booklet explained political parties, the caucus system, and electioneering. He reminded readers that while politicians claim that their art is compromise, "the Christian must not compromise, PERIOD."

Christian Action might have been Briggs's passion, but his legal practice paid the bill. Establishing himself as an independent attorney, Briggs sought cases that involved family issues and issues of religious freedom. He frequently represented churches and church schools against state authorities. In one famous case, he successfully defended leaders of a church who had used switches to discipline children. While Briggs's political opponents sometimes attempted to depict him as a defender of child abusers, his personal life defied the charge. In the course of his practice, he had represented, free of charge, orphaned, abandoned, and abused teenagers. He had been so moved by the troubles of one child whom he defended that he adopted her.

As a parent, Briggs said he struggled to guide his two daughters toward his vision of a Christian life. It wasn't easy, he told me. Columbia was one of the safest cities in the nation, but it had its drug pushers and its juvenile delinquents and its runaway teens. Briggs worried about the movies his fourteen- and nineteen-year-old daughters could rent and play at home on a videocassette recorder. He mentioned that they had just viewed *Top Gun*, a movie about fighter pilots in training. The movie had one, fully clothed, sexually suggestive scene.

"There is a great secularization of society taking place and that's disturbing. I even have a little confession about that," he said. "I allowed them to watch *Top Gun*. Some Christians, fundamentalists especially, say no movies are allowed, none. I don't agree with that fully, but I do feel bad about letting them watch *Top Gun*. But that kind of thing is so much a part of society now it's hard to monitor it all."

Briggs's efforts, whether to shield his daughters or to elect Pat Robertson, were motivated by an overarching sense of religious doom. "God has blessed America abundantly, but we've turned away from Him, and if we cross a certain point, He's going to abandon us," Briggs told me as he steered his car through the University of South Carolina campus. "The Christian movement is a reaction, to things like AIDS and to the fear that God might abandon us." Pat Robertson's candidacy offered America a way back into God's graces, he said. "It was the lie

of the Devil to say that Christians must not be involved in politics,"
he said. "It may be the thing that saves America."

One of the best ways to save America, Briggs had decided, was to
enter into an alliance with Ray Moore and the other activists who had
gathered at the Lizard's Thicket to support Pat Robertson. After that
conference, Briggs went to preachers and conservative Christian activists around the state, many of whom he knew well, and got them
to start recruiting people to go to the caucuses as Robertson supporters.
At the same time Moore tapped his Freedom Council contacts, and
his list of Robertson backers, to add more volunteers. Together Moore
and Briggs had built the framework for a Robertson precinct blitz
statewide. Many of the volunteers had never been involved in party
politics. Some had never even voted. But they were willing to jump
into the caucuses for Pat Robertson.

Robertson arrived in South Carolina just a few days before the state
caucuses. His visit was particularly well publicized on born-again
Christian TV and radio stations, but there had been little notice of
the visit in the mainstream press. So while everyone in born-again
society was pumped up to see him, the rest of South Carolina was
oblivious. Robertson came into town unnoticed and went straight to
a rally at a hotel in downtown Columbia. The rally had been intended
to be just for loyal campaign workers. But when a few GOP regulars
got wind of the rally and wandered by, they were stunned by the size
of the crowd. More than a thousand people jammed the ballroom of
the Radisson Hotel to hear Robertson take a few jabs at front-runner
Bush and to remind the faithful of the importance of the South Carolina race. "South Carolina is the absolute key to the South," he said.

After the Radisson Hotel rally Robertson went to a second big meeting, at Columbia High School. That meeting was closed to the press
and people outside the Robertson fold. However, a few regular Republicans slipped through the crowd and a couple of local newspaper
reporters climbed onto a roof and peered into the windows. Inside,
the meeting turned out to be more seminar than rally, teaching Robertson's local workers the mechanics of overwhelming a precinct meeting. There was even a skit called "How to Take Over a Precinct."

The rallies startled the state's Republican regulars, most of whom
supported Bush and had expected that the 1987 caucus would be as
boring as every one before, with Bush winning handily. With just two
days left before the precinct meetings they didn't have a chance to
organize their own workers, so they went to the press with cries of

foul. William "Rusty" DePass, one of the few Republican regulars who had witnessed the meeting at the high school, told local newspapers that he was reminded of "what a Nazi pep rally might have been like. The group was whipped into a froth, it was a real mob mentality. They were like sheep," DePass told *The State*, a Columbia paper. "It's the craziest thing I've ever witnessed."

I talked to DePass on the telephone and he said much the same thing. He said the Robertson people were not Republicans, but religious zealots. "These people would jump off a bridge if Robertson asked them to," said DePass. "Now, I consider myself a Christian, and a conservative. But these people were so far to the right of me, both politically and religiously, that they were about to fall right off the edge."

When caucus night came, Robertson's people did what they had set out to do. In precinct after precinct they showed up in force and wrested control from longtime GOP regulars. By the end of the night they had just over 50 percent of the delegate spots to a state convention that was going to set the rules for the 1988 contest.

The party convention that followed the caucus was a mess. The regulars invoked a little-known rule, requiring that delegates be registered ninety days before caucuses, to whittle the Robertson force down to about 45 percent of the total. Then the two sides fought to a draw in the struggle over GOP leadership positions. When it was all over, Orin Briggs filed a lawsuit against the regulars over the exclusion of Robertson delegates.

In the weeks following the Robertson surprise, the South Carolina press was filled with reports on the battle of "the Christians versus the regulars." Political columnists in the state referred to Robertson's loyalists as "Revolutionary Guards," likening them to the extremists in Iran's Islamic regime. The Robertson forces fought back. They called the regulars country-club elitists, and even suggested, because several of the disqualified Robertson delegates were black, that there was racism involved.

Amid the rancor and the lawsuits, born-again politics had reached a high point. A TV preacher-turned-presidential candidate had fought the Vice President and an entire state Republican machine to a draw. The Robertson activists had tasted victory and, led by Ray Moore and Orin Briggs, were hungry for more. The longtime Republican loyalists, who had only recently made their party competitive, were bitter and frustrated.

Over breakfast, Ray Moore had told me that he understood the resentment. "We came in and upset their power system," he said. "But we have as much right to be involved as anyone." Moore said the regulars were upset because a group of born-again conservatives who had never played politics before had caught them by surprise. "These people we used, and millions like them, are hearing that they should be involved in politics and, for the first time, they're considering it," said Moore. "Well, they look around for someone like them, a Christian candidate who is a man of God." The difference between the Christians and the regulars, he said, "is inspiration." The Christians believe they work, not for a party or a candidate, but for God.

I had asked Moore where his campaign was strongest. The first place that came to his mind was Spartanburg, a small city of old textile mills in the northwest corner of the state. Spartanburg had an active corps of born-again political operatives working out of a growing church called Evangel Cathedral, he said. Evangel's political organizing was so strong that there was little difference between the church and the local GOP. He made it sound as if Evangel's pastor, Charles Gaulden, could conduct party business with the quorum present at a Sunday service.

The following day, I drove the hundred miles to Spartanburg. The countryside was sparsely populated. I passed heavily wooded hills and farms where crops of tobacco, soybeans, and cotton grew in rich soil warmed by the Southern sun. Spartanburg was one of a string of small cities linked by Interstate 85, which ran east to Charlotte, North Carolina, and west to Atlanta. Evangel Cathedral was on a side road next to the highway. It was easy to find. Gaulden, an associate pastor at Evangel, had told me to look for a construction site and a big frame of steel girders. "We're expanding," he had said.

Gaulden, a tall man with light brown hair and a runner's lean body, met me at the door of the old church building. He had a pair of white hard hats in his hands. He loved the construction project that was taking shape next door and rushed me over to see it. Crews were beginning to tack the metal skin onto the building's steel frame. The framework, made of steel girders that were painted a dried-blood red, formed the outline of a building that was about four stories high, 200 feet deep, and more than 300 feet long.

We parked our cars in the rutted mud in back of the building and walked beneath the girders and onto the smooth white concrete floor. Bright noon sun blazed in through the holes where the façade was not yet complete. Gaulden pointed to where the choir would sit and told me how the congregation would be arranged. He stopped for a moment where the pulpit would be located and gestured upward, at where the balcony would be. For a moment, he seemed to drift off. He spoke as if the church were finished, packed with worshippers, and he were preaching. He even raised his hands and gestured for a moment. I expected him to start a sermon, but then he looked back at me.

"When it's done, the church will seat five thousand, making it one of the largest auditoriums in the state," he said, breaking the silence. "That will make things a lot easier around here at Christmas." The Evangel Cathedral Christmas pageant attracted people from all over South Carolina, he said, as many as 25,000 a year.

As we walked around the building, we talked about politics and about the new church. Gaulden said local born-again Christians began to move heavily into Spartanburg politics in 1979, to help defeat Jimmy Carter. "I guess they felt betrayed by him and people rise up when they feel betrayed by one of their own," he said. After that election, those who stayed active got involved in the anti-abortion movement. They joined a local Catholic group, Spartanburg Citizens for Life, and began confronting local candidates, even those who could have no direct involvement in the issue. Gaulden's partner in the Robertson campaign, layman Jan Johnson, was one of the first conservative Protestants to join the anti-abortion movement. After picketing clinics and debating local candidates, he became intrigued by the idea of using politics to promote the entire conservative Christian agenda. "I'd say Jan got me involved in this, and I'll be in his debt for that," Gaulden said over the noise made by hammers on sheet metal.

From the construction site we drove about two miles to a cafeteria-style steak house where we met Johnson for lunch. A graying man with broad shoulders, Johnson was dressed in a gray sport coat, a white shirt, and a striped tie. He had brought along his son Jeremy, who may have been eleven or twelve years old. We met in the parking lot, walked inside together, and wound our way through the cafeteria line and past the salad bar. When we sat down Johnson immediately launched into his story of Spartanburg and born-again politics.

"In late 1979, a group called Spartanburg Citizens for Life came to our church and made a presentation. The pictures and the facts they showed us just knocked me over. I found out we were killing one and a half million babies a year. Now, I'm not normally a joiner, but I went home and prayed and the answer that came to me was: I got to get involved. Well, it so happened that a man named Ronald Reagan was running for President. I ran as a Reagan delegate in my precinct and won. The next month I went to Washington for a march for Jesus sponsored by Pat Robertson. I was impressed by him the way I was impressed by Reagan."

Inspired by his visit to Washington and Ronald Reagan's message, Johnson worked hard to deliver his precinct to the Republicans in the general election. In 1981 he and Gaulden both became delegates to the state Republican convention. Johnson was elated when he was able to help put the state party on record against abortion. He had been surprised by the stiff resistance thrown up by more moderate Republican regulars, who supported abortion rights. But he still prevailed, and emboldened by the victory, he resolved to help shape the statewide party into a more consistently Christian organization.

"After the '81 convention I was shocked that we almost lost on the abortion issue. I called the local churches and said we had to get Christians involved in all the precincts. The next time around there were eighteen committee slots open and we got eighteen Christians into them." Working the political system "was fun, once I got the confidence," he said.

Jan Johnson's religious upbringing, in a conservative Southern Baptist church, had included regular warnings against political involvement. When he was growing up, in the 1950s and 1960s, separatism was at its peak. The beginning of his shift away from separatism came when he was converted to a charismatic faith in 1973. His first marriage was ending at the time, and he was struggling to get his graduate degree in education at Appalachia State in Blacksburg, Virginia. He had seen some charismatic preachers as he was growing up but, like a good Southern Baptist, he considered charismatics to be overly emotional. But in the middle of his divorce, he started praying more often, asking Jesus to help him. One day, as he knelt in his apartment to pray, he was washed with a sense of peace. He also found himself praying in tongues.

"I was thirty-three then, but I had never been close to Jesus Christ before," said Johnson. He sought out a local charismatic church and he found that his new, more emotional faith helped him through school and the divorce. He came to Spartanburg to run an adult education program for the local school district, and found Evangel Cathedral. The church became his main source of emotional support. He worshipped there, socialized with fellow church members, and even taught a night course on Christian influences in early American history.

"Even in that class, I remember, people saw the system, society, getting more and more secular and less and less Christian," he told me over lunch at the self-serve steak house. "I studied the history books that were available and I saw that they were leaving out God in the history of America. It's a gross distortion and I knew it was a sign that things were going wrong. We also saw that Christians have a chance to save America."

"I grew up in a patriotic family, like most Christians. My father was in the war, and I always had a commitment to my country," interjected Gaulden, who had been silent through our lunch. "But as a Christian I didn't know how far I should go, even if I did feel things were not as they should be in America."

"I developed the feeling that the nation was going downhill," added Johnson.

"Yes, it was an absolute sense that the nation had deteriorated," answered Gaulden.

Both men said they had been bothered by the social unrest of the 1960s and intimidated by the tide of liberal progress. "I grew up in the segregated South, and at the time everyone accepted it. Everyone seemed to want it that way. Then Martin Luther King had those protests," said Johnson. "I thought that was bad. Later I came to see that segregation was wrong and had to be changed, but I thought the protesting was bad."

While the liberal political and social trends of the 1960s frightened Johnson, Gaulden, and the rest of the born-again subculture, they also gave them a model, an example of how moral outrage can blossom into social change. "For the longest time I thought protesting was bad. I associated it with hippies and the anti-Vietnam era," said Johnson. "Then I saw how it could be used against abortion clinics and candidates who support abortion, or against political candidates like Jimmy Carter. Now I know protesting and organizing can be good. It works for our side too."

In his home ward, Johnson had conducted a door-to-door registration drive, carving a 60 percent Republican majority out of a traditionally Democratic precinct. Citywide, Evangel activists shifted the Republican Party toward the Christian Right. "Spartanburg now has forty delegates to the Republican convention," said Johnson. "Of those, twenty-one are from Evangel Cathedral," he said proudly. "Of the six officers at the top of the delegation, four are conservative Christians for Robertson and two are from Evangel Cathedral."

As they organized Spartanburg, Gaulden and Johnson trained other born-again Christians in politics. "We step aside from leadership positions and let other Christians come in and get experience," said Pastor Gaulden. "By 1986 we had a hundred people from our church as delegates to the local county convention. This year we had a hundred fifty," he said. "That's more than one-third of all the delegates. I don't think the party knew there were that many of us."

While they recognized that they had built a classic political machine, both Gaulden and Johnson said their organizing was not so much about partisan politics as it was about morality. "I now know what those people in the 1960s felt," added Gaulden. "There's a cooperation and a freedom that comes when you do something active. I once heard a preacher talk about Christians who avoid the world," Gaulden concluded. "They're like plants growing in the shade. They never really develop fully. It's better to be right out in the sunlight."

The steaks and salad were consumed and Johnson's son Jeremy, who had been quiet during the whole meal, grew restless. I asked the two men about the future of Christian politics. They said the movement was slowly developing national leaders and candidates. And they pointed me westward, toward the city of Anderson, about thirty-five miles down Interstate 85. "Go visit Henry Jordan," said Gaulden. "He's someone who could really put it together for Christians."

Jordan was Anderson's leading surgeon and a growing political force. A losing candidate for the U.S. Senate in 1986, he was preparing to run for Congress in 1988. He was a Vietnam veteran, an Air Force Academy graduate, and director of an organization called the Carolina Conservative Coalition.

After saying goodbye to Gaulden and Johnson, I called Jordan from a phone booth near the steak house. He said he would be happy to meet me at his office the next morning. "I'm all for Pat Robertson," he said. "I'll do anything that might move him along."

With that appointment set, I drove to Greenville, which is about halfway to Anderson. I wanted to meet James Guth, a political science professor at Furman University. Guth was, at the time, one of the most quoted sources for news reports about the Christian Right political movement. He had done a study of Robertson's contributors. The Robertson campaign had raised $7 million, second only to Vice President Bush. The money had allowed Robertson to put seventy-five paid campaign workers like Ray Moore into the field. Only Bush had a bigger campaign staff. Robertson's aides often pointed to the large campaign kitty and the far-flung staff as proof of their imminent success. The claim was like the one made by the believers I met at Second Baptist of Houston; it must be good because it's so big and popular.

The Furman campus was a few miles outside Greenville. I found Guth, a balding, middle-aged man wearing running shoes and shorts, in a two-story brick building. He was sitting in a tiny, white, windowless office tapping away at a computer. He was surrounded by books and stacks of green-and-white computer printouts. "I got some new numbers recently from the Federal Election Commission," he said. "I want to see if they change anything."

Guth had grown up in Wisconsin, in a family that belonged to a fundamentalist church that banned dancing and movies. His personal faith had changed since those days, but, he said, "I still have some affection and appreciation for these people." With that said, he then declared, "Robertson is not going to go anywhere come 1988." Despite Ray Moore's lists and organizing and the fervor of people like Gaulden and Johnson, "the numbers just aren't there for him," he said firmly.

The numbers came from Guth's analysis of who was contributing to Robertson. He had watched the money flow into Robertson's campaign committee for more than a year. He checked contributors' occupations and hometowns and sampled their religious affiliations. Every quarter new reports on donations were issued and every quarter Guth ran his checks. "They show that he simply hasn't broken out of his base among the conservative Christians," he said. "Practically no one who isn't part of that subculture is supporting him with money," added Guth.

In fact, only one segment of the conservative Christian subculture, the charismatics, was really solidly behind Robertson. "He's a charismatic and there are 20 million of them or more, and he's bringing them into the political process," Guth said. "But there is surprisingly low support for him among Baptists and other noncharismatics." Guth argued that the noncharismatics were uneasy with Robertson on religious grounds, rather than political grounds.

The professor presented an insight that had been missed by most of Robertson's political critics. Many politicians said Robertson was too conservative on moral issues, like abortion and school prayer, and that those positions relegated him to the right-wing fringe. But Guth suggested Robertson's religious extremism was much more damaging to his candidacy than his politics. Robertson was a committed charismatic. He had tried to heal cataracts and hemorrhoids on his TV program, and he claimed to have "rebuked" a hurricane, steering it away from his Virginia Beach headquarters with the power of prayer. He had once even tried to pray life into a child who had been killed in an auto accident. Those displays made Robertson unacceptable to many Southern Baptists, fundamentalists, and other conservative, non-charismatic groups, not to mention less religious Americans.

Robertson had done well in South Carolina, Guth reasoned, because South Carolina was an anomaly. It had a higher percentage of charismatics than most states and a vulnerable caucus system. "Look, this state is the only small state where you're going to find a hundred or more activist preachers, and a caucus, and a high number of charismatics, all waiting for him to use them," continued the professor. "But he's just not attracting any other support. So when he gets to a primary state where everyone votes, or a state away from the Bible belt, you may see him drop real fast." Overall, said Guth, the born-again political movement was a selective kind of ground swell. It was a genuine grass-roots reaction to the liberal social change of the 1960s and 1970s. "But it's not the sweeping kind of conservative push they would claim."

Over the long run, Guth suggested, the conservative Christians were being steadily pushed toward more liberal attitudes. They just didn't realize it. "I can make the case based on the kinds of people I grew up with," Guth said. Back then conservative Christians everywhere didn't smoke or drink or dance. They shied away from public life and avoided mixing with other kinds of people. Their separatism helped them stay pure. "Then they started trying to change the world, and to convert people. The irony of it is that they were the ones who got changed. They go to movies, show up at parties where there is drinking. Jerry Falwell has even become friends with Teddy Kennedy. That's the danger in all of this for them. Once you go out in the world and become part of the process, you see that dancing isn't so bad, nice clothes and makeup aren't so bad. Pretty soon, you're the one who has changed and accommodated yourself. It's a powerful leveling process."

As the shadowy campus became dark, Guth said he was going to go running. "They'd probably have a fit if they heard me say it, but I'll leave you with one last thought," he said as we walked out of the building. "These institutions they're building, the colleges and universities and such—they are really mausoleums."

The next morning I drove southwest to Anderson to meet with Dr. Jordan. Anderson, a city of about 40,000, sits in a small corner of South Carolina that juts into Georgia. Dr. Jordan's office was across the street from Anderson's hospital, which was a big, blocky red-brick building.

Jordan arrived dressed in military-crisp blue pants, serious black shoes, and a spotless white shirt. He was a young-looking forty-three, with short brown hair, a clean-shaven face, and an even, bright smile. His hair was cut in a neat 1960s style, with a short bushy fringe of bangs and the hair on the sides just brushing his ears. Jordan shook my hand and led me to the office door. He unlocked it and showed me past a waiting room that was decorated like a small shrine to the doctor/politician. It was filled with pictures of healed patients, bumper stickers, and photos of the doctor with prominent Republicans. As we walked to his inner office, Jordan said he was tired. He had spent much of the night in an operating room across the street, trying to save a teenage girl who had been in an auto accident. "She had a flayed chest," he said, explaining that her injuries radiated across her body, like the spokes in a wheel. She was a mess of broken ribs and lacerations. But by morning it looked as if she would survive. "I prayed over that one," he said.

Jordan's heavy wooden desk was on the left as we walked into his office. To the right was a long couch. Behind the desk was a bookcase filled with medical texts. On the desk was a book entitled *Study Bible*. On a mantel on the far wall was a century-old doctor's bag. Next to the bag was a duck decoy and next to the decoy was a framed picture of Pat Robertson. A Vietnam War memento, a framed certificate of "Hank 'Doc' Jordan's" service in a unit nicknamed "Satan's Angels," was also on the wall. It was signed by every member of the unit, the way high school seniors sign yearbook pictures.

"That macho stuff, like Satan's Angels, was all bull," Jordan said as he sat at the chair behind his desk. "I was scared to death when I was over there."

Jordan's family had come to the New World in the 1730s with John Wesley, he said. His mother's family was related to Robert E. Lee. The Jordans had been doctors since before the Civil War. "My great-

great-grandfather used that medical kit—for the good side, of course, the boys in gray," he said, smiling. "That family stuff is important in the South, but the people who usually try to impress you with it are people whose family doesn't go back very far."

Jordan had grown up in Anderson, the oldest of four brothers, three of whom became doctors. The family attended a Methodist church, he recalled, "but I really didn't know Jesus." The most important event of his early years was his mother's death, which came when he was just fifteen.

"My mom was the one who built us up. She would tell us, 'If you are as good as I know you can be, you'll be all right in life,' and we believed it." She died of ovarian cancer. Jordan said his anger and sorrow about his mother's death led him into a brief period of delinquency that crested when he was seventeen when he was involved in a high-speed car chase. A carload of teenage toughs chased him across town to a friend's house. Jordan ran inside, came back out with a gun, and fired at the car.

"It wasn't long after that that I decided I wanted to go into the Air Force and I wanted to go to the Air Force Academy." Young Jordan had thought he could straighten out his life in the service, find a direction. The military academies are filled, for the most part, with candidates recommended by members of Congress. Jordan lobbied his congressman, finished high in a competitive test, and won the congressman's nomination.

"Leaving the South was traumatic," he recalled. "I had been to Washington once before and to a Boy Scout jamboree in Valley Forge, but other than that I hadn't really left the South. It was a real culture shock going to the Academy in Colorado. Everything I knew was this place, and I guess I still see everything in life filtered through Anderson, through my family and the way I was brought up."

After he graduated from the Academy, the Air Force sent Jordan to Thailand. He arrived the week that U.S. ground troops started pulling out of Vietnam. But the Air Force squadron that he was assigned to continued to fly combat missions. Jordan was a navigator and lived in a tiny shack at the end of the runway. "I wasn't born-again, so I couldn't really read the Bible to help me back then. I would lose friends, the gooks pulverized a buddy of mine from the Academy, and I couldn't even turn to the Bible. We got by on the macho stuff."

When he returned to the United States, Jordan resigned his commission and enrolled in medical school at Emory University, in Atlanta. "They call it the Harvard of the South, but I don't think Harvard's that good," Jordan said. He served a surgical residency at a city hospital in Atlanta and worked at perfecting his skills as a surgeon. But it was not enough. He began to feel an emptiness, an insecurity. At the time, his father, who had become a more devout born-again Christian, was dying of cancer. "He knew he was dying, but he didn't flinch," Jordan recalled. "I knew that he knew something about life and death that I didn't know. It dawned on me that I had really accomplished all my dreams, that I had spent more than thirty years concentrating just on myself, and that it was all useless in terms of eternity. I had fulfilled my agenda but I hadn't sought God."

One night, not long after his father died, Jordan was on an overnight shift in the hospital emergency room. He took a break in the doctors' lounge. He turned on the TV, as usual, but he didn't look for an old movie. He saw TV preacher Jerry Falwell on the screen and, for some reason, didn't change the channel. Jordan can't remember what Falwell had said on that broadcast, but he did recall that he had changed his opinion about TV preachers that night. "After that I started watching Charles Stanley, another preacher. I realized that these men are as smart, or smarter than I am. They spend their whole lives studying one book. Just one book. It didn't happen all at once in the kind of dramatic way some people describe. But I just slowly became humble and I repented of my sins and I accepted Christ."

Jordan sent for the books that Stanley offered on his TV program and immersed himself in fundamentalist theology. He gradually adopted a highly religious view of life. "I felt no fear after I accepted Christ. If I had a patient who was dying, I was able to accept it better." At the hospital he began to challenge doctors who performed abortions. "I was stunned by how it was just accepted by physicians who would fight to save babies on one floor and do abortions on another. I complained to a professor at the medical school, and he said, 'What can I do?' Professors are wimps."

Before long Jordan was buying every book he could find on conservative Christianity. He was fascinated by the idea of Armageddon and was particularly impressed by a best-selling book on the subject by a born-again writer named Hal Lindsey. Lindsey's book, *The Late Great Planet Earth,* outlined Bible prophecies and argued that they predict an imminent battle of Armageddon and the Second Coming of Christ. While outsiders dismiss such books as apocalyptic nonsense, millions of born-again Christians, including Dr. Jordan, subscribe to their theories. Jordan grew more and more animated as he explained to me his views on prophecy and the spirit world.

"The prophecies have essentially been fulfilled," he said. "One is that the gospel must be preached to the four corners of the earth. With TV, that's being done. The second is the reestablishment of Israel. The third is that a number of nations will be against Israel. And the fourth is a revival of the Holy Roman Empire, which we see in the European Economic Community. I was at the Paris Air Show recently with Senator Thurmond. I saw that the European nations are producing weapons themselves and gradually pulling away from America. When I realized that, I said to myself, 'Holy mackerel, this is the end times.' "

To believe most end-times theories, born-again Christians must believe in an active world of good and evil spirits, unseen but powerful beings that interact with people on earth. When he was a Methodist, Jordan didn't believe any of that. Over time, he changed his mind. He came to believe that angels and evil spirits are routinely involved in people's lives. "Make no mistake, Lucifer is on this earth. That sucker's all around us," he said, rocking forward in his chair.

To illustrate the point, Jordan told me about a successful colleague, a surgeon who specialized in repairing infants' hearts. "The guy is a genius, and people really love him. He goes in there and operates on these tiny hearts and his success rate is amazing. He works hard, and if people don't have the money to pay, that's OK too. People love him. But the sucker's a nonbeliever. I've talked to him about it. He just won't accept Christ. Well, I have to figure that his talent is being helped by Satan. It's as if Satan is giving him all this so people will see that someone who isn't a Christian can be successful. Satan's tricky that way. But in the end, that poor sucker is going to hell because he's not born-again. And there's no question there's a hell. It's eternal torment too, like being strapped into an electric chair forever but you never quite die."

God allows Satan and his minions to roam the world, and influence men and women, in order to test them, said Jordan. Those who become born-again Christians pass the test and win eternal bliss.

"We get to rule the universe with Him," Jordan said. Those who, because of Satan's influence or their own fault, fail the test get the never-ending electric chair. As he goes through his life, Jordan can decide that people who don't follow his faith, like the pediatric surgeon, are simply under Satan's mysterious, evil influence. It was clear that he liked the heart surgeon. He admired his skill and he was impressed by his colleague's long hours and the number of fees he waived for poor patients. He was a good person, but he wasn't a believer, so it must be Satan's trick.

I asked why God would make life so complex.

"Life here, the spiritual battle and all, it's an elaborate experiment to glorify God," he answered. "We don't see every part of it, but by studying, especially in the Bible, we learn it's there." He then jumped up from his seat, lunged at a radio that was near him, and switched it on. "It's like that. You hear the music, but do you see the radio waves? No. That doesn't mean they aren't there. You just don't see them. The spirit world is real and you better take it seriously."

Once he had accepted born-again faith, Jordan reassessed both his view of America and his own life. "My sins and what had gotten me in trouble were the same sins that had gotten America in trouble. I was arrogant, happy with myself. I had survived a traumatic childhood. I was a doctor. I had an attractive wife. I was really proud. But that pride was blinding me from being aware of what salvation was all about. People like Jerry Falwell, who I had made fun of, knew something I didn't know. They knew that people like me, and the country, were going to suffer for their pride."

Pride, happiness, and wealth, in the Christian view of history, always lead to evil and suffering. The suffering ends only when sinners repent. Two days before, I had switched on the TV in my hotel room in Columbia and watched Pat Robertson's son Tim describe the cycle on the 700 *Club*. He drew a circle, like the face of a clock, on a chalkboard. At twelve o'clock he wrote "Prosperity," at three o'clock he wrote "Fall," at six o'clock he wrote "Trouble," and at nine o'clock he wrote "Holiness." Man, who is basically sinful, always follows this pattern, he said. Periods of holiness are followed by prosperity, which is God's reward. Then there is a fall from grace, followed by troubled times, which end only with a return to holiness.

The 1980s were a troubled period, said Dr. Jordan. America suffered a fall after the prosperity of the 1950s. Society came to accept the alternative lifestyles of gays, feminists, liberals, and other non-Christians. The result, as he saw it, has been abortion, AIDS, economic decline, and the erosion of America's global influence. "I've seen our country relying too much on our technology, education, and other abilities," said the doctor who the night before had used a high-tech breathing machine to save the girl with the flayed chest.

"We have to regain our biblical wisdom. One way to do that is for Christians to become involved. Staying out of politics is a cop-out. I think God intends Christians to be involved. This country was founded to be a country built on the Bible, not to promote Muslims or Buddhists. I saw it all happening, the gays and the feminists moving in, the whole shooting match. But I know things will turn around. America may be in a time of trouble now, but I think there's a revival building."

Jordan had given me an entire morning of his time to describe his own conversion and theological beliefs. Now he said he was hungry and suggested we get lunch at a small restaurant nearby. We drove past downtown and back out toward the highway to the little cafe, where breaded pan-fried catfish was the $2.95 blackboard special. Over plates of catfish, hush puppies, and fries Jordan explained where the Great Revival, politics, Pat Robertson, and Henry Jordan came together. He explained that he had coordinated a revamping of the county GOP that had left it dominated by born-again Christians.

"The non-Christians think we have twelve out of the forty-eight delegates. We really have thirty-two," he said. "Without trying I've become the leader of the New Right in the state, not just the Christian Right but country-club Republicans too. Heck, I can claim that, because I am a country-club Republican. My wife drives a Mercedes. I'm a successful man here. But I've got one foot in the country club and one in the church. That's what's different this time around. Christians aren't backward poor people anymore. We are accepted members of society."

By joining the Republican mainstream and running for Congress, Jordan hoped to force born-again Christianity into the political process. If he won and the Christian organizing in places like Spartanburg and Anderson led to real power, then nonbelievers would have to take notice. "People are going to say, 'What do these folks have that makes them so successful?' Well, we have Christ. That way, politics will spark a religious awakening. It will serve God."

Jordan predicted that a Christian Right army would follow him and Pat Robertson into politics, wielding the same kind of influence the labor movement had in the Democratic Party of the 1950s and 1960s. Well organized and wealthy enough to fund campaigns, the Christians would go out into their neighborhoods and make the case for Henry Jordan, Pat Robertson, and, finally, God. It would start in the Iowa caucuses in 1988, he said, where Robertson had 100,000 names on his computer list, and 30,000 votes can win a four-way race. It would continue a few weeks later in South Carolina.

"By this time next year, Robertson will be a very credible candidate," he said. "They'll have to deal with the Christian agenda."

Jordan saw born-again political victory as inevitable. Like the TV preachers who called on the faithful to give to God's work by sending them money, Jordan believed his political ambition was God's ambition. A vote for him, or Pat Robertson, would be a vote for God. "This isn't just something I want," he said. "I have no doubt that I'll be in Congress, or the Senate. It's God's calling."

= 6 =

Christian Foreign Legion

ALTHOUGH the Christian Right was, overwhelmingly, a domestic political crusade, its leaders had a vision that went beyond America to include a large but little-known international wing of the movement: modern born-again missionaries. This Christian foreign legion, scattered around the world, had begun to grow in the late 1970s as the American TV evangelists looked for ways to extend their influence. In the 1980s the missionaries were among the most glamorous characters in the born-again movement. Sponsored by the televangelists or local churches (Smithtown Gospel Tabernacle had, for example, funded several missionary "teams"), thousands of born-again foreign crusaders promoted both American-style religion and American-style politics in Third World countries. Ardently anti-communist, they worked to convert the masses to conservative faith and to promote American political ideology. By the middle of the decade, leaders of the Catholic Church in dozens of underdeveloped countries were decrying the encroachment of the Americans. They implored their people to tune out the evangelists' broadcasts and abandon the missionaries' chapels. The Brazilian bishops even charged that the

American missionaries were more interested in right-wing politics than in matters of the soul. They branded the outsiders "Reagan cults."

In the late 1980s, Honduras was on the front line of both anti-communism and born-again evangelism. It was home base for the American-backed Contras, who were trying to overthrow the Sandinista government of Nicaragua, and it was also home to hundreds of conservative American missionaries who had come to fight communism. I went to Honduras in the spring of 1987 to tour the front lines of the missionary movement. Moments after arriving, I discovered how pervasive a presence missionaries had become. I didn't have to look for them. They found me in the milling crowd at Tegucigalpa's dilapidated airport terminal.

"Michael? I'm Allen Danforth," the man said as he grabbed my suitcase. Danforth was one of the missionaries I had telephoned from New York the week before. He had said he might try to meet me at the airport. I never expected he would actually do it. "Welcome to Honduras," he said. "Let me help you get out of here."

After a brief chat with the uniformed officials, who seemed to know him very well, Danforth returned with my passport and guided me quickly through the small dark terminal and out into bright sunshine where he climbed into a metallic-blue van. An American eagle was painted on the canvas that covered the spare tire on the back door. He drove the van down a small hill, past a handful of airport beggars, and into a tangle of streets. To the right, a city of squatter slums stretched toward the horizon. On the left, "*¡Fuera Contras!*" ("Contras get out!") was scrawled in red on a wall. Hondurans were growing tired of the American-backed Contra rebels, who from time to time brought the Nicaraguan Army with them into Honduras as they returned from raids.

"We're seeing more of that every day," said Danforth as he pointed to the slogan. "That's one reason it's so important that we are here, as Christians and as Americans." Danforth paused to turn on the fan to blow fresh air through the van. The air conditioning was broken.

"Religion aside, Honduras is the front line between communism and Texas," he said, shouting over the noise of the fan. The communists were to the south in Nicaragua. The rebel Contras were their opponents. "Communism draws its base of support in poor countries by providing people with their basic needs. The communists do it with things like low-cost medical care. We can be a powerful tool to eliminate that, to head communism off at the pass, in the name of Jesus Christ."

Allen Danforth was the founder of World Gospel Outreach, a $2-million-a-year operation supplying medicine and food to hundreds of families across Honduras. He said his mission work was a gift to God and country. He believed health-care and feeding programs could still the leftist rebellion brewing in Central America. Nicaragua had had its Marxist revolution because the old, American-backed regime hadn't done enough for the poor, he said. He saw the same happening in El Salvador. Honduras could be pacified, he said, with enough aid and enough born-again Christianity.

In practice, Danforth was a Christian fixer, an arranger. He persuaded American charities and corporations to donate supplies to his ministry, and distributed them in Honduras. In typical fashion, he had arranged to be the first person I met, and soon I realized that he would guide my entire tour of Honduras, if I allowed it. Danforth had a complete afternoon and evening planned. I told him I had a reservation at the Holiday Inn, but he took me to the Hotel Maya, a tall white-and-beige building that was full of Americans—mostly missionaries, soldiers, and journalists. "You'll be more comfortable," he said. "I'll cancel the Holiday Inn for you."

The Maya was indeed more comfortable. It was also an island of Americanism. It housed the office for the local Dale Carnegie franchise and on Thursdays hosted the California-based Full Gospel Businessmen's Fellowship, a kind of fraternity for born-again businessmen. On weekends the Maya was usually jammed with American soldiers on leave who were more at ease with English-speaking waiters and American-style food.

After check-in, which Danforth expedited with a visit to the back office, we went to my room. He said we had time for a short break, and then we would have dinner at his mission house with a group of Texans who had come to Honduras to do volunteer work with World Gospel Outreach. The night would end at a special prayer service in Nueva Suyapa, one of the dusty hillside slums on the outskirts of the city. I hadn't planned anything for the rest of the day, so I accepted his itinerary.

A tall, thin man with a bushy mustache and wide blue eyes, Danforth was filled with nervous energy and a likable sincerity. In my room, Danforth sat and talked about Honduras and his work and about his own conversion to born-again Christianity.

"I was raised a Methodist and went to Wake Forest, which was supposed to be Southern Baptist. But that's where I learned secular humanism," he began. "Anyway, I came out of school with a business degree and one goal: to climb the corporate ladder." He chose banking and climbed well, moving from small institutions to larger ones, eventually becoming a highly paid vice president for a bank in Houston. "I had been divorced and I moved to Houston to make a lot of money. I also considered myself an intellectual and I got involved in yoga. Yoga was great physically, but it had a spiritual side that was dangerous."

As Danforth talked, the air conditioning in the darkened room slowly defeated the accumulated heat of the day. He paused after the word "dangerous" to open the curtain. The view included the blue oasis of the hotel pool and the sprawling slum city beyond. The tops of the farthest hills were green, but the nearer ones were dusty brown mounds covered with shacks. The families who lived in the shacks got by on per capita incomes of about $60 per month. When it rained some of the shacks slid off the hills. Danforth sat back down on a plastic-covered orange armchair and continued talking. A pair of black birds landed on the balcony behind him.

"Anyway, it got to the point where I was getting up at four-thirty every morning to do yoga. One morning—it gets brutally hot in Houston early in the morning in the summer—I got up, opened the windows, and sat there meditating. It gets to be like a trance, you know, you just open yourself up to the spirit world. I was sitting there with my eyes closed and I felt there was a presence in the room. I turned to look toward the door, but I couldn't see anything.

"A little while later I felt it again and I said, 'Who's there?' Well, the temperature dropped fifteen degrees just like that," he said, snapping his fingers. "I went to open my eyes and I couldn't move. I felt what seemed like an electrical current running through my neck. I knew there was a spiritual being in the room and I knew it had a purpose. I had reached out to the spirit world and it had contacted me.

"I knew whatever it was was there to possess me. I thought to myself: 'This is awful. This is something really evil, an absolute evil presence.' I kept thinking: 'It's evil. It's awful.' And then I thought: 'If this evil is real, then there must be an equal good, like God.' I started to pray.

I said, 'God, if you show up here, on your terms, I'll follow you all my life.' I was crying. I said, 'If you are real, God, I want to know you.' "

With that, the evil presence vanished. The Houston heat flooded back into the apartment and Allen Danforth was almost a born-again Christian. "I spent the first few days going over the dishonesty in my life. I wept for three days and asked the Lord to forgive me. Eventually I started feeling a love, a love so strong that I knew it was an answer."

Danforth described several days more when he stayed in his apartment, praying. A neighbor then recommended he attend a nearby charismatic Assemblies of God church. There he found others who had had similar spiritual encounters. They spoke in tongues and fell to the floor during the service, seemingly struck down by the power of their faith.

"I cried out, 'God, there are people here who love You like I do,' " said Danforth. "I drove home clutching a Bible to my chest and sobbing with relief to know there were other people like me." Within a few weeks, after intensive Bible study, he declared himself a born-again Christian. "I knew the voice of God," he said. "I heard it in my heart."

All of this shocked Danforth's parents back in his hometown of Palatine, Illinois. He recalled his mother holding up the Bible and saying, "You mean, you believe this fairy tale?" Since then, Danforth says, his sisters have become born-again Christians too. His mother, however, remains outside the fold, despite his persistent efforts to convert her.

Not long after his conversion, Danforth left banking to study for the ministry, eventually becoming an ordained associate pastor at an independent church called Houston Evangelistic Temple. A fellowship allowed Danforth to study foreign missions. In the process he met some Honduran officials who invited him to establish his work in Tegucigalpa. The Hondurans helped with some of Danforth's early aid shipments, adding them to loads of arms that were being ferried from the United States. Gradually he got going on his own. Danforth ended his story and went into the bathroom. I noticed that darkness had begun to fall on hillside slums that were framed by the picture window. When he came out of the bathroom Danforth said it was time to leave.

We climbed back into the metallic-blue van and drove through winding streets and up a hill into one of the city's few posh neighborhoods. This was where we were to meet the Texans who had come for two weeks to work with Danforth and to check on World Gospel Outreach, which they supported with their donations. Danforth had already given them a tour of his territory and had involved them in some small mission projects. A man who was a plumbing and heating contractor had installed a hot-water system for an orphanage. A dentist had spent much of his time fixing teeth in poor neighborhoods.

When we arrived at the mission house, the Texans were preparing to sit down to a meal of macaroni and cheese and soft drinks. It was to be their last dinner in Honduras together. They seemed eager to put their experience in perspective, and the arrival of a journalist who wanted to hear about their stay in Honduras gave them the opportunity to focus their thoughts. When I began asking questions, the group instinctively turned to their leader, their pastor, to speak for them.

"In South Texas people are very much aware that this is the border with communism," explained Rev. Gary Adams, from Liberty Church in Lake Jackson, Texas. "But not everyone gets involved. They know what they know based on the nightly news. But when you come down here, you see it firsthand. It makes it real."

"Christians now sense there's something wrong in the world," added Danforth. "They see the world isn't what it was twenty-five years ago. Twenty-five years ago there was hardly any communist influence in Africa. Today half of Africa is Marxist. In the Far East we're seeing that the domino theory wasn't a theory. It is a fact. Country after country is falling. Now, in the Western Hemisphere, the Monroe Doctrine is laughable. Americans have been lulled to sleep and the Christians are just the ones waking up first."

After dinner, Danforth and the visiting Texans piled into the blue van and drove to Nueva Suyapa. The revival service they planned was supposed to strengthen the faith of the *barrio* residents and reinforce the bond between America and Honduras. On the way over, the Texans joked about being packed into the van like sardines, and sang gospel songs. The targets of their attention, the people in the hills that ring Tegucigalpa, usually met American missionaries in small chapels and church schools. Born-again Americans, along with trained Honduran associates, had opened hundreds of churches and schools across the country. Children attended the schools free of charge, and were usually fed at least one meal each school day. Medical teams made the rounds, holding open clinics once or twice a year at each school. Honduran mothers were eager to send their children to the Christian schools, not only because they would be fed there but also because of the supervision. From the missionaries' point of view, the children were also to be "fed spiritually," as Allen Danforth described it, and many were subsequently drawn out of the Catholic Church and into born-again faith.

Nueva Suyapa was a small neighborhood of one-room shacks terraced into one of the hundreds of brown hillsides that surrounded the city. The people who lived there were squatters who had come in from the countryside looking for work. We drove to the neighborhood on one of the dirt streets that cut horizontally across the hillside. The van pulled up in front of a tin-roofed chapel and the Texans emerged, still singing gospel songs, in English, and throwing candy to the dozens of children who came to see what was going on.

The Americans went into the chapel, followed by the children and dozens of adults who were drawn by the music and the spectacle of our arrival. The church was a single room with white walls and a tin roof held up by heavy wooden beams. The center beam was painted with the message "*Jesús, la Luz*" ("Jesus, the Light"). I sat on a wooden bench between an older man and a small boy who wore a black T-shirt decorated with a life-size picture of a skull and the words, in English, "Mercenaries Never Die."

"Jesus is here with us," began Gary Adams, a tubby man with puffed-up black hair and a bone-white face. A much smaller man, an American with pale freckled skin, red hair, and a red mustache, translated Adams' English into Spanish. "Let us give Jesus the praise. The Holy Spirit is here," said the American.

"Now, I want to talk to you about freedom. God wants his people to be free," said Adams, punching a fist in the air as he said the word "free." "We have all been in bondage, but I'm here to say that Jesus came to set me free. Jesus redeemed us to set us free from sin and to give us eternal life."

By the end of the service Gary Adams had the people of Nueva Suyapa crying "*Gloria a Dios*" and waving their hands in the air. They sang "Born Free" in Spanish, accompanied by a tape recording that blared from a portable stereo. Several answered the altar call, moving to the front of the chapel to pray intently with Pastor Adams and declare that they had been "born again" that night.

Back in the dirt street, the air was cool and the night sky was a soft black sheet flecked with tiny dots of starlight. The Americans piled into the van to ride back to Tegucigalpa. As they wound their way through the streets, they again sang gospel songs.

Danforth drove to the Maya and dropped me off before he took the Texans to the mission house. We made a vague plan to meet again. As I said goodbye, a chorus of "God bless you's" came from the dark recesses of the van.

The next morning I went back to Nueva Suyapa. At eight-thirty, the barrio glowed in dusty sunlight and smoky cookstoves filled the air with the smell of burning wood. Here and there gardens sprouted with vegetables and gangly banana trees. Children played in the streets. Some had nailed the lids of tin cans to the ends of sticks and were pushing them along the dirt. On every street there were tiny shops run out of people's homes. The shops offered soft drinks, a few vegetables, soap, even sewing kits. In one I asked a man standing in a doorway sipping a Coke where I could find the evangelicals, *los evangélicos*. All born-again Christians are called *evangélicos* in Honduras. He responded with a short speech about the many evangelists who trooped through the neighborhood.

"The evangelicals, the Adventists, the Jehovah's Witnesses, I've heard all of them here," he said. "Each one talks and I listen and I can't find much to believe in. In my foolishness I think none of it really changes anything. Only God can judge us all in the end." Then he pointed up the street and added, "But go see Isabel. She's one."

Up the street I found Isabel Godoy de López outside her home, washing clothes by hand in a series of water-filled oil drums. A bus driver's wife, Mrs. Godoy lived in a two-room hut a few streets up the hill from the mission chapel. She had five living children. Three others had died. She said the washing supplemented her husband's income. She said she had gotten involved in born-again Christianity after she sent her children to a local missionary school.

"When they started going to the school there were Americans there, but eventually the teachers were Hondurans," said Mrs. Godoy, a small woman with a deeply creased face. She wore a flowery cotton dress and had a red kerchief on her head. "They taught them, gave them some clothes and lunch, and taught them prayers. At first we sent the children for the material things. But I went down a few times and I liked the prayers. Now I thank God that those material things helped me become born-again."

After she began to attend the school chapel regularly, Mrs. Godoy was invited to join a women's Bible study group. The neighborhood women met once a week to read the Bible and talk. Mrs. Godoy found that the group helped her cope with her husband's alcoholism. "Of course, this makes life easier," she said. "I just give my problems to the Lord. The church gives me moral support, and my sisters pray for me. It makes me feel better. Otherwise, I try to accept the life God gave me."

When asked about politics, about the way peasants in other countries organized for change, Mrs. Godoy said the Bible discouraged political organizing. "We're not supposed to vote," she said. "That is the law of man. Voting is earthly. We're not involved in that."

Mrs. Godoy's faith showed the kind of trickle-down effect the American missionaries had produced in Central America in only a decade. Wherever they went, the missionaries had spread the same end-times ideas. Eventually, the Armageddon outlook was accepted by people like Mrs. Godoy. "We're concentrating on the Second Coming of the Lord. I can't say the day for sure, but the prophets and the things going on in the world today show that He is coming very soon," she said.

Mrs. Godoy said her ideas about the Second Coming and politics came, in part, from a sermon a guest preacher had delivered at the neighborhood church. The preacher had come from El Cenáculo, the big evangelical church in downtown Tegucigalpa. It was a church for wealthy and middle-class Hondurans, she said. Though she had never been there, she considered it the center of the evangelical movement, the seat of born-again authority in Honduras.

I stopped in at El Cenáculo a few hours later. The big church was just a few blocks from the Hotel Maya. And like the Maya, it seemed oddly American. Its pastor, Fernando Nietto, was a Cuban who had spent years working as an evangelist on the West Coast in the United States. In Honduras he had built El Cenáculo into the kind of large conservative church that can be found in most American cities. It was like Evangel Cathedral in Spartanburg or, on a small scale, like Second Baptist of Houston. El Cenáculo had a school, Bible study groups, adult education programs, social events, and even advertised its day-care center in the Tegucigalpa yellow pages.

Allen Danforth had introduced me to one of El Cenáculo's more prominent members at dinner the night before. A medical doctor and former national minister of health, he had told me that El Cenáculo's members were civil servants, professionals, the upper middle class of Tegucigalpa. "You will see, these are the decision makers, the people who set the tone in Honduras," the doctor had said.

On the day when I stopped in, El Cenáculo was hosting an American evangelist named Don Stewart. About five hundred people were in the main sanctuary, where Stewart was preaching. The room was octagonal, with a balcony and a towering stained-glass cross behind the pulpit. There was a crowd of wheelchairs in the center aisle, and most of the people in the chairs were attended by nurses. During a prayer for healing, the nurses pushed the chairs closer to Don Stewart and some in the congregation moved down to the front and knelt or lay on the floor. "If people fall and get hurt, our job is to heal," said Stewart. "Christian love is not a cold, clinical thing. It is healing."

After the service, I introduced myself to Stewart, who said he was beginning to establish himself in Central America. He said he had just been in the Philippines, where he was better known and had filled the 25,000-seat Araneta Stadium in Manila. He said he had time to talk and we went to a small office next to the sanctuary.

Stewart was a tall Southerner with bushy salt-and-pepper hair and a full beard. He said he had given a lot of thought to the worldwide competition for souls, and he had decided that if conservative Christians were to convert the masses, they would have to focus on economic issues. Poor Third World people needed to be given food, shelter, and security before the Bible. "Born-again Christians are finally seeing both the human suffering and the spiritual need in these countries," he said. "We also are seeing that people were opting for a theology that was inconsistent with the gospel. They were headed down the wrong road, mostly because no one was telling them about the right road."

The "wrong road" was the revolutionary movement within Catholicism known as Liberation Theology. Stewart was the first to mention it, but many of the conservative activists I met later in Honduras would agree with his analysis. Liberation Theology, Stewart argued, was communism masquerading as Christian faith. And it was the real enemy he had gone into the field to fight.

Although it was a complex twenty-year-old development, Liberation Theology could be described as a blending of leftist politics and the Bible. Its proponents argue that Jesus Christ was a political revolutionary—the one who threw the money changers out of the temple— and they believe Christianity is intrinsically a movement of the poor. Any other interpretation is viewed, by these radical priests and nuns, as a deformation of the Christian message. These activists were present throughout the impoverished Third World. They backed—a few even

joined—the communist rebels in the Philippines and helped overthrow
dictator Ferdinand Marcos in 1986. Wherever they worked, the leaders
of the liberation movement criticized American power and the capitalist system as the causes of poverty throughout the world.

"I can see why something like Liberation Theology appeals to poor
people," said Stewart, propping his legs on a coffee table in Nietto's
office. "It makes a lot of promises about the poor sharing the wealth
and, like communism, it can sound good. But as an evangelical Christian, I feel that it was attractive, spiritually, only because we weren't
there offering the gospel. Now that we are offering an alternative,
people are coming to Christ."

Stewart saw Liberation Theology as a theology of hate, a belief
system that pitted the poor against the middle and upper classes. Stewart
considered his version of Christianity to be a faith of love, one that
focused on man's vertical relationship with God, not his horizontal
relationships with the world. The Contras understand that, he said.
"They respond to the appeal of the Bible very well." When I suggested
that the Sandinista government also laid claim to Christian inspiration,
Stewart paused for a moment to reflect. "The Contras understand
we're fighting satanic warfare here."

Back in the hotel, I went up to my room and switched on the TV to
find American television evangelist Jimmy Swaggart. Stalking the
stage, microphone in hand, Swaggart was prowling for Honduran
souls. The broadcast was a recording of one of Swaggart's huge revival
meetings in one or another arena in the United States. But Swaggart,
who spoke only English, seemed to be speaking perfect Spanish. The
dubbing was flawless.

Obviously, an American television preacher was unlikely to raise
more than a few thousand dollars each month in a country like Honduras. But unlike in the United States, the money was not important.
In Central America, the TV preachers were missionaries themselves,
more interested in spreading their religious and political views. The
broadcasts were a powerful tool for conversion. Even in Honduras, it
was a rare family that was without a television. Poor families made
time payments, at astronomical interest rates, just to get a small set.
In the evening, most of the squatter shacks that surrounded Tegucigalpa
glowed with the light of the flickering black-and-white televisions.
Tegucigalpa's Catholic bishop had warned about "the drug effect" of
the TV preachers, but they had the most attractive programs on the

air. Swaggart was known to put on a good show and people watched.

The foreign broadcasts served the American evangelists in a number of ways. First, they provided a base of support for the evangelists' international preaching tours. When Swaggart, for example, went to Argentina or Chile or El Salvador, he could be fairly confident that he would fill stadiums with loyal TV viewers. Second, the foreign connections actually contributed to fundraising in the United States. Swaggart's American broadcasts often showed him holding starving children and walking through refugee camps scattered around the globe. The pictures, coupled with pleas for money for Swaggart's foreign missions, netted him millions of dollars.

Swaggart was the most prominent American television evangelist in Honduras. He had a well-staffed office in one of downtown Tegucigalpa's few modern buildings. His Honduran coordinator was a young American named Randall Bardwell, whom I met the next morning over breakfast on the poolside terrace at the Hotel Maya. It seemed one could sit in the Maya for a week and meet almost every American in Honduras. Half of them would be missionaries.

Before he became a missionary, Bardwell was an associate pastor for an Assemblies of God church in Swaggart's backyard, Hammond, Louisiana. The Assemblies of God denomination was one of the fastest-growing in America. Swaggart was the denomination's most prominent preacher, and in Honduras the denomination and Swaggart were virtually one and the same. Bardwell more or less confirmed this when he told me that he took most of his direction from Swaggart's headquarters in Baton Rouge.

Anti-communism, rather than "soul-saving" missionary work, seemed to be the priority for the people back in Baton Rouge, but the two were closely connected. "Brother Swaggart regularly preaches that the world is divided into two camps, Christianity and communism. One representative of Christ, the other representative of the evil one, Satan," Bardwell told me. In the field, Swaggart's missionary forces fought communism with schools, food, medicine, and blankets, he said.

"The number-one goal for us is to evangelize and save people from communism," said Bardwell. "A person who is healthy, well fed, and saved won't need to listen to leftist agitators," he reasoned. "First you soften them up, get their attention really, with a medical van, for example. Then you introduce them to the Lord."

Besides overseeing the medical vans, Bardwell was in charge of a correspondence course on the Bible, eight schools, a string of small chapels, and the Honduran broadcasts. It was through the schools that the Swaggart missionaries encountered most of their potential converts. In three years the school population had grown from 117 students to more than 2,100. Of those, about 1,600 participated in a free-meals program. In neighboring El Salvador the Swaggart school system was even better developed, Bardwell told me. There Swaggart had nineteen schools serving 14,000 children. El Salvador was also the test site for an experimental, low-cost water purification system Bardwell hoped to bring to Honduras. Pure water, a scarce commodity in poor countries, could open an entire community to evangelism.

"Jimmy Swaggart started his missionary work after he came to visit a Christian organization called Feed the Children," he said. "They weren't evangelizing them, and that disappointed him," added Bardwell. "The schools, or the vans, or the courses aren't the important thing. The souls are. If I can take the school money and win more souls by doing something else, I'll do it, because that's the higher goal. Our message is appealing because it's the message of the Second Coming of Christ as an imminent happening. People are ready to leave their misery, so that message is appealing."

Bardwell said that he was nearing the end of his tour in Honduras and that he was exhausted. While the schools still took up most of his time, he said he was excited by an entirely new project the Swaggart organization in Honduras had started. They were sending food, medicine, and other supplies to refugee camps on the Nicaraguan border. The refugees were the object of great concern in born-again America. Some were the families of Contra fighters. Others had been persecuted by the Sandinistas for their religious beliefs. During the early years of their regime the Sandinistas had closed American-style born-again churches because they suspected they were pro-Contra. The members of those churches were jailed, were exiled, or fled to camps in Honduras. "Go out to the camps. You'll see a great revival out there," Bardwell said. "That's where you'll see the results of what we're trying to do."

The camps were clustered in an area two hours east, by car, from Tegucigalpa. I drove there with a translator and guide named Roberta Reina. Roberta had once worked for the Honduran Army as a press aide and she knew her way around the country and the Honduran bureaucracy. Her family, which claimed both a vice president and a presidential candidate, was well known.

The sixty-mile run to the border area went through green valleys and forests and tiny villages. As we drove, Roberta questioned me about life in the States. "I am not one of these people who hate gringos," she said. She said the communist threat in Honduras was real "and the Americans protect us." As we passed small farmhouses and peasants leading burros loaded with firewood, she said that life was not so bad for the poor in her country. "I don't think the people here are so desperate. They just want peace, to be left alone. I think a lot of people are glad the Americans are here," she said. "They aren't happy about the Contra bases, but they think the Americans keep the Nicaraguans out."

Eventually we arrived in Jacaleapa, the village where the main refugee camp was located. The camp sat in a pasture in a small valley about a mile away. Neatly ordered rows of one-room shacks, hundreds of them, were arranged on flat, packed dirt. The shacks were never intended to be permanent homes, but by 1987 some of the refugee families were well into their third year there. Behind the shacks, dozens of large tents provided temporary housing for more recent arrivals. Beyond the tents was a small river, which was used for drinking water and washing. Smoke from wood-fired stoves filled the camp. Laundry hung on lines strung between the little houses. Children played catch with tennis balls, or ran down the one broad muddy street in the camp tugging tiny paper kites behind them.

When we arrived, the man tending the gate in the barbed-wire fence recognized Roberta and swung it open. The Red Cross field director at Jacaleapa, a short, energetic Honduran named César Juárez, met us outside his office. He said there were about 5,600 refugees at Jacaleapa, of whom 75 percent were born-again Christians. Many were converted after they entered the camp, he said. "They can find more social activity and even get more material things if they belong."

Juárez was busy preparing for the arrival of several hundred new refugees, whom he expected within the week. The Contras had begun to mount attacks just across the border, their campaign timed to influence the American Congress, which was then debating whether to continue funding them. Whenever Congress debated funding, said Juárez, fighting increased and so did the population at the camp. He turned us over to Javier, a young man about eighteen or nineteen years old who was a camp leader. He assisted Juárez and the camp doctors with whatever they would let him do. It helped cut the tedium in the camp, he said. It made him feel useful. Javier knew where to look for the people we wanted to see. The three of us walked about the camp trailing children and dogs.

Randall Bardwell had asked me to check on the pastor of the camp church, Ramiro Ballejos, who had been sick. Bardwell hadn't talked to him for more than a week and he told me he was worried about him. We headed for the church, the largest building in the camp. It was a squat wooden chapel made of rough, unpainted pine and perched on top of a concrete slab. At noon the hinged plywood shutters had been lowered to keep the sun and the heat out of the building. A man playing a guitar inside the church said that Pastor Ballejos was at his house, resting.

We found Ballejos sitting on a rough-made stool beneath a sheet of corrugated metal that jutted past the roof of his house to shade a small yard. A light breeze carried the smoke from the cooking fire away from the house. A young boy, who looked to be about ten years old, sat on the ground next to him, sometimes leaning against him. Ballejos explained that the boy had been born with a crippling disease. He could not speak or walk. His legs were withered sticks and he breathed heavily through his mouth, making loud sucking noises. He stayed close to the pastor, as if this would bring some healing or safety. Ballejos said he himself had suffered partial paralysis—one side of his body had been affected—the week before. The camp doctor had been unable to determine the cause of his paralysis, Ballejos said, but the symptoms seemed to be disappearing.

Ballejos had left his home in Nicaragua because he had been accused of helping people travel illegally to Honduras. He wouldn't say whether he had in fact been smuggling people out of the country. But he admitted that after one twenty-five-day stay in a Nicaraguan jail he did give the Sandinistas a fabricated list of names of supposed Contra supporters. Then he fled north himself.

In the camp, Ballejos' sense of the theological meaning of the Nicaraguan struggle had deepened. Now, he said, he saw the Contras and the Sandinistas through the filter of biblical prophecy—specifically, through the American conservative view of biblical prophecy. Ballejos said the Nicaraguan exiles "have been picked out of our society by God to show that we evangelicals are the chosen people." While the chosen sat on the sidelines in Honduras, in Nicaragua God would let the Sandinistas grow in power. "Communism needs to flourish in Nicaragua because it is part of the prophecy of God. It is part of the suffering we have to take for man's sins. God is letting the communists flourish as a punishment. But the final war [Armageddon] will come and that will be when communism is finished. And that is an event that is happening soon, I think."

This prophetic view seemed to afford the people of the Jacaleapa camp the same comfort that apocalyptic stories have provided to isolated Christian communities for centuries. Most of the people I met in the camp seemed to agree that, even though the Sandinistas were consolidating their power, God was about to intervene. The Armageddon battle, beginning with the Russians in the Middle East and spreading around the world, was coming soon, they said. But before it happened, born-again Christians would be "raptured" into the heavens to safety.

"The only refuge from this big war is going to be Jesus Christ," Ballejos said as he rose from his chair to lean against the fence that surrounded the small yard. "No organization, not the Contras, not the United Nations, not politics, is going to protect you. Only Jesus Christ can. That's why last week we had seventy-nine people accept Christ. We're going to expand and expand his church until there are only Christians and communists. And the Christians will be saved."

In the meantime, Ballejos said, his duty was to convert as many people as possible and fight the communists any way he could. "That's why the real Christians are the Contras," he said. "In the Bible the people of God, the chosen people, do take up arms to defend their country."

We left Ballejos and walked around the camp, speaking with some of the people in the tent city. The few Catholics complained that their priest visited only once every month. They were planning to build a chapel, they said, but the funds for materials were long overdue. This was in stark contrast to the camp's Assemblies of God church, which had become, with its lively services and material aid, the principal social institution of the camp. For the time being, in Jacaleapa the religion of comfort was the religion that, like the medicine and blankets, came from America.

Outside one of the shacks a young man named Porfirio Alemán said he had just been converted. "I was a Catholic, but the Sandinistas were Catholics too and look at how they turned to communism," he said. "The evangelicals teach us to have faith in God, that God and the fulfillment of prophecy will save us. I believe that now. I really do." Alemán said he was nineteen years old and had been in the camp for two years. I asked him if he thought about his future, about what kind of life he would like to live outside the barbed wire. "I really haven't thought about it," he replied. "I don't really need to."

For the isolated born-again Christians of Jacaleapa, life was simply waiting. Waiting for the end of the Contra war, or waiting for the end of time. They lived in a refugee camp surrounded by barbed wire in a country that really didn't want them. So, with the help of American-style born-again faith, they built their own reality inside the fence, a reality that included an avenging, rescuing God and salvation in the end time.

Driving back to Tegucigalpa, I mentioned to Roberta that I had heard about another kind of settlement in Honduras, a kind of religious commune where Americans had established a permanent home. "Oh, I know where that is," she said. "Those people are almost famous here. We'll go tomorrow."

I had heard about the Mennonites of Honduras from a minister named David Bontrager. Bontrager was executive director of an organization called Christian Missions to the Communist World, Inc., which sent money, supplies, and Bibles to anti-communist Christian missionaries from, as its advertising declares, "Argentina to Zambia." CMCW's mission statement includes four goals: "to deliver Bibles, to aid families of Christian martyrs, to bring to Christ leftists and communists, and to warn Christians in the West of the dangers of communism." Bontrager had described a Honduran mission settlement run by a man named David Peachy: "a good Christian man and anti-communist." Bontrager had visited Peachy and had given me directions to the settlement.

The next day Roberta and I headed north, looking for Bontrager's milestones and finding every one. Seventy miles out of Tegucigalpa, in a valley of parched rolling hills, we saw a big American-style farm-house, an irrigation pond, neatly ordered fields of corn and other crops. It looked as if nineteenth-century rural America had been set down in the Honduran countryside. The people who walked the long dusty road that wound through the complex could have been Pennsylvania Dutch, except that most of them had the Latin features and brown skin of Honduran peasants. The bearded men wore long-sleeved white shirts, dark pants, wide-brimmed hats, and suspenders. The women wore long dresses with long sleeves.

That morning, most of the settlers were gathered in a small white clapboard church set atop a hill planted with fruit trees. A few people walked slowly through the orchard, up the hillside, and into the church. The doors and windows were open and a man's voice could be heard. Someone was preaching loudly, in Spanish.

Outside, a bearded old man sat in the bed of a pickup truck, half listening to the sermon that drifted out of the church. He said his name was Fermín Mejía Gómez, and that he had been drinking himself to death when he came to the Peachy farm. The Mennonites had welcomed him and put him to work. Within a week, he said, "I felt changed. The money I used to make I would drink. Now I don't. The Christian doctrine says, 'Don't spend your money on what is not bread.' "

Mejía Gómez explained that each man who declared himself born-again and joined the group was given a horse and a piece of land to work. He said the farm had a small dairy, and that the Mennonites sold seed and supplies to neighboring peasant farmers. The group also made money by selling bread, which was baked by the Mennonite women and trucked to Tegucigalpa twice each week. Together, these enterprises provided a living for every member of the community. "This is the best life you can have," Mejía Gómez said proudly.

The sermon had ended while Fermín was talking, and people had started leaving the church. Among them were several American-looking women, in Mennonite dress, who carried what were apparently Honduran infants. David Peachy, a tall, spindly man with short blond hair, strode stiffly to the door of the church and called out, "Hello." He was not surprised to have visitors. After all, the settlement was a kind of tourist attraction and middle-class Hondurans and curious Americans often made day trips to the farm, where they could expect to be welcomed.

Peachy was middle-aged but had the stiff bearing of a man twenty years older. He walked the half mile to the main house, with Honduran men, women, and children following several paces behind. I asked him how many people lived in the settlement, and I inquired about the half dozen American women I had seen leaving the church holding babies. He said that about a hundred Hondurans and twenty Americans lived on the farm. Another twenty people, orphaned children, lived in a special house on the grounds. The orphans were bound for America, where Amish and Mennonite families would raise them. The American women were there to meet their new adopted children and learn something of their origins. There had been scandals recently in Honduras involving the sale of "orphaned babies" who were either abducted on the streets or purchased from their parents, he said. "Our adoption service is monitored and sanctioned by Honduran officials."

When we got to the house, Peachy stepped onto the porch, arranged some chairs in a circle, and sat down. He sent a young Honduran boy to check on lunch. "I know what most of the questions are, so I'll start by explaining our clothes," he said. Like the other men, he was dressed in a starched white shirt and suspenders. "They are a symbol of our modesty," he said. "We don't think that what we wear on the outside is very important.

"Now, I imagine you want to know how this place came to be," he went on. He explained that the community had been founded in the late 1960s by Amish missionaries from Indiana. The Amish are even more old-fashioned than Mennonites. They avoid all machines, electric lights, even radios. In the United States they survive in old, self-contained communities in Pennsylvania and the Midwest. The Honduran mission had been an experiment: the Indiana Amish had wanted to see if their way of life could be spread around the world.

When they came to Honduras, the Amish brought the huge draft horses which did the work of tractors back in the United States. The horses, which required special care and feeding, never adjusted to the Honduran climate. Some of them died of illness brought on by the heat. Eventually the remainder were slaughtered. The Amish settlers survived, but they never adjusted either. "They found that mission work and Amish life just don't mix that well," said Peachy. "You can't spread the gospel successfully while holding, almost religiously, to these old customs."

Peachy recalled that he had first learned about the farm in Honduras when its founders stopped at his farm in Pennsylvania to rest on their way to Central America. He had long thought about working as a missionary and had kept in touch with the Amish pioneers. In 1970 he left his thriving farm near Harrisburg, and with his wife and five children went to join the group in Honduras. The Peachys traveled by ship from New York and then rode buses across the countryside. "It was one of the longest journeys I could imagine at the time," he recalled. "It was a real test."

When he arrived in Honduras, Peachy found that the Amish community was in turmoil. Several of the missionaries had adopted the Mennonite faith, which shared the simple Amish piety but had fewer restrictions on the use of machinery and electricity. Then Amish himself, Peachy also converted when he saw that the stricter Amish lifestyle would not succeed in Honduras. Gradually, all of those who didn't convert returned to the States and what had started as an Amish experiment became a Mennonite outpost.

Under the Mennonites, the farm began to prosper. Gradually it recruited new residents from among the poor in the region. Peachy said such people might otherwise have been swayed by the communist agitators who were active in the area. "It's clear that Christ did not give us any revolutionary agitation in his teachings," he said. "The Bible says to pray for the government but that the church has no place in the government. The early Christians were separated from politics and so should we be."

The Peachys' children had all been raised on the farm and educated in the mission school. By the time I met David Peachy, all of his children were grown. Two of his sons were on their way back from the United States, accompanying a cargo of new farm equipment. Peachy's wife was in the United States. A grown daughter, who had recently come back to Honduras, prepared and served our lunch. She would not speak to me, though, despite my encouragement.

Peachy offered us lunch in the kitchen of the main house. We were joined by two other visitors. One was a twenty-three-year-old Jewish man who had been staying on the farm for weeks. He introduced himself as David and said he had been traveling, by bus and by foot, for the better part of the year. The other was a Mennonite farmer named Ira Huber. Huber was in his sixties, much shorter and much rounder than Peachy. He sat quietly, speaking only when he wanted more to eat. Huber had come to bring his daughter, an unmarried woman in her forties, back to his home in Ontario, Canada. Not only was there little talk over lunch, but, more striking still, only the men sat down at the table.

The lunch we ate was huge—heaping plates of sausage, beans, rice, and vegetables—and Peachy pointed out that it was more substantial than anything the local farmers would likely ever see. The locals knew that life was materially better on the Mennonite farm, and that fact served to attract them, he added. "Christ said, 'I came that you might have life and have it abundantly,' " Peachy said. "I feel that he means it to happen for man right here and now, that he have abundance. We can show people a better way of life here, where there is enough for people to enjoy and share without being selfish. They have peace with God."

After lunch we walked over to meet a recent convert, a woman named Virginia Bonilla, who had moved her family into a cottage that stood at the end of a long dirt lane under a very large oak tree. When we arrived, Mrs. Bonilla's fourteen-year-old daughter was in the garden, holding a red flower and leaning against a fence. She called her mother, who came running out of the house to invite us inside. At first Mrs. Bonilla was reluctant to talk. She wanted Peachy's permission. When he gave it she spoke briefly of her life on the farm. She told of a faith that was essentially a bargain. She had traded her independence for security.

"We forget about earthly things," she said, standing in a bare kitchen. Flies buzzed about her and a dog wandered in and then out again. "We have the fear of God and when you fear God you just can't do everything that you want." At the settlement David Peachy controlled access to cars and trucks and money. Nobody left without his permission. While Mrs. Bonilla couldn't do as she pleased, she and her children had most of their material needs met.

"I used to have to walk from my old house to as far as Mr. David's house to get water," she said. "Now I have it here, at the house." Smoothing her dress, she said she had been "full of vices" before she moved onto the Mennonite farm. Now she was living a Christian life, and was praying for her family to be converted soon, "because I feel the Second Coming is about to happen." Mrs. Bonilla said she never left the farm. Of course, she had no money of her own and no means to leave. Her world stretched only as far as the preacher's big house.

On the road back to the main house Peachy recalled that he had had to drive only one person off the farm. This was a young man who had been flirting with the women. He once borrowed a truck, and some money, and went to Tegucigalpa "for no apparent reason at all. The problem was, he wasn't really born-again," said Peachy. "This is the best life for a person who is born-again."

David Peachy believed the isolated, restricted life he had created in Honduras was a special Christian alternative to the evils of communism. He hoped it would be an example and would spread across Honduras like the expanding Kingdom of God. As I looked back down the road at Mrs. Bonilla, who stood alone under the expanse of the oak tree, it seemed as if the Christian crusaders had reached their ultimate goal of born-again utopia. But in the name of Christ and anti-communism, the people who lived there had created an authoritarian system of their own. And it was difficult to imagine how, even under the rule of the dreaded communists, their lives could be much more restricted.

=7=

Heritage USA

T HE PILGRIMS—2 million in 1981, 4 million in 1985, 6 million in 1987—had to come in along Interstate 77, the highway running like a spine down the middle of the Carolinas. From the north they would stream through Charlotte, and into the suburbs, past the roadside factory outlets for local pottery, towels, and linens. They would pass the giant amusement park called Carrowinds, where a looming, twisting roller coaster could be seen from the highway. The roadside signs along the way advertised new housing developments, where some of the houses sold for upward of a quarter of a million dollars.

About an hour south of Charlotte, just over the South Carolina state line, the pilgrims would turn east on State Highway 21, which cut through rolling hills of white dogwood, emerald-green pastures, and orchards crowded with peach trees. Three miles down, just past a bend in the road, the pilgrims would see, bigger than life, billboard images of TV evangelists Jim and Tammy Faye Bakker smiling down at them. They welcomed the faithful to Heritage USA and the PTL (Praise the Lord) television show. Just past the giant billboard of Jim and Tammy, a long driveway led into born-again America's sanctuary. Inside Heritage USA were the condos and houses, shopping mall,

theaters, hotels, campgrounds, and amusement park that made up
Christian America's refuge from the outside world.

It was ironic that the Christian Right crusade would start to unravel
here in 1987, with so many victories seemingly at hand. The Alabama
textbook decision had just been handed down. Pat Robertson's political
machine, well lubricated with donations, was picking up speed. And
as the furious response of the Latin American Catholic bishops showed,
the born-again foreign legion was winning a worldwide battle for converts. It was fair to say that by the mid-1980s American conservative
Christianity was a powerful, credible social and religious force growing
stronger every day.

  Then a scandal took place that was, symbolically, the beginning of
the downfall of the born-again Christian movement. This fall from
grace had actually begun seven years before in a Florida motel room.
By most accounts, evangelist Jim Bakker went there for a fast and
heated extramarital fling with a twenty-one-year-old church secretary
named Jessica Hahn, who had come to Tampa, Florida, from Long
Island to watch Bakker participate in a local telethon.

  By Hahn's later accounts, the encounter was violent and devastating
to her. She said she had been fed a spiked drink and then Bakker
essentially raped her, leaving her to be assaulted again by one of his
fellow preachers, John Wesley Fletcher. Hahn, who would later appear
to be all too willing to profit from this episode, said she had been
traumatized by Bakker's assault. Whatever the truth of this, the PTL
ministry paid her off to keep the events secret.

  The payments, which were made over several years, amounted to
hundreds of thousands of dollars. But in 1987 the story came out when
a lawyer connected with Hahn apparently leaked it to one of Jim
Bakker's rival TV evangelists. Hahn kept quiet for a short time, but
even as Bakker continued to deny that anything happened, she began
to dole out bits of information to the press. Eventually she told all and
became an instant, if fleeting, celebrity.

  The more Bakker denied the charges, the bigger the scandal grew.
In tight-fitting jeans, stiletto-heeled boots, and heavy makeup, Hahn
fed her story piecemeal to the reporters who camped at her doorstep.
The revelations spurred other reporters to investigate PTL and the
Bakkers. Within months they found that Jim and Tammy and many
in their ministry's top management had all but looted PTL's bank

accounts. Millions of dollars were said to be missing, and the press was full of reports of the Bakkers' financial excesses, ranging from the vacation homes to an air-conditioned doghouse, to Tammy's extraordinary expenditures on jewelry and cosmetics. By late April 1987 the scandal had landed Jim and Tammy on the covers of both *Time* and *Newsweek* and had forced them to retreat to their home in Palm Springs, California.

But while the Bakkers hid, the pilgrims continued to come to South Carolina. Despite the uproar, or perhaps because of it, PTL officials reported they were taking in more money than ever. Jim and Tammy's followers remained steadfast, at least for the moment. Nonetheless, it was clear that born-again America was struggling with the first real crisis of the 1980s revival. Moreover, to those who had followed the historical course of revivalism in the United States, the sexual nature of the scandal was familiar. After all, in the 1930s Aimee Semple McPherson, the most popular evangelist of her time, had seen her movement destroyed when it was revealed she had been having an illicit affair. Similarly, Billy James Hargis' immensely successful ministry had been destroyed in the 1970s amid allegations of various sexual improprieties. This time, the question was whether this politically powerful and more sophisticated version of born-again Christianity could weather a crisis which in its perennial nature had the quality of nemesis.

I decided to go to Heritage USA on Easter weekend, a time when I could expect that the charismatic Christians, who made up the bulk of the Bakkers' followers, would be most focused on their spiritual lives. The Bakkers, PTL, and, indeed, the entire born-again movement had suffered an enormous loss of prestige and were threatened with the incipient possibility of a real decline of their power. It would be interesting to see how the hard core of the faithful were holding up.

When I arrived, I drove through the condo developments and past the shopping mall, and followed the signs to the television studio. It was housed in a three-story, brown stucco building set in a grove of southern pine and fronted by a huge parking lot. Several big white satellite dishes sprouted from the back lawn. At the time PTL had the best satellite network in Christian television. The network fed Christian programs, twenty-four hours a day, to more than 1,400 broadcast and cable TV stations around the world. In front of the TV building the parking lots were filling with buses and cars. At the same time, groups of people walked down from the surrounding campgrounds and filed into the TV center.

The lobby of the studio, a space the size of half a basketball court, was called the Hall of Faith. On the walls were thousands of two-inch-long brass plates engraved with the names of donors who helped build the complex. There was a large American flag hanging on one wall and near it was a framed oil painting of a baby's face. Under the painting a small sign read: "My greatest argument against abortion!—Jim Bakker." The lobby was filled with more than a thousand people waiting to see the live broadcast of the daily *PTL Club* program.

Given the vital link that the TV show provided for the Bakkers and their followers, it was not surprising that attendance at a live broadcast would be the highlight of a visit to Heritage USA. The program was the locus of the Bakkers' relationship with their supporters and their most significant fundraising tool, providing them with as much as $100 million each year. At about ten minutes before ten, the doors to the studio were opened, letting out a cool blast of air conditioning. The audience filed inside, filling the rows of blue cushioned seats. Everything in the studio—the walls, the chairs, the curtains—was pale blue.

Normally the live broadcast would have begun a few minutes later, but ten o'clock came and went and it soon became clear there would be no program. Eventually the PTL singers, three men in blue blazers and three women in blue dresses, came out to announce that because it was Good Friday there would be no program. Ron, a young man with bushy brown hair who seemed to be the leader of the PTL singers, reassured the audience that they would, nevertheless, be entertained. He began by reading aloud the schedule of events published in that day's *Heritage Herald*.

"Of course, there's a baptism going on in the Heritage Grand Hotel pool at 2 p.m. today. Just wear something that's thick, so that when it gets wet, it's not thin."

Many in the audience tittered, but no one laughed.

"Tickets are available for a horse carriage ride." He paused to think. "Seems to me if you're willing to ride around looking at a horse's rear end, it should be free.

"Anyone here on their honeymoon? Well, stand, if you can!"

Ron threw his program in the air, the crowd laughed nervously, and then a barrel-chested older man in a white windbreaker, a blue sweater, and white pants strolled onstage. In the pause, I leaned toward the couple to my right and introduced myself. They said they were Barbara and Dennis Clausen, of Kutztown, Pennsylvania. "Could you tell me who these people are?" I asked.

"That's Doug Oldham," Barbara Clausen explained. "He's a wonderful singer. He's had a hard life himself. But the Lord picked him up."

"Good morning, folks," Doug Oldham boomed from the stage. "You all awake? Some of you look half dead. Now, I know it's raining and we've haven't got the *PTL Club* for you today, but that's no excuse. Wake up!" Doug Oldham introduced Raleigh and Furn Bakker, who were sitting in the front row. They are Jim Bakker's parents. The crowd applauded politely. "You ladies have to watch ol' Raleigh," joked Oldham in his sonorous baritone. "He loves to hug and squeeze. But don't worry. Furn keeps him in line most of the time." It was the cleanest kind of sexually suggestive joshing, and the audience loved it.

Raleigh and Furn—an elderly pair who waved slowly and then sat down—were the closest the audience would get to Jim and Tammy Bakker that day. At another time, Jim and Tammy would have appeared to help entertain the faithful and remind them, as they had so often, that "God loves you, He really does." Jim would be expected to preach. Tammy would be expected to sing. But Jim hadn't preached for weeks, and Tammy shared his seclusion.

As Raleigh and Furn sat down, Dennis Clausen, who was sitting next to me, said what was probably on the minds of half the people in the room: "I bet they're mad at Jim."

"I bet they forgive him," answered his wife.

Onstage, Doug Oldham announced that his records were sold in the lobby next to Tammy Faye's. Then he sang about angels who protected Christians from harm. In the middle of the song Oldham stopped singing and said, in a hushed voice, "God's our father, you know. He promised He'd stay with you. Thank God for all the angels He puts around you."

When the song ended, the audience applauded warmly. Ron, of the PTL singers, came back down to the front of the stage and asked who in the crowd might be celebrating a birthday. An old woman rose from the front row. Ron jumped down, ran to her, and held his microphone in her face. "I'm Ella Mae Hodges," she said, "and I'm ninety-five years old today." Ron pulled the microphone back and said, "Isn't that wonderful. Let's try and find a prize for her!"

Ron then rejoined the rest of the PTL singers on the stage and conducted a gospel version of *Name That Tune*. The orchestra would play a few notes, and people in the audience yelled out the name of the song. The prize was Tammy's latest album of gospel songs.

After a while, Ron ended the game, announcing that it was time to collect donations. Ushers handed out cardboard buckets for what Ron called the "Love Offering." Doug Oldham started clapping his hands, and said, "We always applaud for the collection here. We know it's an opportunity to show the Lord what is in our hearts." Only a few people joined in the applause, but just about everyone reached for his or her wallet or pocketbook. Ron reminded them that the amount they gave would be a measure of their "faith and love for God."

As the cardboard buckets were passed along the rows of chairs, Oldham went backstage for a moment, returning with a box. When he returned, he ceremoniously opened it and took out a soft doll with curly blond hair. "You partners are doing a wonderful job, keeping us afloat while we're having problems. Our mail is up, our donations are up, you're keeping us afloat. Now, this doll is a Christian doll and if you just press her belly button she'll sing gospel like you've heard here today." He held it up to show the audience. "I have to tell you she's available in the lobby where Tammy Faye's records are sold. I know she started out at over twenty dollars, but if I'm not mistaken, she's just ten dollars now."

While the buckets still traveled from hand to hand, Oldham told a story about a deaf man who hated deaf people until he became a born-again Christian. "Now his bitterness is gone and that man runs a school for the deaf, praise the Lord," he said. Then he brought out a sixteen-year-old singer named Lana Young, a slight-looking girl with long brown hair. She sang a song called "How Great Thou Art," and as if to emphasize Oldham's story about the deaf man, gracefully translated the words into sign language as she sang them.

The buckets had been picked up by the end of the song. The show was over. "Goodbye, God loves you," the PTL singers cried above the applause.

I walked out of the studio with the Clausens, who turned to climb a hill. They said their motor home was parked a few hundred yards away, under the tall pines at the Sugar Creek campground. They hesitated when I asked to come along. Then Dennis said, "Well, I guess it would be all right. Come on and we'll sit and talk for a while."

Their daughter, Jennifer, and their three sons, Andrew, Jeffrey, and David, ran ahead. We walked slowly along the eight-foot-wide asphalt path through the campground, a heavily treed warren of pathways and vacation trailers. Barbara, a tall, thin woman with short, wavy red hair and a fair complexion, started to talk about the Bakkers. She sounded like a faithful fan reviewing the story line from a favorite soap opera as she recalled the details of the Bakkers' lives: the time Tammy Faye became addicted to diet pills, or when Jim failed to show up for his daughter's birth. The details spilled out of her like a memorized poem, in monotonous double time.

"All the stuff in the media, we all knew about that for years. If you watch the show you know the Bakkers were having trouble with their marriage. Why, Jim wasn't even there in the hospital when their children were born. That must have been terrible for Tammy. I remember when our last child was born we did natural childbirth and I could never have done it without Dennis. Well, after that they were obviously having marital problems and then Tammy got hooked on over-the-counter medicines. But they were getting back together. The affair Jim had was a one-night stand and it happened six years ago, but now it's in the media and it's really hurting them. It's hurting us."

The depth of Barbara's knowledge about the Bakkers surprised even Dennis. He looked at her with his eyes wide open. "How do you remember all that?"

"If you watch the show," she explained quickly, "you know these things."

We reached the Clausens' campsite and Dennis stopped to unlock the door to their small motor home. "You know, as we drove in here we missed their presence," he said. "Usually you could expect you might see Jim and Tammy on the grounds, or on Main Street. They usually greet us PTL partners," Dennis went on. "I had a tear in my eye when I walked on Main Street and knew they weren't here." Dennis went inside the camper to get a sweater. It was cool under the trees. Barbara and I settled into folding chairs that were arranged around a picnic table.

"It's like having this happen to a member of your family. It hurts," Barbara continued. "But you don't turn your back on them, do you? I'm not going to be unforgiving."

Forgiveness seemed to be the main theme at Heritage that weekend. On one wall of the TV studio thousands of letters had been pinned to a fifteen-foot-high painted heart bearing the inscription "Forgive." At the entrance to the park, rows of flowers had been arranged to spell out the word F-O-R-G-I-V-E-N. In the Heritage Grand Hotel the telephone operators, who worked in a small glassed-in office on the second floor, had taped a sign on the glass: "Forgive."

"The Devil tempts those who walk close to God," Dennis said as he returned and sat with us. A struggle with Satan was considered a badge of honor in born-again circles. Dennis had fallen too, I would learn. He knew what it was like. The Clausens said they had followed a long road to their born-again faith and they were holding on. The Bakker scandal had not shaken their faith in born-again Christianity.

The Clausens were both born Lutherans, she in Pennsylvania and he in Iowa. They both had stayed in the Lutheran Church until just after they were married. They were teachers back then, and their first jobs were in California. As young adults the Clausens became religious seekers. Dennis cautiously explained that in the 1970s he dabbled with the occult. For a time he was even a follower of a supposed spirit named Seth who spoke through a woman in Elmira. He attended spirit readings and conventions for followers of the occult. He even planned to move back East because he believed in psychic Edgar Cayce's prophecy that one day the western part of the United States would sink into the Pacific.

In the meantime, Barbara said, she had had an experience in which she felt she talked directly with God. She then began to pray daily, although she did not join a church. But when the Clausens moved to Dennis' native Iowa, where he had decided to study chiropractic, Barbara got involved in a local born-again church in Davenport. As she immersed herself in Bible study and prayer, she became born-again. But, at least from her point of view, Dennis was still being courted by the Devil. She prayed for him, hoping he would drop his interest in psychic phenomena and come to church with her.

"I thought I was ahead of everyone else. That I had found God," said Dennis, nervously smoothing his deep blue V-neck sweater. Dennis started to doubt his belief in psychics when he happened to see a former Edgar Cayce believer on the *700 Club* TV show. The man had suffered a series of illnesses and personal tragedies that ended only when he became a born-again believer. "He said, 'Get rid of all those occult books, they're the Devil's, get rid of them.' I did it. I ran around the house pulling them all down, put them in a bag, and threw them out."

By the time Dennis had graduated from chiropractic college and the family had moved to Kutztown, Pennsylvania, Barbara had started actively challenging Dennis' beliefs. She persuaded him to accompany her to the charismatic church she had joined. And over the course of several months of her proselytizing, he eventually was convinced that he had been wrong about Seth and Edgar Cayce and he embraced his wife's born-again Christianity. In retrospect, Dennis believed his exploration of the occult had been a flirtation with the Devil. "There's a lot of demon power among those people," he said matter-of-factly. Born-again Christianity, reinforced by Jim and Tammy Bakker, had saved his soul. "I thank the Lord," he cried, wiping away a tear, "that I'm out of that now."

At the time of Dennis' conversion, in the late 1970s, the Clausen family started watching the *PTL Club* and began contributing. Heritage USA was being developed, and the Bakkers offered special deals to contributors who sent money for the construction. The deals were actually time-shares—reserved, prepaid vacations—that were tax-deductible. With a payment of $3,000, the Clausens got one week's stay per year at the Heritage Towers Hotel for the rest of their lives. Of course, the twenty-one-story hotel had still not been completed in 1987, and the scandal over Jessica Hahn had caused construction to be halted entirely. Until the hotel was finished, the investors were receiving three weeks' parking privileges at the campsite. "Thank goodness for the camper," said Barbara.

At the time we met, the Bakker–Jessica Hahn scandal was in practically every newspaper and TV news broadcast in the country. Jim and Tammy had stepped down from their posts as leaders of PTL and Heritage, and the future of the big hotel, the unfinished golf-course condos, and everything else at Heritage USA was in doubt. "Satan's responsible for it all," Dennis Clausen said when I asked him about the trouble. Just as he was behind Edgar Cayce and Seth, Satan was responsible for Jim Bakker's problems. "Satan has fought everything that has been done here. Every project has had troubles, but with faith we have overcome them. Satan didn't want the TV studio built, and the creditors were at the door, but we saved it. It's the kind of thing the Bible says will happen in the end times, when the forces of evil mass against the forces of good." The Clausens said they weren't troubled by the scandal because the battle of Armageddon and the return of Christ were imminent.

"In the meantime, there's not much we have to do about things but wait," said Dennis. "First there will be troubles like this, and then one-world government, and then the end of time followed by Christ's millennium." I asked whether their children had been taught about the prophecy and believed it. "They know about it. But they are saved," he answered. "They know they'll be with the Lord and it will be better there."

Dennis got up from his chair and went into the camper. He returned with a camera and started taking pictures of me and Barbara. "Don't pay any attention to me," he said. "Just talk."

The first thing Barbara said was: "My first fiancé was killed." She said it happened in 1959 when she was a college senior about to graduate and marry. Three months before the wedding day her fiancé was fatally injured in a freak explosion at his highway construction job in upstate New York. It was to be ten years before she would meet Dennis, fall in love again, and marry.

Dennis then rejoined the conversation. He said that he had spent his childhood shuttling from house to house, often living with relatives, while his father struggled with alcoholism. "Oh yes," Barbara recalled, "I grew up with alcoholic parents too."

Just then the Clausens' children returned, breathless, from a pickup game of basketball. They wanted lunch. Rising to say goodbye, Dennis wiped his eyes. "Boy, we really talked, didn't we?" he said. "Hope it wasn't too much. Anyway, when you write about Heritage USA, say it's awfully nice to have a place where Christians can go and feel safe and relaxed. That's what I feel about this place. You can come here and feel safe."

I left the Clausens' campsite and walked through the woods, past a recreation hall for children and a small man-made lake, to the center of Heritage USA, the hotel/shopping complex. I sat on a white wrought-iron bench near the revolving doors of the Heritage Grand, the luxury hotel that was attached to the shopping mall. Behind stood the unfinished Heritage Towers Hotel.

The day was cool, but not cold, and when the sun broke through the clouds it brought instant warmth. I watched the doorman greet a busload of pilgrims. Straight and tall in his plumed hat and gray-and-white uniform, he looked like a heavenly version of actor Robert

Preston in the film *The Music Man*. One after another, more than thirty middle-aged, mostly overweight women tumbled out of the bus. The doorman wrapped each one in a big hug. While he greeted, bellhops, less regally uniformed, wrestled mountains of luggage into the lobby.

"Praise the Lord! Welcome home!

"My, my, what a heavenly host of young, beautiful ladies. Praise the Lord! Welcome home!"

I got up and followed the ladies through the revolving doors and into the lobby. The Heritage Grand looked no different from many large modern hotels. The lobby, four stories high and lavishly done up in marble and glass, served as a courtyard for four floors of hotel rooms that rose on all four sides. The ladies barely broke stride. They moved past the glass case displaying the china doll dressed like Tammy Faye Bakker on her wedding day. They ignored the check-in desk, where golden letters on the wall behind the clerks proclaimed: "Jesus Christ Is Lord." They bustled right by the woman playing classical music on the ornate 107-year-old Steinway grand piano. Just as Ron of the PTL singers had promised, there was a baptism going on in the swimming pool at the far end of the lobby. And a seminar on makeup and hair care was starting in an adjacent shopping mall called Main Street USA. The group divided. Some headed for the baptism, where they could applaud and praise Jesus. The rest turned toward Main Street searching for the beauty show.

I chose the baptism, moving close to the railing around the lobby pool so I could hear the pastor. A crew from the Canadian Broadcasting Corporation was filming the event. The sound man had taped a microphone to a long metal rod and he held it over the edge of the pool to capture what was said. The cameraman positioned himself behind the pastor and panned across the expectant faces in the water before him. The CBC producer told me she was there because the *PTL Club* is popular in Canada and Canadians are interested in the Bakker-Hahn scandal. "They've made such an effort to make this place seem luxurious," she said as she looked around.

A young preacher strode, fully clothed, into the shallow end of the pool. Hundreds of onlookers jostled to get a view. Some lined the railing around the pool. Others peered down from the four floors of balconies above. Behind the preacher, nine baptismal candidates shivered slightly in their bathing suits. There was a ten-year-old girl, an elderly man, five middle-aged women, and two young men. Behind them a pair of glass elevators carried guests to their rooms on the floors above the pools. To the side, silver scraped on china and ice tinkled in glasses in the lobby cafe, where lunch was being served.

"Lord, we ask a special blessing on this girl," the preacher began, wrapping his arms around the one child in the group. "Let everyone who sees her know she loves Jesus Christ. I baptize her in the name of the Father, the Son, and the Holy Spirit." Flashbulbs popped, the faithful applauded, and the preacher dunked the girl under the water, lifted her to the side of the pool, and wrapped her in a towel. So it would go, for all nine. A short prayer, a dunking, a towel, and applause.

After the second middle-aged woman was baptized, I decided I wouldn't be missing anything if I checked out the beauty show. I walked across the lobby, through the entrance to the shopping mall, and past a vendor selling popcorn. There, about a hundred folding chairs were arranged in front of a small portable stage. On the stage a smiling, motherly-looking woman in her forties was cutting a teenage boy's hair. A second woman, glamorously dressed in a pale blue silver-studded dress, silver shoes, and wide silver necklaces, applied makeup to a teenage girl's face, all the while lecturing the assembled multitude on bases, eye shadow, lipstick, and wrinkle creams.

"Now, ladies, if your face breaks out when you first use Tammy Faye, it means the makeup is working," said the glamorous blond woman in the blue dress. "But if it lasts more than a week, consider discontinuing." She dabbed a cotton ball into a jar and moved it over the girl's eyes. "It rejuvenates the skin cells around your eyes. This is the same as Estée Lauder, but theirs is thirty-five dollars and Tammy Faye is twenty-seven dollars. A full line of Tammy Faye is available right here on Main Street."

The crowd applauded and then many moved on to shop on Main Street. Main Street was built to look like an idealized nineteenth-century village. The stores resembled Victorian shops with heavy molding and many windows. Overhead an arched ceiling was painted sky blue and simulated scudding white "clouds" were projected in convincingly realistic patterns of cumulus formations. Behind the Victorian-style façades, which were painted pale green, pink, and blue, lay that vaunted paradise of Christian consumerism: a Christian record shop, a Christian bookstore, a men's shop, a women's boutique, a hair salon, Tammy Faye's cosmetics shop, an ice-cream stand, even a sweet shop called Der Bakkers' Bakery.

In the Main Street bookstore I found volumes on everything from biblically inspired dieting to child rearing, where the emphasis seemed rather excessively oriented toward corporal punishment. A wide variety of Bibles and "Jesus Loves Me" mugs, T-shirts, and hats, were available in the gift shop. Parents could also buy their children sets of plastic shields, helmets, and swords called "The Full Armor of God." There were no bargains on Main Street; indeed, ticket prices did not even include the 10 percent surcharge, called an offering, which Heritage USA levied on every purchase. There were, however, small signs that told bargain hunters to search out the Goody Barn, a warehouse hidden in the trees nearby, where gifts, books, and clothes were available at reduced prices.

The shoppers who inspected Bibles and turned over mugs to check prices were well dressed, middle-class, and mostly white. Most wore plastic identification cards that marked them as members of one or another of PTL's donor organizations. The cards certified that they were entitled to discounts on their purchases and free admission to certain events. The lowest-ranking were the PTL Partners, who donated small amounts monthly. Then there were the 1100 Club members, who had each contributed a one-time $1,100 donation. There were also Silver, Silver 7000, and Gold Club cards, which were issued to those who had given even larger amounts of money. For the most generous, there was the Victory Warrior Club.

Some of the shoppers were college kids, many of whom were wearing sweatshirts with the words "National Spring Break Getaway" printed on the front. It was incongruous to see, on Easter weekend at Heritage USA, this reference to spring break, a time when American college students traditionally head south for hell-raising vacations synonymous with drunkenness and wet T-shirt contests in Florida bars. But in 1987 the PTL organization was holding its second annual alternative spring break, a weekend of planned Christian events, for born-again college students. The turnout was small by Fort Lauderdale standards; only a few hundred young people had turned up.

At Bentley's, a brass-railed Main Street restaurant, I joined two young men who were wearing these "Getaway" sweatshirts. Michael and Rick Domingo came from Alexandria, Virginia. They were brothers, seventeen and nineteen respectively, and shared the same Spanish-Asian features. They were quite willing to talk about Spring Break Getaway and Heritage USA. But as we started to talk, the subject they broached was not their holiday, but rather something more serious: Rick Domingo's crisis of faith.

"The basic thing is this: there's a trade-off between having sex and having eternal life," Michael said sternly. Michael had been baptized that morning. "I'd have to say that at this moment, because I understand that I am the more serious Christian," he said.

A high school senior with a passionate interest in physics, mathematics, and computers, Michael Domingo seemed to revel in his own sense of certainty. "I follow the straight and narrow path," he boasted.

Rick was taller and more athletically built. He described an academic record that was hardly sparkling. He had taken the last semester off from Central Michigan University, where he had been a psychology major. He said that his course work had made him doubt his religious commitment and that, in any event, his friends were probably all in Fort Lauderdale drinking beer at that moment. The problem for Rick was that he no longer believed that sexual abstinence was a good, in and of itself.

"I feel I'm going to marry my girlfriend one day, even though she is Catholic and not born-again," said Rick. "Given those circumstances, I don't think it's so serious to have had sex. I don't think that means I'm going to hell."

"God's more important to me," Michael interjected, at which point Rick shrugged and, turning to me, remarked, "We haven't gotten along that well lately."

Michael added hastily that, like Rick, he too had a Catholic girl-friend, but that he wouldn't consider having sex until after marriage, and he wouldn't consider marrying someone who wasn't a born-again Christian. "It's like AIDS," he said. "God is weeding out the good and the bad. You have to control yourself."

Both of the Domingos agreed that their values had been shaped mostly by their mother, who was a born-again Christian. Their father had abandoned the family when they were young, and she worked and raised them on her own. That experience left the boys with a healthy respect for working women. "Marriage is fifty-fifty," said Michael. "And communication is everything in a relationship," said Rick. But then Michael added, "Of course, in God's eyes, the man is the head of the family. He's held responsible."

The Domingos were, first and foremost, believers in the Christian life, PTL, and Heritage USA. Looking up from their hamburgers, and across the hotel lobby, they pronounced the place "beautiful" and insisted it was not a resort but rather was a Christian retreat dedicated to God. Rick said he had come to Heritage that Easter with a clear purpose. "I'm trying to get straight with the Lord," he said. "Maybe it can happen here."

The food was gone and the waitress looked up from the cashier's station, where she was reading *The New Pocket Testament and Psalms*. She brought the bill. The Domingos paid, and they were off for a volleyball game with the spring-breakers. I asked if there was any chance of romance with the young women at Spring Break Getaway. "Oh no," said Michael. "That's not what we're here for."

That night I saw the Domingos in the crowd at the opening of the annual run of the Heritage USA Passion Play, the story of Christ's betrayal, crucifixion, and resurrection. The play was performed in a large outdoor amphitheater made of cement which was colored to look like red clay. Opening night was sold out. While most productions of the Passion Play adhere to the biblical story, the Heritage USA version included an appearance by a flesh-and-blood Satan who spoke directly to Jesus. He came in a flash of light and a puff of smoke, and exited the same way. Heritage also added God's voice to the play. It boomed out at Jesus from a loudspeaker in the rear of the theater.

The production had an elaborate set: a temple, Jerusalem hillsides, Calvary, and even Gethsemane. There were live goats and camels and sheep and a cast of hundreds. In the end Christ rose from the dead illuminated in the glare of quartz-halogen stage lighting. After the play, most of the faithful retired to their campgrounds or hotels. But the spring-breakers finished their evening at a Christian rock concert held in the TV studio. On Good Friday, the somber day when Christians around the world recalled the crucifixion, when "the world" was hounding Jim and Tammy Bakker, Heritage USA rocked on into the night.

Saturday morning brought showers, which delayed the season's opening of Heritage Island, a complex of water slides that was the main recreational attraction of the resort. Built in the middle of a small lake, Heritage Island was a hill-shaped landfill covered with a maze of twisting fiberglass chutes. Bathers hopped into the chutes, which carried fast-running streams of water, and whooshed along into pools below. The park also had a wave pool the size of half a football field. Alongside the pool were stretches of sand that made up an artificial beach.

To an outsider, it seemed curious that the mood that Easter weekend was dampened only by the rain. That morning, the *Charlotte Observer* had led with an article revealing that Jim and Tammy Bakker had been paid $1.6 million in 1986, and more than $4.8 million in all during the previous three years. Even by the standards of television ministries, the sums were astronomical. Jerry Falwell, who by any measure was a preacher of equivalent stature, had been paid $100,000 by his church in 1986. The *Observer* report made PTL and Heritage USA look like giant cash cows, fed by millions of believers and milked by the Bakkers and top ministry officials. And the paper suggested that as the ministry approached its crisis—with the Jessica Hahn secret slowly leaking out—high officials in PTL grew more greedy. Richard Dortch, who had become the stand-in host of the *PTL Club* when Bakker left, took $270,000 out of the operation in the first few months of 1987 alone. Another of the Bakkers' close aides, David Taggert, had made nearly as much in the same period.

But although the papers and the news broadcasts outside may have been filled with these revelations, nothing seemed to penetrate the consciousness of the community of faith at Heritage USA. Certainly, no one was reading the newspaper at Bentley's, where I had breakfast, and the television set in the restaurant was tuned to the PTL Network. People seemed to be talking about the Passion Play, or about the rain and the postponed opening of Heritage Island, but not about the Bakkers' increasingly precarious situation.

After breakfast, I walked out the back door of the Main Street mall and passed the site where what was to be the world's biggest Wendy's hamburger shop was being built. Even around the construction site, there was no litter on the ground.

In the parking lot next to the half-built hamburger castle, I met two women, a young one pushing an older one in a wheelchair. The younger woman said her name was Jean Pense and she introduced her mother, Joyce. Jean wore a green-checked flannel shirt and blue jeans. The drizzle matted her hair, sending tiny rivers of water down her neck. Joyce wore a blue nylon windbreaker and green slacks. She had pulled the hood from her jacket over her head. The Penses said they were looking for their car, an old olive-green Chevy Nova. As we walked around, looking for the car, the Penses offered me their assessments of born-again Christian life, Heritage USA, and the Bakkers' plight.

"Well, let's start right with this," Jean said, holding her cigarette out and looking at it. "Now, there will be some people here who say we can't be Christians because we smoke." She put her cigarette back in the corner of her mouth. "They're wrong. There's nothing in the Bible about smoking. But we wait until we're outside, away from people. We don't want to ruin the atmosphere for anyone."

In fact, Jean and her wheelchair-bound mother were themselves part of that atmosphere. Many disabled and sick people came to Heritage USA hoping they might be healed. People in wheelchairs seemed to be everywhere on the grounds, and it was not unusual, said Joyce, for other visitors to stop and pray over her, trying to will a miracle of healing. "Healings do happen in our time," said Joyce.

I told her that in all my contacts with Christian America, I had not met one person who had been miraculously cured of a serious illness.

"The reason is that it's not all that common," said Joyce. "Sometimes a person just isn't ready to be healed, and sometimes the Lord has other plans for people."

Joyce had had polio, and despite frequent pilgrimages to Heritage USA, and constant prayer, she remained paralyzed. But she continued to believe. And she recounted a small healing miracle of her own, which helped her keep faith. She said she injured a toe so severely "that the crack made me certain it was broken." It so happened that a TV preacher told a story about the healing of his own toe that day and Joyce prayed along.

"I was healed," she said.

"And I know plenty of others who have been healed as well," added Jean.

We then talked briefly about the Bakker scandal.

"It felt like a death in the family," said Joyce. "The newspapers are all out to get the Bakkers. They don't understand what PTL and this place are. They are like home to us."

"And besides, who among us hasn't sinned?" Jean chimed in.

Neither of them seemed much concerned about their donations being used to buy Jessica Hahn's silence or luxury items like the Bakkers' air-conditioned doghouse. The Penses' connection to the Bakkers and Heritage was strong. People there were kind to them. That morning a hairdresser in the Tammy Faye salon told Jean she would cut her hair at home and charge her much less than the salon charged.

Jean insisted that they would continue to spend all of their vacations at Heritage. Glancing over her shoulder at the unfinished Heritage Towers Hotel, she noted that she had invested enough to earn a few free nights per year once the place was finally built. In the meantime, the Penses would stay in one of the budget motels out by the interstate, and they would drive the Nova to Heritage every day.

At home in Virginia, the Penses lived on Joyce's small income from office work and on what they could net from the sale of leather goods— belts, wallets, and handbags—which they made. Joyce pulled a small wallet, a sample of her work, from her purse. It was smooth and shiny, decorated with bird designs. The two women said they dreamed of one day establishing a leather shop near Heritage USA and settling in the area. Jean explained that she had already quit her job "by faith," which meant she had simply walked out, trusting in God to provide. I recalled a woman I once met who had told me that she routinely backed her car out of her driveway every morning "by faith," trusting that God would clear the traffic. "Doing things by faith," said Jean. "It's the way to get where you're going."

The Penses' dream, to live at Heritage USA, had already come true for the more than 1,000 residents of the on-site developments. Leaving the Penses, I drove over to one of the developments, Mulberry Village, which I had passed several times on my way through the front gate of Heritage USA. The houses were low, wood frame buildings with picket fences and clapboard siding. They were painted pale pinks and yellows and greens, the colors of after-dinner mints. I parked at the entrance to the development and followed an older couple into a real estate office.

Inside the office, which doubled as a model home, Vivian Gilbert, formerly of Drayton Plains, Michigan, greeted browsers as warmly as seriously interested prospective buyers. She was a tall, silver-haired woman dressed in a neat black suit, a white shirt, and red beads. She was quick to fill me in on the details of the development. Condos and houses cost between $59,000 and $149,000, she said. Most of the buyers were retirees, like Mrs. Gilbert herself. They came to feel safe, she said. At least that's why she had settled in Heritage USA. To make her point about security, she told me a story about the night when burglars almost robbed her house in Michigan. Her husband, who had since died, managed to frighten them away. "But they ripped a screen and pried open a basement window before we heard them. That gave us quite a scare. We decided we would eventually move away."

The Gilberts had begun watching the *PTL Club* and contributing in the late 1970s. They both worked for General Motors at the time, he on the assembly line that made buses, she sewing automobile upholstery.

As the conversation turned to life at Heritage USA, a tall older man who had been inspecting the model home stopped and cocked an ear. Outside, the rain stopped and the sun flashed its light through the front window of the model home and onto Vivian Gilbert's shiny hair. "Of course, there's no place that's perfect," said Mrs. Gilbert.

The browser edged into the room.

"And I have been a little disappointed by what has been going on. It seems like the Bakkers were making quite a bit of money while most of us who live here, and contribute to PTL, live on a little bit of nothing. That's disillusioning."

Visibly angry, the browser interrupted. "Is he a reporter or something? We don't need any reporters around here. They've done enough, thank you. That's the problem here. If we had this place back in Knoxville, we'd know enough to keep our mouths shut. We'd know how to protect it and hold on to it."

From a back room a woman, sounding like the man's wife, called out, "Now, Chester, quiet." She appeared and they left. Chester slammed the door.

Vivian rose to see me out. "Are you a born-again Christian?" she asked, moving toward the door.

"No, I'm not."

"Well, I'll pray for you. And I mean that in the best way."

"Thanks. I know you do."

The sun was coming out again as I went back to the center of Heritage USA and I decided to take a walk around the lake. I stopped at a small dock where a young man and a young woman in shorts and Heritage USA T-shirts were at work lining up two-man paddle boats. They said the water park would probably open the next day. When I asked them about the PTL scandal, the young woman nervously excused herself. But the young man—he said his name was Joseph Grennan and that he was nineteen—was willing to talk. But he wanted to ask the first question. "Are you an atheist? I'd love to meet one." I answered that I was somewhere between an agnostic and an atheist, and that I was interested in his view of PTL and Heritage USA.

"God built this place, not Jim Bakker," he then volunteered, "and even with what's going on, PTL is not going to disappear. It's God's, and man can't take it away." Grennan became angry as he talked to me, and asked, "Why don't you go interview rock stars who bite off the heads of animals or people who make millions of dollars selling drugs? This place is worth it if even one person going down the water slide is saved in Jesus' name because of us."

Grennan said he was from suburban New York, but that his family had moved to nearby Pineville, North Carolina, when his father was hired to do communications work for the PTL Network. "I used to fight. I mean a lot. But that was because I wasn't saved and because of New York. It's too far gone in the ways of Satan. It's much better here. And my opinion is that the Bakkers deserve what they can get, because they have saved souls from hell and that is a priceless gift." The water park, built at a cost of $10 million, is a "ministry," he said. "It is all worth it—the water slides, the Bakkers' salary, everything— if one person who comes down that water slide makes a decision to come to Christ, to be born again."

Looking up from the dock, I saw Barbara and Jennifer Clausen pedaling two bulky rental bikes along the asphalt pathway that circled the lake. The clouds were breaking up, and Barbara and Jennifer were obviously enjoying the sun and the exercise. They were smiling. I left Joseph Grennan and ran up the gangway to the lakeshore. Barbara's and Jennifer's cheeks were red and they were slightly out of breath when they rolled to a stop in front of me. "Have you seen the paper today?" I asked.

"No. Why? What's in it now?" said Barbara, her face darkening.

"Well, it says the Bakkers were paid a lot of money, $1.6 million just for last year. They don't know if it came from the PTL Partners or from the proceeds of this place. What do you think?"

"Well, I haven't seen it, so I can't say I believe it. I generally don't believe the papers," she said. "But even if it's true, maybe they deserve it. I don't know. That's a lot. What would they need that much for?"

During our long talk the day before, the Clausens had said they dreamed of one day selling all their possessions and spending their retirement as missionaries abroad in service to God. "People don't need much, really," Dennis had said. I told Barbara about Joseph Grennan's view, that a soul saved is worth whatever the Bakkers were paid. "That's the reasoning they tell us," agreed Barbara. "I'm just not sure where you draw the line."

That night, at a concert given by Christian singer David Meece, it was easy to see what it was about Heritage USA that people like Joseph Grennan and Barbara Clausen valued. Meece, an attractive, curly-haired man in a studded rocker's jacket, preached smoothly between songs that portrayed Jesus Christ as a superstar. "No matter how far you've fallen, there's always a choice you can make for Jesus. 'Cause, you know, when God forgives, God forgets. That's the crux of Christianity," said Meece. Then he asked if anyone in the audience would like to tell a story of redemption.

Rick Domingo rose from a long row of young men. "I was off the path. I admit it," he told the hushed audience. "That's why I came here. But after being here for a couple of days, going to the concerts and all, I'm back on the path now. I'm right with the Lord."

The audience burst into applause. All along the row where Domingo sat, hands shot into the air and he slapped them like a running back accepting the ritual high fives from his teammates after a touchdown. Everyone was on the same team. It was high fives all around; another soul saved.

The rain stopped, for good, on Saturday night. Easter Sunday was warm and bright. The dew burned off the grass before 7 a.m. In the lobby of the Heritage Grand, the piano player was gone and the doorman was idle, and I waited for Joseph Grennan, the nineteen-year-old paddle-boat tender. We had made a date for breakfast. He said he was interested in talking more. "I've never really sat long and talked with someone like you," he had said.

An hour past the time we were supposed to meet, I gave up on Joseph Grennan. I wondered if he didn't want to think about my questions, or if his family had discouraged his contact with someone so close to the reviled media. At Heritage USA, the media played the part of the scheming Pharisees in the Bakkers' real-life Passion Play.

While I had waited for Grennan, Easter-morning pilgrims had jammed the restaurants on Main Street. The ten o'clock service was billed as a musical extravaganza, and the believers, who had been warned to get to the massive Heritage Church early, were heeding the warning. I could see that I wouldn't be able to get a table for breakfast, so I left Main Street, wandered the giant parking lot, found my rented car, and drove down the long, winding entrance road to look for a restaurant. I passed the condo high rise under construction and the guardhouse where a counting machine clicked off each time a car went by.

Out on the state road, about two hundred yards from the Heritage USA entrance, I passed a stocky, middle-aged black man mowing the grass at a tiny church. He was dressed in jeans and a navy blue windbreaker. Curious, I pulled into the semicircular dirt driveway and parked on the grass, between the small brick church and an old white wood frame building that looked like an abandoned one-room schoolhouse. I wanted to ask him how a little church survived in the shadow of born-again America's TV playland.

I sat in the car for a moment while the man finished mowing. When he turned the machine off I got out, introduced myself, and asked him about his church. His name, he said, was Robert Mobley, and he told me that no one at his church had ever even thought they were competing with Heritage USA. Instead of talking about PTL, he offered me a history lesson about Mount Zion African Methodist Episcopal Church.

Mobley said that Mount Zion AME Church was founded just after the Civil War, probably by freed slaves. Mobley's relatives were among them. Most of the early members worked for Spring Mills in nearby Fort Mill, South Carolina, making cotton fabrics. Through several rebuildings, the small church with the white wooden steeple had stood for more than a hundred years.

Mobley walked me down a grassy, tire-marked path to the overgrown graveyard in back of the church. The name Spring was on many of the older gravestones. At one grave Mobley smiled and read aloud: " 'To the memory of William Byrne, a loyal servant to the white people of Pineville, N.C.' That tombstone had always bothered me," he said, "until I found out the guy was a distant relative. It made me laugh."

Across the yard, beneath one of the few new markers, lay Robert Mobley's wife, Annis. He explained that she had died suddenly in 1979 of pancreatitis. "She knows I loved her. You know, you never really get over something like that, but you got to go on." In the same year Mobley lost his best friend, an older man named Jeff Williams, who is buried near Annis.

As we walked through the graveyard, the tall grass swishing against our legs, Mobley talked about his friend. "We used to fish together. I don't hunt, because I can't kill things that way. You know, he died without ever telling me his secret. He died without telling me how he caught all those fish. Then one old-timer told me to put the weight down at the end of the line, and the hook and bait up higher. You have to put the bait where the fish can see it. That was Jeff's big secret." He laughed.

On that Easter morning the three black congregations in the Fort

Mill area planned to worship together first, and then return to their home churches. There would be a picnic lunch and an Easter egg hunt at the Mount Zion AME, Mobley said. He had driven down from Charlotte, where he worked as a police sergeant, to attend Sunday services at his home church. "They spend millions on that place across the road, and then some of their own go wanting. They come into the police department, having spent their last dollars to get here, and we have to get them to Traveler's Aid to get them a bus ticket home.

"The way I look at it, you don't just go to church to have a good time and feel good about yourself every Sunday. My definition of being a Christian is getting control of my life, and then helping my fellow man, being something more, something better."

Mobley's dream was to buy a sod farm, raise grass for a few years, and then build small homes on the property, to be sold at low interest "because people have so much trouble finding a place to live these days. That's being born-again. It's an attitude about others. It's not just getting baptized and moving on."

We had walked back to the front of the church. Mobley put the lawn mower in his truck. It was getting close to ten o'clock. I knew the musicians were tuning up across the road, at the huge Heritage Church. The grand Easter service was about to begin. I said goodbye and shook Mobley's hand. As I drove down the short dirt driveway I looked in the rearview mirror. Robert Mobley was hiding colored Easter eggs behind the trees that shaded his little church.

At 9:45 the Heritage Church was packed full. The PTL singers were warming up in front of the fake columns stage right. The organist was limbering her fingers stage left. More than a hundred robed singers formed a chorus that cascaded down the center of the stage, and the PTL orchestra, augmented by members of the Charlotte Symphony, was tuning up in the pit. The orchestra's tones made the plastic folding chairs that lined the back wall vibrate. Just inside the door, an usher directed a stream of worshippers out a side exit and toward the nearby TV studio. There were no more seats available in the main church. The service would be shown in the studio on a giant TV screen for the latecomers. I went into the studio and sat in an empty row of blue chairs.

The service seemed to be missing some spark. Later, the Clausens, who sat behind me in the TV studio, told me what had been lacking was the presence of Jim and Tammy Faye Bakker. Without the Bakkers, the crowd felt no electricity, no excitement.

What I had missed was a discussion of the crisis whirling just past the guardhouse at the main gate. Sunday's newspaper had brought even more bad news: Falwell was calling Bakker's pay "indefensible," and the PTL board was heading for a showdown with a group that was trying to bring the Bakkers back. On the day when Christians celebrated the resurrection, I expected some mention of the resurrection of faith they hoped to fashion out of the disaster. It didn't come. Instead Rev. Richard Dortch, who had replaced the Bakkers as the host of the PTL show, gave what amounted to a pep talk. "Stop that needless worry," he commanded the faithful. "Most of our problems in life are really imaginary."

After the service I walked over to Dogwood, another of Heritage USA's residential areas. I had not really expected to talk to anyone; Heritage families would be gathering for Easter dinner and I was just touring the grounds. But as I walked around, I passed a small apartment building where Adelle Percocco, a middle-aged woman with blond hair and an open, smiling face, called out a friendly hello from the sun deck of her condo. I walked over to talk to her. After a few minutes she invited me in.

The Percoccos' home was small, just a living-dining room, a kitchen, and two bedrooms. When we came in, William Percocco, Jr., a dark-haired man of about thirty who wore a crisp white shirt and a striped tie, was fussing over the Easter dinner. He waved hello and went back to stirring gravy. William Sr., a short, heavyset man with bushy eyebrows, shook my hand and sat back down on the living-room couch. No one introduced me to another dark-haired son, who had Down's syndrome. He sat on the floor and listened to Christian music on a small radio while everyone else talked.

The Percoccos were from suburban New York. Adelle said she declared herself born-again after watching TV preachers in 1977. Soon her husband, William, also gave up the Catholic faith in which they had both been reared and the family joined a born-again church. They said they had been regular PTL viewers and contributors for more than five years. They moved to Heritage from New York when William Sr. retired in 1984. "This is the best place for a Christian person to retire. You are safe. You have Christian neighbors and activities," said Adelle. "We considered Florida, but when we visited here, we fell in love with the place."

As Adelle talked, William Sr. went to a back room. He returned holding a postcard. It was a picture of him playing the part of a blind man given sight by Christ in the Passion Play. I suddenly recognized him as one of the Pharisees in the production Friday night. He had a large Roman nose and a thick mustache. The postcard shook in his left hand and he jabbed it with his right index finger to punctuate a brief speech. "Look at this." Jab. "Every year I'm in the play." Jab. "It's wonderful here." Jab.

William Sr. and Adelle said they weren't bothered by the Bakker sex scandal, and thought that maybe Jim and Tammy deserved the $1.6 million. "People who retire to Florida," said Adelle, "don't have the Lord with them, as we do here."

With that, William Jr. dropped the knife he was using to carve the roast chicken. He reached into the refrigerator, retrieved a bottle, and poured a glass of wine. "I'm no longer in this, and for them it's fine," he said. "But I think everyone involved in this mess should be punished, held responsible. That's all I'm going to say."

A knock on the door brought a neighbor, Steven Zito, who had been invited for Easter dinner. "Italians stick together, even at Heritage USA," Adelle Percocco said with a smile. The dinner was not yet ready, so the Percoccos suggested that Steven show me his condo and tell me why he lives at Heritage.

A handsome man of twenty-one, Zito had bright blue eyes and carefully trimmed dark hair. Muscles bulged under his T-shirt. As we left, he explained that he worked for "a Christian construction company," one where the staff prayed before major decisions and the boss asked prospective employees if they were born-again. We walked next door, past a pickup truck with oversized, mud-covered tires and into his small home.

Zito said that his teen years had been focused on drugs and loose sex. All that ended during his senior year in high school, when he returned to Christ during the first Spring Break Getaway, in 1986. "I don't want to live out there," he said of the outside world. "The world is sin and you have to be careful." Steven said he was waiting for Armageddon and the "rapture" when born-again Christians would be lifted out of the battle zone into heaven. Until then, life on earth was better under the protection of Heritage.

It seemed unusual to me that someone would uproot himself and change his life after one weekend at Heritage, but that was not the most remarkable part of Steven's story. The most startling element of his born-again testimony was his version of Joyce Pense's "stubbed toe." It seemed that when Zito was about twelve, his baby brother escaped from a diaper changing and ran naked through the house. Jumping from chair to chair, he waved a winged plastic toy rocket. Suddenly, as he dodged and weaved, he fell.

"It looked like he had almost cut his penis off," Zito told me, his voice dropping to a whisper. "We rushed to our doctor. He took one look, called the hospital, and we hurried over there. All the way over I was praying that he wouldn't lose it. When we got there they put a butterfly stitch on it and sent him home. That was it. It was a miracle. The prayer healed him."

Zito's phone rang. It was Adelle. It was time to eat. I said goodbye. Steven gave me his phone number. "Call me, anytime. I never get tired of talking about the Lord."

I walked back to the center of Heritage USA, where the water slides had, at long last, been turned on. The South Carolina sun was warm, and families who had waited all weekend were flocking to Heritage Island. The coconut scent of suntan lotion and the music of a Christian rock band floated on the breeze all the way to Main Street. On the island, children splashed in pools and flew down the fiberglass chutes. Teenagers and adults basked in the sun.

I found Barbara Clausen dipping her toes in six inches of water at the shallow end of one of the island's man-made lagoons. She was wearing a hot-pink tank suit and big sunglasses. She said her children were "roaming free. It's something I would never let them do in Kutztown."

We talked about the weather and the water slide, and Barbara asked if I had heard anything new about the Bakkers. I told her the Sunday paper had reported that Jerry Falwell believed the payments to the Bakkers were "indefensible." Barbara recalled a PTL show when Bakker had explained that there were two or three people in the media determined to bring him down. "I guess they must be feeling pretty big right now," she said.

The conversation turned to the Bakkers' suffering, and I mentioned that Jim Bakker had admitted that he and Tammy were receiving frequent psychological counseling. This was something unusual, because most born-again Christians rejected psychological help. Surprisingly, Barbara Clausen said she believed in it. "I just recommended it to a friend of mine whose daughter seems anorexic. Now, Jimmy Swaggart would say I'm wrong to do it. But I think there are times when it works. At least you can go a few times to find out what's wrong and then work on it yourself."

As we leaned against the fabricated rocks that ringed the lagoon, Barbara wondered aloud about church leaders who faltered. She said the pastor of a large Christian church in Kutztown was widely known to be a homosexual and he was rumored to be soliciting young boys. "But people still go to the church. I don't understand the way people are sometimes," she said.

Just then Dennis, his camera strapped around his neck, arrived from the other side of the island, where he had been taking pictures. He was wearing a red, white, and blue cap with the McDonald's hamburger chain logo on it. Some of the PTL Partners were circulating a petition to ask the ministry's board of directors to reinstate Jim and Tammy, he reported. He had signed it.

Turning to leave, I told the Clausens I had to get to Charlotte for a flight home. I thanked them for their help. They had been open and kind. Before I was ten feet away, Barbara called out, "You don't happen to have today's paper, do you?"

"It's in the car. You can have it."

"No, that's OK," she said. "Maybe we'll take a drive outside and get one."

= 8 =

Southern Baptist
Civil War

THE PTL SCANDAL, in all its titillating detail, captured the public's attention. But while Jim Bakker's sex life and Tammy Bakker's fondness for luxury consumer items may have seemed like the most serious threat to the born-again revival in America, it was not the only threat that had arisen. In that same summer of 1987, while Jessica Hahn was monopolizing the airwaves, a simmering, decade-old conflict within the Southern Baptist Convention, born-again America's largest and richest church, had come to a head. At the center of this controversy was not a picayune sex scandal or a conventional tale of misappropriated funds but a struggle for control of the core of the born-again movement itself.

On one side of this Southern Baptist civil war was the dominant fundamentalist faction, led primarily by the pastors of the largest megachurches. These fundamentalists, who called themselves the "conservatives," had demanded that all church officials, including seminary professors, accept and promote "inerrancy," the belief that every story and image in the Bible was literally true. The conservatives were opposed by the "moderates," a smaller group of liberal intellectuals and moderate preachers who thought that some parts of the Bible, such as the story of Adam and Eve, might be fables.

In 1979 a conservative minister, Adrian Rogers of Memphis, became president of the denomination. He was swept to power by a highly organized group of fundamentalist preachers who were intent on returning the church to more conservative theology. The fundamentalists had held on to the church's top post ever since. Every year a few more conservatives were placed in important church jobs. And every year the moderates grew more bitter. By 1985 the struggle had become so serious that the moderates, who claimed 40 percent of the church membership, were talking about suing for a share of the church's assets and starting a splinter denomination. The threat of a schism had frightened church leaders into creating a Peace Committee to try to save the church. The committee was ordered to report its findings, including ways to save the denomination, at the 1987 Southern Baptist Convention in St. Louis.

This meeting (both the church and its annual meeting are called the Southern Baptist Convention) is the biggest church gathering in the world. Each year more than 25,000 delegates, called messengers, are sent by their congregations to elect officers and listen to reports on everything from foreign missions to Sunday-school texts. But this time it was clear that the real agenda of the convention concerned a showdown between conservatives and moderates that could no longer be avoided.

All the important business of the 1987 meeting, the Peace Committee report and the election of the church president, was to be crammed into the convention's opening session on Tuesday. The day before, the politicking had already been in full swing. In the pressroom that Monday, I joined a crowd of about two dozen reporters surrounding a man who looked remarkably like Jimmy Carter. He had Carter's worried-looking blue eyes and ash-blond hair, and his jowls were creased with the same deep lines. He spoke a bit like Carter, with a measured, even drawl.

"This is a battle between reason and science and fundamentalism," said Glenn Hinson, a liberal professor from Southern Seminary of Louisville, the oldest and most prestigious Southern Baptist seminary. Hinson was a leader of the Southern Baptist Alliance, a 1,000-member group that was exploring the idea of starting a splinter church.

"It's the same battle that has been fought for centuries. They are trying to make this the Catholic Church of America," Hinson continued. "Taking the Bible so literally that you even use it for science is not Christianity. Inerrantists say the world is ten thousand years old, no older, because that's what they think the Bible says. Well, the Bible doesn't claim to be scientific. It doesn't claim to be inerrant, but these people want to say that it is. Really, they want to say that their view of the Bible is infallible. Like papal infallibility, that just goes against what Baptists are all about."

While Hinson talked, a young man of about twenty, wearing a dark brown suit and a blue striped tie, pushed into the clutch of reporters. Breathing hard, he squeezed beside a tall TV cameraman. He stood on his toes so he could look past the TV camera and focus on the professor. Meanwhile Hinson made his point about the earth's age and said that the biblical stories of creation shouldn't be taken literally. Then he said the same about Adam and Eve. "It can't be assumed they were real," said Hinson. "Faith doesn't demand that you simply suspend reason."

With that, the man in the brown suit spoke up. "Now wait a minute," he said. "Are you saying that Adam and Eve were not real people?"

The television cameras were turned away from Hinson and trained on his challenger.

"Well, I'm saying that the Hebrews approached the truth through stories and parables," answered the professor.

"Oh, really?" the man in the brown suit said as he pinned a delegate's name tag on his lapel.

A reporter asked, "Who are you?"

"I'm Craig Cox, associate pastor of First Baptist Church of Cache, Oklahoma. And Baptists believe that Adam and Eve were real. Everything I've read and can understand says that."

Cox's voice grew louder as he spoke. A boyish figure with short brown hair and a smooth face, he stood defiantly erect, his strong chin jutting out. The muscles of his jaw bulged as he clenched his teeth.

"You, Professor Hinson, are wrong," he said, jabbing his right index finger out at him.

Professor Hinson's voice trembled a bit as he answered. "Well, if you look at it historically, long before the Old Testament the Hebrews had stories like Adam and Eve to explain man's origins," said Hinson. "They were more symbolic than actual."

"Has God convicted you of that?" Cox shot back. "Or is that just your opinion?"

As Hinson began to answer, several reporters complained about the interruption. Someone from the Southern Baptist News Service, which ran the press center, summoned the hotel security guards, who grabbed Cox by his arms and asked him to leave. As the guards led Cox to the door, Professor Hinson called out an invitation to meet later to continue the discussion.

"I'd be happy to meet you. Just call here at the hotel."

"No need," Cox called back as he left through the lobby.

Indeed, Craig Cox had no reason to talk at length with Glenn Hinson. At the 1987 Southern Baptist Convention, Cox was part of a confident conservative crusade and Hinson was on the defensive. With the reelection of fundamentalist president Rev. Adrian Rogers a near-certainty, the conservatives were poised to consolidate their control over every board and committee in the 14.6-million-member denomination. They were ready to seize the seminaries and the Sunday-school board, the Southern Baptist missionaries and the largest publishing house in the world. Many conservative leaders were saying that Rogers' reelection would be followed by a purge. They warned that all the moderates who still worked in seminaries and other church institutions would soon be asked to leave their jobs.

In the pressroom, Professor Hinson continued answering questions while at the same time trying to leave. He agreed to meet with me at the end of the convention, after the battle for the presidency and the report of the Peace Committee. "Just wander around the convention," Hinson advised me. "You'll start to see what's going on here. It's pretty obvious."

After Hinson left, I found Alvin C. Shackleford, the head of the Baptist press office, who gave me a press pass and told me, "There won't even be a contest for the presidency this year. The conservatives have it. People may just be too sick and tired of it to fight anymore." He said he was glad the St. Louis Cardinal baseball team was in town. "Usually it's our luck to have the convention at a time when the team's out of town. This year I'm going to try to get to the game."

Shackleford pointed me toward a back room at the press center, where another expert on the Southern Baptist crisis was holding forth. James Hefley, writer in residence at Hannibal-LaGrange College and author of *Truth in Crisis*, Volumes 1 and 2, which chronicle the continuing power struggle, was issuing his assessment of the Baptist battle. Tall and thin with dark curly hair and blue eyes, Hefley sat on a stool with his hands jammed into the pockets of his blue sport coat.

He said that in the 1960s liberals and moderates had dominated the church and filled its institutions with left-leaning people. But then, as conservative sentiment grew within the church in the 1970s, the fundamentalists were able to challenge the status quo. Finally, in 1979, they won the convention presidency. Since then, the conservatives had been able to gain control of most of the boards that governed the institutions. But they had been frustrated to discover that the bureaucracy, the professors and office workers, would take a longer time to clean out.

"But remember, this is not really about politics, I don't think. I really do believe it's theological," Hefley said. "It's some kind of reaction to modern times. They want to return to a pre-1950 theological climate, as if that will make all the modern problems go away." But in this fundamentalist drive Hefley saw a great danger. He warned that if the conservatives were too aggressive, they could cause a hemorrhage of members.

"If this move to the right happens too quickly, they are going to cause a split. The first to go will be the brighter moderates who want to serve the church. As it is right now, seventy-five percent of the candidates for the ministry in the United Methodist Church in North Carolina are former Southern Baptists. That shows you something about where the best and brightest are going."

Hefley was also worried about the ripple of scandal that was emanating from PTL. He said the outside world was "getting the wrong idea about Christianity. There's been too much conflict, too much of a focus on money and control in all of Christianity." Other born-again leaders shared Hefley's concern in 1987. Jerry Falwell had said that the PTL scandal "had hurt the entire cause of Christ." Hefley agreed. "In view of PTL, I think we need something like a Peace Committee, and we need to make sure this doesn't look like just a big power contest," he said.

(While Hefley had been talking, the Peace Committee was secretly meeting somewhere in the city, and, we would all later learn, the deliberations were going poorly. The Peace Committee had succumbed to the same kind of bickering that it had been created to stop. Voting had fallen into a pattern, with a slim conservative majority dominating every ballot. They were gradually pushing through a report that would support inerrancy and create a "watchdog committee," something like an inquisition, to review the beliefs of seminary professors and others, to make sure they were properly conservative. Some of the moderates on the committee were threatening a walkout.)

Across from the hotel where Hefley was giving his briefing, the pre-convention meetings were being held in a boxy cement-and-steel building called the Cervantes Center. It had a huge lobby where the Baptists had set up a lemonade stand and some tables for distributing the convention bulletin. In the center of the lobby was a long escalator that led to the second floor. Past the escalator was the entrance to the main convention hall, a meeting room the size of three football fields which was filled with thousands of wooden folding chairs. A 200-foot-wide elevated stage had been built along the long back wall of the auditorium. Near the front of the stage, on the audience's left, was the rostrum for speakers. Behind it were several desks. To the right were chairs and music stands for an orchestra and a choir. Looming over the stage and everything else below were three gigantic television screens.

On the second floor I walked through a maze of promotional booths. Some were displays for colleges and seminaries. At others, salesmen offered tours of the Holy Land, audiovisual aids for Bible study groups, even prefabricated church buildings. The second floor was also where delegates would find two small meeting rooms that had been turned into bookstores. In these rooms were thousands of books, all on Christian topics, stacked on tables and piled on the floors. There were leather-bound Bibles, Christian self-help books, and even religiously oriented novels by born-again Christian writers. One of the books given prominent display was *God's Way to Health, Wealth and Wisdom*, written by Adrian Rogers, president of the Southern Baptist Convention.

Downstairs, the pastors' meeting was winding down and many of the participants were leaving. I walked out with the crowd, but instead of joining the flow of people that streamed toward the waterfront restaurant row, I walked a few blocks across town to the Kiel Auditorium, an old municipal opera house. The Kiel was the site of a kind of counterconvention, called the Forum. Conducted by and for the moderate faction, the Forum had been running opposite SBC sessions since the beginning of the conservative power push.

The opera house was a Depression-era hall with an old red velvet curtain, a high ceiling, and small box balconies on either side of the stage. The place was nearly full when I arrived, but I found a seat next to a middle-aged couple, who introduced themselves before I could sit down. They were Pastor Edgar Farrell and his wife, Betty, of First Baptist Church of Black Mountain, North Carolina. She wore a neat blue dress and a strand of pearls. He wore a blue-and-white plaid jacket and a blue tie. Graying and soft-spoken, they made an unlikely picture of the kind of heretics whom fundamentalists blamed for the decline of church and country.

I asked the Farrells about the inerrantist campaign and the rumors I had heard about the squabbles among the members of the Peace Committee. "We think the Peace Committee is important because this division is serious," said Mrs. Farrell. "But even after this long, we don't understand what the real disagreement is all about. The funny thing is, we think we're very conservative, Bible-believing people. We're as conservative as anyone. But we do think someone might have a different view and still be a Christian, still be a Southern Baptist."

Mrs. Farrell argued that the moderate position on inerrancy, which made belief a matter of personal choice, was more consistent with Baptist tradition. "Baptists have never believed in having a lot of documents and orders saying what people should and should not believe," she said. "It's the personal, vertical relationship with God that counts. That's what makes Baptists different from the Catholic Church, where there's a powerful hierarchy and lots of rules."

In general, the moderates in the Southern Baptist Convention were more open to historical interpretation of the Bible. Their theology left a place in heaven for those who were not born-again Christians, and it allowed for scientific insights in the matters of evolution and the earth's beginnings. Pastor Farrell, who said his congregation supported his liberal theology, seemed wounded by the course of events in the SBC. "We come to the Forum to get away from the circus atmosphere," he said bluntly. "The Forum is less like a political convention."

Edgar Farrell had been pastor of his church for more than twenty years. When he started, he recalled, the church was the center of community life. "As with most communities, that's not the case now," he said. Immigrants from the North, economic growth, and improved education had all brought competing values to North Carolina, he went on, and the church was no longer the dominant social center in most communities. "The result is that young people start thinking on their own a lot earlier than they used to," said Farrell.

The conservative crusade was an attempt to stop the social trend, to mandate that the changes stop. "That's not going to work," he added. "The only thing that will work is to change ourselves, to keep our message relevant. Otherwise, we're going to lose more and more people.

"What a lot of very conservative people don't understand is that the whole structure of society is changing. They may have growing churches now, but changes will happen where they are too. We can't expect every teacher in a public school to be a Baptist. We can't expect every influence on our children to be from Christian people. We have to learn to adapt and to accept others."

A few people had walked onto the stage while Pastor Farrell was talking. But before the Forum program began, Betty Farrell leaned across her husband to make one last point. She had shared his work and she understood it, she said. "I can also be a little less diplomatic. It all boils down to this: we don't have to all think and act alike to be Baptists."

The afternoon speaker at the Forum was Rev. John Hewitt of Asheville, North Carolina. A young man with thick salt-and-pepper hair, Hewitt did something none of the speakers I would later see at the Cervantes Center did: he poked fun at Southern Baptists. Hewitt began with a story about a deacon at his first church, in Elmburg, Kentucky. The man had insisted that the world was flat because the Bible referred to "four corners" of the earth. And he had said that American space missions to the moon were television hoaxes. Hewitt recalled that when he used the Bible to argue with the man, the man's answer was always: "Preacher, that may be Bible, but it's not Baptist."

Repeating the refrain, Hewitt described church controversies over vestments, kneeling rails, and the use of wine for communion.

"I wanted to use different vestments. They told me, 'It may be Bible, but it's not Baptist.'

"I said I'd like install kneelers, like the ones used in Southern Baptist churches in Dallas.

"The people in my congregation thought kneelers were only in Catholic churches. I reminded them that knees were invented before Catholics, but they were not amused.

"Kneeling may be Bible," he said, pausing to smile, "but it's not Baptist."

Turning serious, Hewitt argued that the SBC faced a sure schism unless it could accept diversity, "unless some congregations could use wine for communion while others used Welchade. We have made it easy in this country to be a Christian, but very difficult to be a Southern Baptist.

"Seven years ago we also had our convention at the Cervantes Center. There was a bitter fight then too, and I walked out of the convention dejected, with my head down. Tonight, when you lay down your head in convention weariness, pray for a miracle of insight this week. And if at the end of the week you are still discouraged, remember, this was only a Baptist meeting."

On Tuesday morning, the convention hall slowly filled with messengers. Some came equipped with pillows and picnic baskets. Others staked out large sections of the wooden chairs for family and friends. By eight-thirty, when the choir and orchestra began their "Music for Inspiration," even the standing room in the back of the hall was crowded. After the music, President Adrian Rogers, a tall, tanned man in a dark suit with a red handkerchief tucked in his pocket, introduced a series of honored guests. The first was June Scobee, the wife of astronaut Richard Scobee, who was killed in the explosion of the space shuttle *Challenger* in 1986.

Mrs. Scobee, a small woman with curly brown hair, looked tiny on the stage, but she was a huge, imposing figure on the TV screens overhead. She asked the delegates to support the construction of an educational center that would be a memorial to the astronauts who died when the *Challenger* exploded after takeoff. The center would simulate life in space for groups of children who would visit for a week at a time. "Pray for us as we move toward reaching our goal of bringing children together from all over the world to learn about our universe," she said. "Pray for us that the Lord's will be done, that we have the courage to reach our goal."

The delegates applauded, a few even cried, as Mrs. Scobee left the stage. Adrian Rogers moved quickly to the podium to say a prayer on her behalf.

"In the name of Jesus, we bless and pray for June Scobee and we thank the Lord for the memory of her husband. In Jesus' name, amen."

After that, another preacher, Paige Patterson of First Baptist Church of Dallas, came to the microphone. Patterson had been instrumental in the conservatives' original efforts to win the SBC presidency and in their continuing control of the denomination. He was part of the group whom the moderates called the "Texas Mafia." The leaders of the Texas Mafia included Patterson, Ed Young of Second Baptist of Houston, and Patterson's boss, W. A. Criswell. Patterson would be a constant presence on the stage during the convention, hovering around Adrian Rogers much of the time. But his official duty was to serve as the master of ceremonies, opening the meeting and then moving things along.

"Lord, corporately we admit to the need for Your wisdom, in order that we may reach out to the four billion lost people on the face of the world," said Patterson. Patterson then announced the attendance, 22,438, and introduced the next speaker. "He's a believer in our Lord Jesus Christ, an author, a leader, a statesman, and a very fine singer and writer of gospel music, Missouri governor John Ashcroft."

Ashcroft moved quickly to the lectern and began speaking even before he was close enough to the microphone. The first words that came out of the loudspeakers were: ". . . and of course we are brothers and sisters in Christ." Ashcroft began his short speech by praising God for "the fact that our nation is on the mend. Inflation is down. Interest rates are down. Thank the Lord," he said.

A few people in the audience yelled out, "Amen!"

Ashcroft said that, as the "salt and light of the earth," the Baptists had a solemn duty "to fashion and shape this nation." And sounding much like an inerrantist preacher, he urged the assembled delegates to accept the view of the Bible as God's literal truth. "It is God's word. The truth. And truth is welcome." Ashcroft ended with a song he had written himself called "Thanks for the Power." The refrain was:

Make me strong, Lord Jesus!
Give me power!
Give me strength, dear Lord
To do Your will.

After Ashcroft, Earnest Eudy, a Texas evangelist, delivered a welcoming speech that would set the tone for the business part of the convention. Eudy laid out the fundamentalist complaint, suggesting that the Devil was behind all the liberal theological developments of the last century. Thus the battle between inerrancy and modern theology was a battle between good and evil.

"Satan's goal is to rip the Bible from common Baptist people. He clips the wings of faith with the scissors of reason," he said. A tall, thin, middle-aged man with a craggy face, Eudy punctuated his sermon with broad sweeps of his arms. "When scripture speaks," he cried, jabbing a finger into the air above his head, "God speaks!"

Eudy declared that Christians needed the comfort of believing that the whole Bible is literally true. "You laymen, did you ever feel intimidated by the criticism? Well, did you hear about the dear old grandmother who is hard of hearing? The doctor told her he could cure her.

"She said, 'There'll be no operation.'

"Everyone wanted to know why.

"She said, 'I'm seventy-nine years old and I've heard enough!' "

Warming to his finish, Eudy brought the crowd to the deathbed of a believing Christian whose comfort was the Bible's promise of salvation.

"Don't take this book away from a dying person," he said, raising his Bible in the air. "One of these days you're going to die. What kind of book do you want for your pillow when you die?"

With Eudy still speaking, and a long line of greeters scheduled to follow him, I went up to the second floor. Hundreds of moderates, it soon turned out, had left the hall as well. They stood in small groups talking, wandered among the seminary displays, and browsed in the bookstores. The second floor was obviously going to be their shelter from a morning of inerrantist diatribes.

At the display booth for Southern Seminary, Glenn Hinson's school, I struck up a conversation with a professor named Raymond Bailey, who taught preaching. He was a big man with a bright face and shining dark hair that he wore slicked back. Sitting there at the desk in front of the display, Bailey seemed comfortable, smiling constantly and calling, "Hi, y'all," to people who passed by.

"This is, at bottom, class warfare," said Bailey as he rocked his chair behind the desk. Bailey divided the Southern Baptist denomination into two social groups. One was composed of the more educated Baptists of old Southern cities such as Charleston, South Carolina. The other group was closer to the working-class, rural roots of the church. These more conservative believers formed the church's powerful middle class. Many could still be found in small towns and on farms. But others had, over the past twenty years, migrated to the growing cities of the Sunbelt, such as Houston and Tulsa.

"In the 1960s people's illusions about America were shattered. And the social norms were disrupted. There was integration and the Vietnam War followed by Watergate," said Bailey. "People, especially those from the old rural middle class, were very upset with all that. What's happening now is an attempt to recapture the sense of security that many people felt they lost. They really do want to go back to the 1950s."

Rod Byard, a teacher from Southeastern Baptist Theological Seminary, joined the conversation, suggesting that the conservative surge was fed by a fear of technology. As Byard spoke, muffled applause and the convention speeches echoed in the background.

"Everything moves so quickly today. People feel out of control," said Byard. "We have the means now, with atomic bombs, to end the world. That makes people hunger for security, for certainty. They see computers, and they don't understand them. They hear reports on TV about faraway places and they can't incorporate what they see." As the world becomes smaller, Byard said, religious absolutism became more difficult to maintain. The fundamentalist drive within the Southern Baptist Convention was a desperate attempt to preserve the believer's sense of "chosenness." "You can't have assumptions about other people being evil, or something less than you, when you see their faces, their children, on your TV screen at night," he said. "That's what is upsetting these people."

Byard spoke as if he were describing a subject opened for scientific inquiry, not something that was part of his own life. There was a touch of condescension in his voice, a knowing understanding of the frail egos of simple believers. Many conservatives understood Byard's analysis. Some even agreed with it. But they also knew that they were winning the battle for control of the church.

Leaving Byard and Bailey, I rode the escalator down to the convention floor. Just outside the door to the main hall stood Karl Davis, an old-fashioned traveling evangelist from Fort Worth. A gregarious, overweight man with wavy red hair combed back from his forehead, Davis said he worked mostly in the South, preaching in little churches for whatever the collection would bring. Tall and imposing in his dark brown suit, Davis stood at the door looking for people he knew and shaking their hands. It was a good way to remind pastors that he was available for revival meetings, he said. Davis also said, rather proudly, that he was part of the Texas Mafia. I asked him to explain the conservative cause and he just started talking.

"The moderates say this fight is about power, about politics. Well, that's not it at all," said Davis, shouting so he could be heard over the noise of the convention. "This is about theology and culture, about what being a Baptist really is."

Davis said that historically Southern Baptists had maintained a firm belief in the literal truth of the Bible, despite Darwin and the Scopes trial and the kind of theological arguments raised by the people at the Forum. "We were the keepers of the flame, the remnant in America," he said.

Davis was, for the most part, correct. The Southern Baptist Church was founded by British colonists who left England in the seventeenth century and believed that America was a Protestant promised land. Through the nineteenth century Southern Baptists generally believed that America's founding and its expansion proved that God was promoting His chosen people: born-again Christians. That belief began to fade after World War II, as the church opened new congregations around the country and Southerners grew wealthier and more educated. The church moved closer to mainstream society and away from its Southern fundamentalist roots. By the late 1960s the SBC was assuming liberal positions on civil rights and poverty. Some Baptist preachers protested against the Vietnam War. And many Baptists even drifted theologically toward the less literal reading of the Bible popular among Episcopalians and liberal Roman Catholics.

"This happened mostly in colleges and seminaries," Davis said, reaching up to loosen his bright yellow tie and revealing a huge silver ring with a turquoise the size of a half-dollar. In the 1950s and 1960s the seminaries, which had been filled with the brightest scholars the convention could hire, were training young preachers to read the Bible in historical context. Many academics, including some at Baptist seminaries, taught that few, if any, of the quotes the Bible attributes to Jesus are accurate. Some even argued that Jesus may not have existed at all.

"I was taught to doubt the Bible when I was at Oklahoma Baptist University," said Davis. His loud monologue had started to attract a crowd, and he began speaking as if he were delivering a sermon. Davis recalled that in one of his college classes a professor had taught the theory of evolution and had attempted to discredit the Bible's stories of creation.

"Well, I got so upset that I stood on my desk and cried out, 'You'll have to answer to God for that.' " Davis said it was then that he became a fundamentalist activist. He joined a student group that produced a scathing criticism of the doctrinal strayings of their professors.

"Philosophers and professors can dispute the existence of God," Davis continued, clapping his hands to emphasize the word "God." "But this is a complex world and people need something to believe in.

"Take hell. Well, I can use words and say that hell isn't real. There's lots of fancy theology you can use to explain hell away. But the words don't make it go away. Hell is still there. It's in the Bible and I believe it. So what good does it do for the seminaries to tell students it might not be real?"

As Karl Davis made his case outside the convention hall, his voice rising and falling to accentuate important points, the small circle of onlookers grew to a crowd of more than thirty people. He took off his glasses and wiped his face with the back of his hand.

"We have been inward-looking as a people, but if we turn outward, we have to have the courage to speak the truth," he said to those around him. A passerby patted him on the back and said, "Amen, brother."

"It was the 1970s before we started to wake up," Davis continued. "When we did, we noticed that we Baptists, like the whole country, were drifting in the wrong direction. Take abortion. That's wrong and yet Southern Baptists hadn't been active enough in opposing it. And I'll tell you why I know it's wrong. They found me, when I was a baby, in a Dumpster in McAlester, Oklahoma. Luckily I was adopted and raised right. If there was legal abortion back then, I probably wouldn't exist right now. You wouldn't be talking to me. Think about that."

Davis said that conservative Baptist leaders were appalled by abortion in particular and more generally by the liberal drift of American society, but they were most frightened by the liberal excesses inside the denomination's seminaries and colleges.

"We were afraid that if too many preachers went out with this historical interpretation, the very central theme of Christianity, Jesus' standing as God's son, would be attacked," said Davis. To combat the liberal theology, the conservatives promoted inerrancy. "Inerrancy, as a matter of Baptist teaching, may be the only way to protect Christ from being reduced to a mythical figure, like the ancient Greek and Roman gods," said Davis. "That's the way we saw it. We felt that Christ himself was endangered by this liberalism."

If their campaign for inerrancy was to work, the conservatives had to be careful not to expose the faithful to the troublesome details of scientific developments and the new historical research that had been done on the Bible and its origins. So at every turn in the debate they had avoided discussing the specifics of such questions as the age of the earth. Instead they focused on their belief that the Bible was given to man by God and, therefore, must be perfectly accurate.

"That's how we've kept this under control," Davis said. "This has to remain just a contest between Bible faith and doubt."

Davis concluded by telling, in hushed tones, the story of a professor at OBU who had asked students to consider the possibility that Jesus Christ had had homosexual experiences. "I won't tell you the professor's name, but that just shows you how, even when I was in school, the colleges and seminaries were drifting."

While Davis was talking, inside the hall, political-style nominating speeches were beginning. I left Davis and walked onto the crowded convention floor and found a seat next to Jerry Speers, a young pastor from Northside Baptist Church of Columbus, Georgia. Speers sat quietly, balancing his ballots on the tips of his fingers and turning them over and over. The ballots, pink and beige computer cards, were used only for votes on the most important convention business. Simple resolutions were voted with a show of hands. But the president was elected by ballot cards, which would be quickly processed through counting machines.

Speers, sitting at the end of a row far from the elevated stage, watched the speeches on one of the giant TV screens. A solid young man with dark hair, a heavy brow, and dark eyes, he was dressed in a red, white, and blue striped sport shirt, casual blue pants, and heavy black shoes. At thirty-four, he was already a relaxed veteran of Southern Baptist Conventions. This was his ninth, and he approached it like a savvy baseball fan who didn't need a program. He was accustomed to the political-style speeches and the technological razzmatazz. He smiled when, up on the big TV screen, the picture lagged behind the audio, throwing the speaker's lips out of sync with the sound that came from the overhead loudspeakers. "That happens every time they use those screens," he said, laughing. "Technology sure is something, eh?"

Speers watched impassively as Adrian Rogers was nominated by Pastor Ed Young of Houston's Second Baptist Church. Tall, handsome, and well dressed, Young looked like a movie star. His strong voice, amplified many times by the sound system, echoed off the back wall of the big auditorium.

"I nominate the president of our convention, Adrian Rogers," began Young.

A wave of applause washed the huge auditorium. Eventually about three-quarters of the people were standing and applauding. Young raised his hands to quiet the multitude, and continued.

"We are all tired of feuding, fussing, and fighting," he said. "With the election of Adrian Rogers we can move on to Kingdom business, because Adrian is a Kingdom man."

Someone a few rows behind me muttered, "Yeah, Adrian is a king."

Jerry Speers stood and applauded.

After Ed Young's nominating speech, a preacher named Charles Redmon nominated the moderate's candidate, Richard Jackson of North Phoenix, New Mexico. Redmon spoke as if he were reading Jackson's résumé, describing his career as a pastor and noting that Jackson was happily married and had three children. "He has a heart of compassion and a zeal for souls," Redmon said. "Richard Jackson walks where mainstream Southern Baptists walk, and if it is God's will, may this convention elect Richard Jackson president."

Jerry Speers literally sat on his hands while Redmon spoke, and he didn't join the scattered few who had stood to show their support for Jackson.

When the ushers came around, Speers cast his ballot with one of the computer cards he had been holding. He had supported Rogers the year before in Atlanta and he voted for him in St. Louis too. He said the convention was slowly moving back to Bible basics, but there was still some ecclesiastical housecleaning to be done, and Rogers was the man to do it.

"In the 1960s and 1970s there was a kind of confusion that set in, in the world and in the church," said Speers, who had attended his first convention in 1979. "A lot of it was caused by a movement to the attitude of 'I'm OK and you're OK,' " added Speers. "That ignores the fact that you might believe something different than me or that, in the end, none of us is really OK."

Traditional, conservative Southern Baptists earnestly believed that people are definitely not "OK," said Speers. From Adam's fall in the garden it has been clear, to Baptists, that man's nature is evil. Being "born-again" doesn't absolve a person from sin, but it is, in Baptist belief, an irrevocable ticket to heaven. In a way, becoming born-again makes your status as a sinner manageable, said Speers. But it doesn't make you "OK."

"In the 1960s there were a lot of things that were not OK that everyone just seemed to accept. Living together without marriage. Homosexuality. Sexual promiscuousness. It's even been accepted that teenagers will have sexual activity. Well, it's not biblically OK to do those things and we've got to stand up and say so. The scriptures teach the way to be happy in life. To live any other way is to be unhappy."

The inerrantists realized the wrong turns taken in the 1960s, said Speers. Society had become permissive and so had the church, with scholars arguing over even the most basic tenets of faith. "That cannot be tolerated. If you allow people to believe there's any error in the Bible, you open the whole thing up to criticism. How are you going to decide what is true and what is not? Which parts will be the word of God and which parts will be stories?"

While Speers talked, the results of the election were being tabulated. It took less than an hour for the convention computers to process the more than 20,000 cards and determine that Rogers had won by a three-to-two margin. He became the first man ever to be elected Southern Baptist president three times running, and his election marked the ninth consecutive conservative victory.

A staunch inerrantist, Adrian Rogers was a man who seemed to embody two of born-again America's major obsessions: certainty and success. His church, Bellevue Baptist of Memphis, was one of the largest and richest in the denomination. But Rogers' reach stretched beyond Memphis. He hosted a syndicated TV show that reached millions of homes on cable networks and he had written a series of upbeat books. His latest, *God's Way to Health, Wealth and Wisdom*, was part of a trend in conservative Christian publishing: books that promised that worldly success would follow born-again faith.

When the convention delegates were told that Rogers had won, they erupted in cheering and applause. Rogers walked across the stage waving to the adoring crowd. Though fifty-five years old, he carried himself with the sure bearing of the 1950s Palm Beach High School football star who had been voted most likely to succeed. In a short speech he made clear his commitment to the pursuit of born-again orthodoxy:

"Southern Baptists," Rogers told the cheering convention, "are old-fashioned, Bible-believing Christians that believe that hell is hot, heaven is sweet, sin is black, judgment is sure, and Jesus saves. That's who we are."

After the election, Rogers went to the press center at the hotel across the street. At the news conference he was humorless. "I am grateful to God that Southern Baptists are coming back to who they are," he said. He defended his recent appointments to convention boards—all 100 were from the conservative camp. And he complained about being called a "fundamentalist." The term was used to describe people like the Ayatollah Khomeini, Iran's religious ruler, Rogers said. "It has become a pejorative term."

Back in the convention hall, rumors about the Peace Committee's report rippled through the delegates. The supposedly secret report was to be voted on at 8:30 p.m., but by three o'clock copies of it were circulating and the moderates were already complaining that a kind of fundamentalist manifesto was being rammed through the convention. The document called on Baptists to follow a rigidly conservative reading of the Bible. It recommended a ban on meetings to discuss church politics, and it called for the creation of a watchdog organization that would police church officials' beliefs.

While the fundamentalists believed they needed the watchdog committee to begin to review the religious purity of seminary professors, moderates saw it as a Baptist inquisition. As the scheduled vote approached, two prominent moderate members of the Peace Committee resigned in protest and others looked for ways to delay the vote. But the convention was being run by the conservatives, and the moderates could find nothing in the rules that would allow them to stall. Eight-thirty came, the report was read to the messengers, and eight people were permitted to address the convention. Two of them tried to table it, but were ruled out of order. Others offered amendments that would have watered the report down, but they were all defeated. By nine o'clock Rogers called for a vote, officials estimated that the show of hands favored approval, and the conservatives had won again.

Then something strange happened. With the conservatives celebrating and many of the delegates heading for the exits, a thin young man wearing a plaid shirt went to one of the microphones that had been placed around the hall. At Southern Baptist Conventions delegates are supposed to be equals and are allowed to speak if they wish. Rogers looked down from the podium, saw the man at the microphone, and called on him to speak. The young man began to read from a piece of lined notepaper, which shook in his hand.

"Now that we've done this here tonight, I propose we erect a seven-hundred-foot-high solid-gold replica of the King James Bible at Southern Baptist headquarters in honor of our newfound discovery of the meaning of being a . . ."

The microphone went dead.

"The messenger is out of order," said Rogers. The convention was adjourned and the messengers left the auditorium.

The following day was something of a letdown, and none of the events at the Cervantes Center drew many messengers. Mostly they concerned reports about missionaries, financial statements of various agencies, and updates on their activities. I called Craig Cox and Glenn Hinson and they agreed to back-to-back interviews in the coffee shop at the hotel where they had had their confrontation.

When Craig Cox arrived, he was accompanied by John Hancock, the pastor of his church, First Baptist of Cache, Oklahoma. Hancock said that he had taken Craig Cox under his wing, made him an associate pastor, and helped him with his Bible studies.

While Pastor Hancock spoke freely about his work and life back in Cache, Cox was guarded with the details of his life. He wouldn't talk about his parents. "I'd need their permission for that," he said. And he refused to discuss his childhood.

Still, from Cox's sketchy replies to my questions I was able to make out a faint outline. He said he had been born and raised in Cache, in a poor family. He had made it through public school without distinction, and then joined the Marines. He had been disappointed by the Marines, though. He thought the discipline and organization were lax. So after three years he quit, went back to Oklahoma, and worked at odd jobs. He decided to become a preacher after he met Pastor Hancock. He was now dividing his time between Cache and a small, independent Bible college in Georgia.

"I had illusions about the Marine Corps," Cox said. "There's this stuff in the Marine creed about God and all that, but only a small minority in the Marines was Christian." When I asked him how he viewed his country, he said, "America is headed downhill, spiritually, physically, and militarily. Look at the rise in divorce, the increase of drug abuse, the financial instability of the family, and the immorality even in the government. It's obvious things are going sour. Fortunately, if you're born-again, God will take care of you. But I'm worried about the rest of America."

From the descriptions Hancock and Cox offered, I could understand why people from Cache, Oklahoma—population 2,500—could believe that America was going downhill. They said their town was struck by the agricultural recession that began in the late 1970s and then staggered by the decline in oil prices that had taken place in 1983. Despite improvements in the national economy, unemployment in Cache was still around 15 percent. The wheat farmers, whose acreage surrounded the town, had seen a decade of losses, and none of the oil wells in the area were pumping.

"Things are bad back home," Pastor Hancock said. "A lot of people are struggling."

Hancock traced the economic woes of Cache, and the theological woes of the Southern Baptist Convention, to the same source: "America's turn away from God. It all happened in the 1960s and '70s," he said. "There was a liberal swing, America fell away from God, and there was a movement toward liberal theology. Anyway, starting in 1979, at least in the Southern Baptist Convention, we started to change things. And one of the things we realized was that our own seminaries have hurt the Christian cause. They've been part of the whole problem. They turn out pastors who don't believe in the Bible the way we do, and they preach in congregations and spread the ideas they have learned. We had to put a stop to it."

The confrontation with Professor Hinson was part of "putting a stop to it," said Hancock. Sitting next to him, Craig Cox seemed to grow uneasy as Hancock mentioned Hinson. He tore his paper napkin and rolled pieces of it between his fingers. In a matter of minutes the whole napkin was reduced to a pile of paper twists. Cox hesitated when I asked him why he had confronted Hinson. He said he had heard Hinson was going to speak to the press and he wanted to be there to confront him if he believed he was misinterpreting Baptist belief. In retrospect, however, Cox was clearly uncomfortable about what had happened.

"I realized who he was. I had heard of him before," he said. "He is a known leader of the church, or at least he claims to be. He does have a lot of influence and popularity. And I don't have the intellectual depth he has. But I sense a lack of spiritual depth in him. I sensed that God would see me through it, even though I didn't have his intellectual experience."

Cox's distinction reflected the long-standing conflict, among many born-again Christians, between "head knowledge" and "heart knowledge." At the convention several preachers had proudly displayed the Bible and declared, "I don't understand it all, but I believe it all." It's a view that reinforces a childlike, all-or-nothing approach to God and the Bible. There was also a widely held belief among conservative Christians that once a person becomes born-again, he is suddenly able to understand the Bible. Craig Cox said as much. Patting a leather-bound Bible bearing his name embossed in gold, he said, "It brings about a spiritual ability to learn more about God. God has convicted me, for example, with the knowledge that the first eleven chapters of Genesis are absolutely true. This is His word, literally. I don't understand it all, but I believe it and obey."

Cox's criticism of Hinson rested on his own assessment of the professor's spirituality. "Dr. Hinson," said Cox, "is not really a man of God. I love Dr. Hinson. And I will pray for Dr. Hinson. He needs it because those who do not know Jesus are getting the worst of things now. People like Dr. Hinson have, somewhere, somehow, been deceived. My prayer and my hope is that God will never let me be influenced by anything outside His word," he said. "It might be sometime after Jesus comes again, but eventually Dr. Hinson will know everything. Like me, he will be held accountable and I would hate to be in his shoes."

An hour later, Glenn Hinson arrived for a late lunch at the same table. He was wearing a plain gray suit. He had placed in his lapel a silver pin, made to look like a sword bent at a 90 degree angle. He pointed to it and explained that he edited a Baptist journal called *Peacemaker*. As we sat down, Hinson was approached by several people who had been at other tables. They were not aggressive critics but rather fellow black sheep liberals. "Don't let them say he doesn't believe," said a former student who was pastor of a church in Virginia. "The thing that moved me the most during a lecture he gave was the devotion he said before we started."

Hinson said he had not been surprised by Craig Cox's reaction to his press conference. "I'm kind of a marked man where these so-called defenders of the faith are concerned," he said. At the convention a year before, one even shoved him in frustration during an impromptu debate.

"The odd thing is, I really understand where they're coming from, because I'm from there too," he went on. Hinson had grown up on an isolated farm in the Ozarks. His boyhood was filled with the same fundamentalism that Craig Cox carried from Cache. For Hinson, going to conventions was like going home to challenge his family's values and ideas.

Hinson was born in 1932. His great-grandfather was a Baptist preacher and so was one of his uncles. His father was a car dealer in St. Louis. Some of his first memories were of the car lot, where, at four, he had learned to read by deciphering the names of the cars on display. Although his father couldn't maintain a marriage or a family life, he could succeed in business even during the Depression, when many others failed. He was a brilliant man, with a fourth-grade education, who was troubled by alcohol, Hinson recalled. "He was an atheist when sober, but a fundamentalist when he was drunk." His father and mother divorced when Hinson was five years old. His mother took him and his brother, Eugene, to the Missouri Ozarks region, where they rented a small farm for six dollars a month.

On the farm, young Hinson was raised by his mother and an aunt and uncle who, in 1987, still lived in a house on the property. His mother had been a religious seeker, maintaining her Baptist ties while dabbling in local folk religion in what was called the Spiritual Church. As a boy Hinson accompanied his mother to services in both churches and to spooky séances conducted by local seers. At age six Hinson began his education in a one-room country school. His teacher was a young high school graduate who had never before encountered a first-grader who could read. "Her influence probably led me to academia," said Hinson. "It certainly wasn't my family. They were the kind of people, like many here, who believe you'll 'get ruint' by college. My religious background probably led me to the seminary."

Just as the seminary had challenged and transformed others, it helped turn Hinson into a critic of his own culture. He was exposed to science, history, and theology in a way that made him question almost everything he had learned back in Missouri. Geology and biology, with their evidence of evolution and creation, posed difficult questions, which orthodoxy was unable to answer.

"Inerrantists say that we have to ignore all the rational science and reason and believe the world is only ten thousand years old," Hinson said. "That's a central issue. But I don't think science means you throw out the Bible. It just means you have to think more carefully about what the Bible really is. I think you can believe the Bible is authoritative on faith and morals, but you don't have to impose a literal interpretation on Christians that forces them to deny science or reason. People won't accept that anymore."

Hinson compromised with science, fashioning a theological approach that allowed him to be a faithful Christian in the modern world. But the process of reconciling his traditional faith with modernity had been so difficult that he worried about how others would cope.

"I decided my vocation would be training Baptist ministers to work in this world, with modern ideas." Hinson stayed at Southern Seminary, helping to guide literally hundreds of students through the process of reconciling faith and reason. Along the way he came to be a symbol of liberalism in the church. Outspoken and almost as certain as the fundamentalists, he became a target for their attacks. In the past year one group had even mounted a campaign to have him fired from the seminary. They complained because Hinson had taught that Christ may have believed that the Bible prophecy of Armageddon would be fulfilled in his lifetime. It was a popular position among modern Bible historians, but it was also an idea that showed Christ, and the Bible, to be less than prescient. Hinson's accusers took their complaint all the way to the seminary's trustees.

"Of course, they assured me that it was nothing personal," said Hinson. "Whatever achieves their goal seems to be OK for these people. That makes me, my job, my family, marked enemies." Ultimately, the trustees backed Hinson, "but it made for a very difficult year for me and my family," he said.

While he had been shaken by his battles with the fundamentalists, Hinson tried to examine the Southern Baptist civil war as a historian. "The decision on the Peace Committee report was the most momentous decision the convention has made in this century," he said. "It's fascinating to be here, now, in the middle of it."

The Southern Baptist civil war had erupted, Hinson said, because many Baptists have been frightened by the twentieth century. Christian America never really recovered from the Scopes trial, he said. When the social change of the 1960s and 1970s came, "they were too shocked to respond right away. Now, in the 1980s, the conservative view has come on strong. People are insecure, and conservative leaders play on the insecurities to develop a following."

Starting in 1979, the fundamentalist revival had fed on the pent-up fear and anger of those who had not been part of the various social revolutions of the 1960s and 1970s.

"But now what are they reaping after their crusade?" asked Hinson. The PTL scandal had recently revealed the limitations and dangers of the big TV ministries. And the turmoil in the Southern Baptist Convention threatened to break the mighty church apart.

"No one wants to imagine that. I don't even like to consider it, because it's my church too," said Hinson. "But for that very reason, a lot of people are not going to be part of what the fundamentalists are doing." He said that if the moderate group, the Baptist Alliance, didn't call for a formal split, with millions of Baptists leaving en masse, the doctrine of inerrancy would force moderates to gradually leave the church and become Methodists or Episcopalians. Either way, the result would be a smaller, less sophisticated Southern Baptist Convention preaching an increasingly anachronistic message.

"If seminaries are stripped of modernism, who will teach students how to reach modern man?" he wondered.

Glenn Hinson had been one of the activists who tried to halt the vote on the Peace Committee report. He had warned that it would push too many people away from the church and move the denomination away from its traditional commitment to what Baptists called "the priesthood of the believer." All of his efforts failed.

In view of the moderates' recent defeat, Hinson's assessment of the larger conservative Christian crusade was surprising: "We're seeing the end of the conservative dominance right now." The PTL scandal and the bitterness of the 1987 Southern Baptist Convention were the harbingers of doom, he said. "They are being discredited and the next part of the historical cycle will be a new, liberal enlightenment."

American history has been punctuated by bursts of liberal religious action called "periods of awakening," said Hinson. "A period called 'the Great Awakening' led to the notion of human liberty that developed in New England from 1730 to 1760." Another "awakening" followed the taming of the American frontier in the early nineteenth century. Each enlightenment followed periods of social stress and brought liberal theological ideas that helped people through traumatic social changes. "All of these awakenings followed a period of confusion, such as we had in the 1960s and '70s, and a time of religious searching, which we have now."

When the liberal awakening arrives, the Southern Baptist Convention, dominated by conservative leaders, would hunker down to resist it, refusing, like Craig Cox, "to be influenced by the outside world." "Then," said Hinson, "the world may just leave the conservative born-again Christians behind, as it did after Scopes."

= 9 =

The Last Crusader

THE VICTORY of the conservatives at the Southern Baptist Convention in St. Louis was, it turned out, a Pyrrhic one. Although Adrian Rogers had been securely ensconced as the Baptists' national leader, within weeks his wing of the church leadership began to suffer a series of defeats. First they lost control of several state governing boards, the most important of which was the large and rich North Carolina convention. Then in September they lost a key struggle for control of Mercer University, an old and prestigious Southern Baptist institution. Student protests and faculty opposition thwarted the conservatives' efforts to pack the board of trustees. By autumn it was clear that Rogers and the rest of the inerrantists were losing control of the church at the local level. The moderates, seemingly vanquished in the big battle at the national convention, were taking the church back in a series of small skirmishes.

Meanwhile, each month Jim and Tammy Bakker sank to a lower level of ignominy. In July, PTL went bankrupt; in August, a grand jury launched a mail-fraud investigation; in September, hundreds of PTL donors filed a class-action suit demanding their money back. By the end of 1987, the Internal Revenue Service was demanding that

PTL pay $65 million in back taxes. The Bakkers embarked on a "fare-well tour" of major cities.

And though the Bakkers were the most prominent symbols of the decline of the Christian Right, the signs were suddenly everywhere. Throughout the year the born-again movement stumbled from one defeat to another. The federal court of appeals overturned Judge Hand's decision in the Mobile textbook case. Jerry Falwell's Moral Majority, once considered the most powerful political group outside the Republican and Democratic parties, was disbanded for lack of support. And for the first time, every one of the major televangelists was losing money, cutting airtime, and firing staff. It was no longer simply a question of a foolish statement by Oral Roberts or the particular venality of Jim and Tammy Bakker.

By the start of 1988, the movement was in crisis, although the media continued to treat the born-again crusade as the same seemingly invincible force that it had been through much of the decade. In fact, the magnitude of the movement's disarray was clear to those inside fundamentalist circles. Thus, Pat Robertson's surprising victories in the early presidential caucuses of 1988 not only drew national attention to his campaign but meant that this charismatic preacher increasingly came to incarnate all the fading hopes of the Christian Right.

Robertson had shocked the political experts by finishing second in the Iowa caucus. He beat Vice President George Bush and nearly upset front-runner Senator Robert Dole of Kansas. The press was filled with reports about Robertson's "secret army" of 30,000 conservative Christians who had swamped the Iowa caucuses. Born-again Christians, many of whom had stopped sending money to evangelists, responded with massive donations to the Robertson campaign. Seemingly without warning, Robertson had become a serious candidate and the Christian Right crusade had found its potential savior. The last, best hope of the Christian Right crusade, he brashly predicted a similar showing in the next test, the New Hampshire primary. A strong showing in New Hampshire would confirm him as a serious candidate for the presidency and restore the credibility and power of the Christian Right crusade.

I went to New Hampshire on February 14, two days before the primary, to watch Robertson try to save the crusade. As I crossed the New Hampshire state line on Interstate 95 in Seabrook, I began to see dark blue "Pat Robertson for President" posters standing in stark relief against the snowy landscape. The farther north I traveled, into the more conservative central part of the state, the more Robertson posters appeared. They littered the roadside like confetti, far outnumbering the placards for Bush and Senator Robert Dole, the front-runners.

About fifteen miles east of Concord, in a little town called Epsom, I passed an old white house that was decorated like a Robertson campaign bus. There was a huge Robertson banner on the side of the house, and in the driveway stood a sixteen-foot-high wooden horse plastered with Robertson posters. In the yard was a mock graveyard filled with white wooden crosses. On each cross was written the name of a communist country.

An old woman, her white hair tied back in a bun, answered my knock at the front door. Her name was Barbara Anderson and she told me that many passersby stopped to ask about the horse. In fact, she admitted, that was the whole idea. "Come in. Come in and have some tea," she said, wrapping her blue cardigan around her as a shield against the cold air coming in the open door.

Mrs. Anderson led me through a large, dark kitchen where an old couple sat eating soup at a long table. As she reached for an already hot kettle, she explained that she had turned her house into a boarding home for elderly pensioners and teenaged foster children. Mrs. Anderson complained about state safety and health inspectors, who were threatening to close the place down. The house was apparently a fire hazard.

"They have too many rules, too many regulations," Anderson said crankily as she handed me a cup of tea. "The old people and the young people seem to get along nicely. Things work here. That's what matters, not regulations."

The small room that served as Mrs. Anderson's study was crowded with books, stacks of papers, two desks, and three old typewriters. It was the office for her boarding home and headquarters for her one-woman political campaigns, which, she told me, were always for conservative causes and candidates.

"Now, I'm an old Episcopalian, and I don't go much for this born-again religion," Barbara Anderson said as she settled into a swivel chair behind one of the two desks in the room. Her voice was gravelly and slow.

"What I am is an old-fashioned, conservative go-getter. I like Pat Robertson because he's not controlled by the politicians or the establishment. You can register your protest against business as usual, against the liberals, by voting for him. I don't think of him as a TV preacher. He's a politician. Look what he did in Iowa. That was politics and I'm impressed."

Mrs. Anderson was, as the newspaper clippings she showed me demonstrated, a well-known political gadfly. She had made her "Trojan horse" in 1978 to protest the second Strategic Arms Limitation Treaty. She had kept it on the front lawn ever since, changing the signs on its flanks to indicate which cause she supported at that particular moment. She said that she usually decorated the horse with her favorite candidate's name early in the primary campaign. But this time around, she had had trouble choosing a candidate. She had been impressed by Robertson's positions on issues but had been skeptical about his wider political appeal. But after Iowa she saw him as a serious candidate. Only days before, she had signed up to chair the Robertson campaign in Epsom, so the posters that plastered her horse were of very recent vintage.

I asked Barbara Anderson about Pat Robertson's religious ideas, especially about his attempts at healing and "rebuking" hurricanes. She said the supposed miracles made her a bit uncomfortable, but not enough to keep her from supporting him. "All I know is, he's the only one talking about the issues I care about, about the awful stuff you see on TV and about drugs. He's talking about abortion and communism and taxes. He could do well heeeuh," she said, dropping the *r* in her last word, revealing a genuine New Hampshire accent. People are going to be surprised, she predicted. "Pat Robertson's going to do a lot better than anyone expects."

It was about one o'clock in the afternoon when I left Barbara Anderson's house and headed to Berlin, where Robertson was to appear at a rally at the Assemblies of God church. Berlin was about ninety miles north of Concord and sixty miles south of the Canadian border. When I reached the edge of town, I stopped at a gas station–grocery store and asked the clerk inside for directions. He said the Assemblies of God church was just a mile away. "It's a new building on the right side of the road," he said. As I went out the door he called out, "Praise the Lord!"

The clerk's farewell surprised me. I had grown up in New Hampshire and had covered several presidential primaries there. I knew Berlin and I knew that a decade earlier the town would have been about as far from born-again faith as Robertson could get and still be in America. Dominated by French-Canadian immigrants, it was one of the most

Catholic places in the country. But by 1988, it seemed, the Christian Right crusade had burned its way even through towns like Berlin. If grocery-store clerks said "Praise the Lord" in Berlin, perhaps Pat Robertson did have a chance of pulling off an Iowa-style surprise in New Hampshire.

The Assemblies of God church was set on a rolling, wooded piece of land across from a truck repair garage. It was a large building, so new that the shingles were still raw and unweathered. The church was surrounded by a large dirt parking lot, which, as I arrived, was quickly filling up with cars and trucks. Three TV technicians were pulling cameras and sound equipment out of a van and hauling the stuff into the church. The snow squeaked and crunched under their boots as they struggled up the hill.

Inside, the church was a simple white sanctuary with large windows and a high ceiling. Bright TV lights were already trained on a small altar and wooden lectern. About two hundred people were there, a gathering big enough to make the place feel crowded. A very nervous-looking, skinny young man with a pale face and dark hair hovered in the vestibule. He wore a dark blue suit and a blue plastic button that said "People for Pat." His name was Tom Fava and he was the pastor of the church, which had grown from about forty families to a hundred and twenty in the past two years. "That's not a bad size," he said, "given that there's only about three thousand year-round residents up here."

While we talked, Fava greeted the people who came through the door, pressing Robertson campaign literature into their hands and holding out a basket that was filled with "People for Pat" buttons. "This is something, handing out political buttons in a church," he said. Fava said he had once felt conflicted about mixing religion and politics. "And I thought Pat Robertson's first calling was the ministry. I think that is the highest calling there is," he explained. Fava said he had changed his mind about Robertson when a state senator named Mark Hounsel invited him to view a video that the campaign had produced to inspire its workers. He was inspired.

"Now I know the Lord brought me to New Hampshire for a dual purpose," he said. He noted that the state, with just one million people and its first-of-the-season primary, played an enormous role in national politics. "You can't come here and not be political, so I have to see that He brought me here to both spread the gospel and support Pat

Robertson. I think the two can work together, that people will be exposed to the Lord through the campaign."

I mentioned Barbara Anderson, who, though not a born-again Christian, had been drawn to Robertson's candidacy. "That's what I'm talking about," he said, glancing through the doorway at a caravan of cars and vans that was pulling into the parking lot outside. "When the heathen get a taste of what Pat Robertson says, even the heathen will vote for him. Then they may also consider his stand for the Lord too. That way, even if he doesn't win the White House this time around, he's going to win a lot of people for Christ with this campaign. The campaign is like an evangelistic tool. I'm talking about a political campaign that's a religious revival too."

Outside, Pat Robertson was arriving. He came up the hill accompanied by Meldrim Thomson, the archconservative former governor of New Hampshire. As Robertson and Thomson came through the front door of the church, someone switched on a tape player and the strains of "The Battle Hymn of the Republic" filled the sanctuary. The people in the church stood and began applauding. The candidate walked down the center aisle of the church, shaking every outstretched hand and grinning for the cameras. A stocky, middle-aged man of medium height, Robertson was dressed in a blue blazer and a red-and-blue-striped tie. He had bushy pewter-colored hair and twinkling blue eyes. He seemed confident, even exuberant. As he worked his way down the aisle, he called out to everyone and no one in particular.

"I feel something happening in New Hampshire," he said, turning toward the cameras and grinning. "Can't you feel it?"

The tape player was turned off. Robertson stepped behind the lectern and raised his hands to quiet the audience.

"Monday night I was so humbled by the Lord," he began. "In Iowa He gave us a smashing victory. We beat George Bush, the Vice President of the United States, who in 1980 defeated Ronald Reagan in Iowa. Now in New Hampshire comes the big one. The eyes of the nation are here. All America wants to know: 'What is the Granite State going to do?' Well, I've been giving a very simple message in this campaign, that I want America to be number one again. I want the greatness of America to be restored through moral strength."

People in the audience called out, "Amen!"

"Ladies and gentlemen, we don't have a political problem in America. We have a moral problem.

"And I want to support the American family. If the family falls apart, the nation will fall apart. These children are our greatest treasure," he said, gesturing toward a row of children seated to his right. "We owe them the best education in the world in a crime-free, drug-free, disciplined environment."

After reciting the list of states where he had confounded the political experts, Robertson breezed through his policy positions. As President, he said, he would be tough on the Russians and the welfare cheats. He would turn Social Security into a private pension system and outlaw abortion. For about ten minutes he sounded like any other conservative politician. But when he got to the heart of his campaign message, a warning about America's moral decline, the politician suddenly disappeared, replaced by the evangelist.

"Either America is going to get back to deep-seated faith in God or we will go deeper and deeper into moral decay," he said.

A few more "Amens" were sounded by the crowd.

"If America declines, the experts will say there is no other way, the answer will be to move America away from sovereignty to a one-world government, a one-currency economy. I'm not going to let that happen. But you have to help me. We have to leave New Hampshire with enormous strength if we are going to continue the fight."

The music was turned on again and the audience stood and cheered. In the back of the church, where I stood with the traveling press, I heard one reporter ask a colleague, "What is he talking about? One-world government? One-currency economy?"

To an outsider, Robertson's rhetoric made very little sense. Certainly it had nothing to do with conventional politicking, even as practiced by staunch conservative Republicans. But for this church audience of born-again Christians, his allusions to end-times prophecy were the core of the message, the thing that had drawn them to his candidacy in the first place. Unlike the reporters, they understood Robertson's reference to Armageddon prophecy. For what he was really saying was that the best way to save America from the end times was to make him President.

It took less than twenty minutes for Robertson to speak, press the flesh, and leave. Suddenly there were no Secret Service men, no TV cameras or lights. The church became quiet as the crowd quickly dispersed. I joined two young men, members of the church, who stayed behind long after the Robertson motorcade had pulled away. One of them, Steve Tremblay, was the twenty-year-old assistant pastor of the church. The other was Mike Saucier, who introduced himself as a tinsmith and a born-again Christian. Both were from Catholic, French-Canadian families. Both had been introduced to conservative Christian faith by watching satellite TV. The long New Hampshire winter offered few diversions for the people of the north country. Satellite TV was one of them. I asked them whether the Robertson campaign was mainly a political campaign or a religious crusade.

Tremblay, a thin man with tousled black hair, paused for a moment and then said, "He's trying to bring people to Christ. That's the first thing. Maybe a campaign like this is a new way to do it. They'll think they are getting a political message but, before you know it, they'll be coming to Christ." Tremblay said he expected Robertson to win New Hampshire. He was going to go door to door in his neighborhood to help the cause.

"You really think he's got a chance?" asked Saucier, who wore a checked flannel shirt and new-looking blue jeans.

"He's got momentum. Look at Iowa," answered Tremblay. "That's what they say is the most important thing, momentum. I think he's got it. I really do. The country is ready to turn back to God too. I feel that. We've been going on man's way too long now. It's time to go back to God's way."

I said goodbye, pulled on my coat, and went out into the night. On the drive south to Concord I listened to a candidates' debate on the radio. Bush and Dole dominated the discussion. It was a rather bland, even boring debate, with the questions drifting from the federal budget deficit to defense policy, until the subject of the recently completed Reagan-Gorbachev arms treaty was raised. Then Robertson jumped into the discussion with a stunning claim.

"Some information came to me that the Soviets, in violation of the so-called Khrushchev-Kennedy accords, have put some SS-4s and SS-5s in Cuba, which are intermediate-range nuclear weapons," said Robertson. "Somehow, in all this brilliant negotiation that these gentlemen are so proud of, they've left out that treaty. It seems like, to me, nukes pointing at the United States are more vital to our security than nukes pointing to Europe."

The debate moderator, Edwin Newman, seemed startled by Robertson's assertion. "You say you have learned that Soviet SS-4s and SS-5s have been placed in Cuba?" he said, his voice rising with incredulity.

"Twenty-five of them, 4s and 5s," answered Robertson. "That's

correct. You can check it. This may be a major flaw in that treaty.
We should certainly look into if there are nukes in Cuba."

After the debate, the radio commentators tried to figure out what
Robertson had said, and why. They agreed that he was obviously
making a grandstand play, trying to squeeze Bush and Dole out of the
morning headlines. But more important, they agreed that what he had
said—about Soviet nuclear weapons in Cuba—was probably not true.
It was not the first time Robertson had been caught bending the truth.
In the previous weeks he had sparked a string of small controversies,
which began when he had told a story about a woman who got AIDS
from kissing her impotent husband. The press hounded him to back
up the AIDS story, demanding that he present some evidence that he
was telling the truth. He didn't. Then there was Robertson's claim
that, through a reading program he had sponsored, a second-grader
had learned to read at a seventh-grade level in just three weeks. No
one could find the little girl. There were more questions—about Robertson's claim that he had "rebuked" a hurricane and about his charge
that Planned Parenthood was trying to build a "master race" through
the sterilization of "blacks, Jews, mental defectives, and fundamentalist
Christians."

With each gaffe, Robertson grew more defensive. At one campaign
stop he yelled at reporters, "I'm not going to do your own research for
you. You do it!" During a tour of a New Hampshire rifle factory, he
had even grabbed a gun and half jokingly trained it on the press corps.

By the next morning it was clear that Robertson's grandstand play over
the missiles had backfired seriously. The Reagan White House angrily
refuted Robertson's claim about the Soviet missiles. So did the Pen-
tagon. There were, it seemed, no nukes in Cuba. Robertson had
captured the front-page headlines, but not in the way he had intended.
Each article not only ridiculed his claim but recounted the many half-
truths and misstatements that had characterized his entire campaign.
Suddenly it was open season on Pat Robertson, who began to look so
weak that his opponents even felt free to mock his brand of Christianity.
At a breakfast meeting in Dover, which was broadcast over the radio,
Delaware governor Pierre du Pont complained about the weather, and
then suggested, "Perhaps Pat could do something about it."

On that Monday, I followed Robertson through a final day of cam-
paigning in New Hampshire. His itinerary was designed to keep him
away from reporters while still getting him onto the nightly news. It

began with a walk on Main Street in Rochester, a run-down old mill city in the eastern corner of the state. While Robertson bustled along, reporters followed him down the sidewalk. After being pelted with questions, he finally answered.

"I'm not going to back off of it," he said of the missile remarks. "I'd be happy to have someone prove me wrong."

Meanwhile, his campaign staff passed around a "clarifying statement" which suggested that Robertson had meant to say there were missile launchers in Cuba, not actual missile warheads. Yet when asked if he had made a mistake, Robertson kept saying, "No, I haven't. I meant what I said."

The Robertson caravan left Rochester and worked its way westward, stopping at gas stations, general stores, and post offices in nearly every small town he passed. When he reached Concord, Robertson went to the state capitol, a sturdy, Bulfinch-designed granite building with a small gold dome, to address the legislature. The supposed high point of the day, the speech was his stock campaign address, which amounted to a recitation of the nation's woes, the warning about the one-world government, and the conclusion that "the trouble in America, underneath all the problems, is moral decay." The text was dull. Robertson was flat. And the assembled senators and representatives were politely unreceptive.

Afterward, a state representative named Wayne King told me that every presidential candidate, Democrat and Republican, had addressed the legislature. Robertson, he said, had received the coolest response of all. "Jesse Jackson, who some of these guys think is a communist, got more applause," King said. "Something is going wrong for him, that's obvious."

Robertson's troubles were confirmed by George Roberts, a former Speaker of the New Hampshire House turned lobbyist. "There aren't that many born-again Christians in New Hampshire, so I don't see how he's going to have a secret army here," Roberts told me. "What he doesn't understand is that New Hampshire voters are very savvy. We've had the big primary up here for a long time and people are used to looking at these guys very critically. He's not standing up to that very well."

From Concord, Robertson and his entourage moved on to Manchester. The procession led to a gym that was in a small shopping center on the outskirts of town. The place was barely big enough for a boxing ring and a dressing room. Nevertheless, more than a hundred reporters, cameramen, and campaign aides jammed into the few feet of space around the ring and dutifully waited for the photo opportunity. Robertson was going to box with the gym's owner, a born-again Golden Glover named Mike Sampson.

In the crush around the edges of the gym the reporters complained about how they were being manipulated. It was one of the most ridiculous scenes of the campaign: a fake boxing match, for the benefit of the TV cameras, held in a gym so small that none of New Hampshire's voters could get inside.

But even as they grumbled, the press faithfully recorded Robertson's entrance, through a back door, to the triumphant strains of the theme from *Rocky*, the Sylvester Stallone movie about an underdog fighter. Dressed in a nylon exercise suit, with a towel wrapped around his neck, Robertson smiled stiffly as a pair of bright red boxing gloves the size of small throw pillows were laced on his hands. He took a few swipes at the air and then touched gloves with his opponent, a muscular young fellow who was attentive to the point of being worshipful.

When the bell rang, the two men lumbered around the ring trying to look as if they were fighting but taking care not to hurt each other. Sampson jabbed at Robertson's gloves. Then he drifted in close, allowing Robertson to flutter a punch against his head. The room was filled with the shriek of motorized still cameras and the flash of strobe lights. Sampson dove to the canvas. When he bounced up, he said something about Robertson knocking down George Bush on election day. When the one-minute round was over, Robertson, red-faced and puffing, hugged Sampson and then slipped between the ropes to go to a dressing room. As he left, he was showered with questions about the Cuban missiles. He ignored them.

With the sun setting, the Robertson campaign roared off for Pelham, on the southern border near Massachusetts, and Robertson's last speech before New Hampshire voted. I followed the caravan to a country club where about a hundred people were gathered in a pine-paneled banquet room. The mood in Pelham was much more reserved than it had been the day before in Berlin. There was no recorded music. Robertson just walked in, trailed by the few reporters who hadn't stayed behind in Manchester to file their stories about the boxing match. (The photo opportunity worked. It was featured that night on all three TV network news programs.) In Pelham, Robertson again predicted victory.

"Something is happening here in the Granite State," he told the audience. "I can feel it."

But there was no excitement in the room. No one stood and cheered. Robertson gave an abbreviated version of his "moral decay" speech, quietly shook a few hands, and left. Something was happening in New Hampshire. Robertson's campaign was dropping like a rock down a well.

The next day, election day, was cold and clear. A big turnout was predicted. The first signs of Robertson's defeat trickled out of some precincts in the southern half of the state shortly after the polls closed at eight o'clock. The contest between Bush and Dole was tight, and the four other candidates—Robertson, du Pont, Congressman Jack Kemp, and former Secretary of State Alexander Haig—were clustered far behind them.

I started the evening at the new Clarion Hotel in Salem, where Jack Kemp's campaign held its election-night party. There, about a hundred well-dressed, high-spirited young people ate scallops wrapped in bacon and drank imported beer. They were New Hampshire's yuppies, less polished perhaps than their Boston counterparts, but nevertheless remarkably well off and cosmopolitan. They watched the returns on giant-screen TVs and cheered each time one of the precincts showed Kemp finishing third, behind Bush and Dole. The second-tier candidates—Kemp, du Pont, and Robertson—were battling for the conservative mantle, I was told. Bush and Dole were both considered moderates, so whoever came out of New Hampshire in third place could claim to be the darling of the Republican Party's hard Right.

After half an hour at the Clarion, I drove the twenty miles north to Manchester. There an older, more moneyed crowd filled a storefront that had been Pierre du Pont's headquarters. Du Pont's campaign committee was running out of both time and money. The volunteers ate tuna sandwiches and watched the election reports on several TVs that were scattered about. Their man's share of the votes hovered around the 10 percent mark. His chances of winning even third place were remote. One of du Pont's aides, who was half drunk by nine o'clock, told me he had spent the day with some Bush campaign aides, angling for a job.

I left Manchester shortly after nine and drove to Concord and the old Highway Hotel, where Robertson had rented a huge ballroom. The Highway, as it was called, was an old political landmark. For years it had been the only place big enough to accommodate the press and staff of a presidential campaign. But the Highway had lost most of its campaign business when new hotels were built in Salem and Manchester in the late 1970s. By 1988 the old place had gone to seed.

When I arrived, the cold night air was quickly freezing the water that had collected in the parking lot from melting snow. The lot was like a skating rink. I shuffled across it, holding on to cars as I went. Most of the cars were decorated with "Robertson 88" bumper stickers. Half of them also had the kinds of stickers I had grown accustomed to seeing in church parking lots—"Jesus Loves You" or "Christian on Board."

While the Highway's exterior had retained its New England charm, on the inside the wallpaper was peeling, the lighting was dim, and the carpets were frayed. I followed a long hallway to the entrance to the dark, dusty hotel ballroom. There, hundreds of born-again Christians milled about, sipping soft drinks and watching the primary election returns on big-screen TVs that were positioned around the edges of the room. Recorded music was playing and the place had been decorated with balloons and streamers. But the people were not celebrating. Robertson had received less than 12 percent of the vote, half of what he got in Iowa. He had fallen from Iowa challenger to New Hampshire also-ran. I talked briefly with Mark Hounsel, who was the only member of the New Hampshire Senate who had backed Robertson. I asked him if the Jim and Tammy Bakker scandal had hurt Robertson's chances.

"He tried to get away from that image, to distance himself from it, but the press wouldn't let him," said Hounsel, who was a tall, slightly overweight man in his mid-thirties. "They always called him a television evangelist, trying to keep that label on him. He never was given a chance as a candidate." I asked if Robertson's many gaffes had also contributed to his defeat.

"That didn't really hurt us as much as the fact that there just aren't that many active Christians up here yet," answered Hounsel. "But it's not over, you know. New Hampshire's not the end."

Robertson appeared in the ballroom at about ten o'clock and acted, astonishingly, as if nothing had happened. He shook hands, smiled as he always smiled, and again pledged to fight "moral decay." He summarily thanked his dispirited campaign volunteers and then warned the other candidates that "the next battle will take place in South Carolina, my backyard." He departed, leaving behind a crowd of crestfallen born-again activists.

*   *   *

While New Hampshire had been a disaster, Robertson's hopefulness was not all bravado. The next tests were in the South, in states where there were strong conservative Christian communities and substantial Robertson organizations. Even outside political experts, in the Republican Party and in the media, predicted he might finish first in South Carolina. After all, he did have a strong base of support there among born-again Christians and an excellent grass-roots organization, led by able political activists like Orin Briggs and Henry Jordan.

But while Robertson had left New Hampshire with some reason for hope, it didn't last long. A few days later, another scandal, involving yet another TV preacher, would rock the born-again movement. This disgrace would contribute further to the failure of the Christian Right crusade and seal the downfall of the Robertson presidential campaign.

Evangelist Jimmy Swaggart had always been the most audacious of the born-again evangelists. A cousin of rock-and-roll singer Jerry Lee Lewis, Swaggart was very much like him, a dynamic, overpowering performer who banged out his own honky-tonk style of gospel music with an energy that turned many in his audience into screaming groupies. His evangelistic crusades were great sweaty displays of passion and hellfire preaching, and his message was highly moralistic. Ironically, no one talked about the evils of sex more than Jimmy Swaggart. In fact, he had leaked much of the information that had caused the PTL scandal and then was one of the Bakkers' most vocal critics. Swaggart had called the Bakkers a "cancer on the body of Christ" and had demanded that they resign from the ministry. There were more scandalous discoveries to be made among the big-time evangelists, he had warned at the time. "I believe they will come out. But they won't come from me."

Swaggart's prediction was half right. There were more "sins" to be rooted out: his. Rumors of Swaggart's sexual strayings began to flow out of Baton Rouge, where Swaggart was headquartered, just three days after the New Hampshire primary. At first the TV networks merely reported that Swaggart's denomination, the Assemblies of God, was investigating charges against him. A day later it was revealed that the charges involved sexual misconduct and that another minister, Marvin Gorman, had incriminating photographs. Gorman had apparently turned the tables on Swaggart. Just two years earlier, as Gorman was starting his own TV ministry in New Orleans, Swaggart had divulged evidence of Gorman's philandering to denominational leaders. As a result, Gorman was defrocked. But apparently he was not defeated.

After getting an anonymous tip about Swaggart, Gorman stalked his enemy, eventually cornering him outside a motel room and snapping the photographs.

Five days after the New Hampshire primary, Swaggart flew to Springfield, Missouri, in his private jet, went before a special board convened by his denomination, and confessed everything. He had learned something from the Bakkers. He wasn't about to let the fall of Jimmy Swaggart consume a year or more. That Sunday, he went before his congregation of 8,000 and tearfully begged for their forgiveness.

Standing before the TV cameras, tears streaming down his face, Swaggart cried and begged forgiveness from his wife, Frances, his family, and his flock. "I have no one but myself to blame," the handsome blond preacher said. Frances looked on with a frozen smile. Swaggart's son Donnie, tears running down his face, mouthed the words "I love you" to his father.

"I do not plan in any way to whitewash my sin," Swaggart continued, his voice shaking. "I do not call it a mistake, a mendacity, I call it sin." Pacing back and forth across the altar, Swaggart asked missionaries abroad and the hundreds of thousands of donors watching on TV to forgive him. "I have sinned against You, my Lord," he said, crying copiously. "And I would ask that Your precious blood would wash and cleanse every stain until it is in the seas of God's forgiveness."

In the audience, people cried and called out, "We love you," as Swaggart wept and begged. They stopped the service twice with standing ovations. After the service, Swaggart disappeared past the gates of his estate. Scores of believers remained in the church, crying. Some of them lay on the floor, their bodies heaving with sobs.

Over the next week, the intimate details of Swaggart's sexual transgressions—including Gorman's photos—slowly emerged in the press. It turned out that Swaggart had met regularly with a prostitute in a seedy motel called the Travel Inn in New Orleans. The prostitute, a woman named Debra Murphree, came forward to describe a year-long string of encounters with Swaggart, who had paid her to strip and pose for him. She said Swaggart never had intercourse with her, but he did once pay her to wear a short dress with no underwear and ride around with him in his Lincoln Town Car. Some press accounts quoted sources who said Swaggart had been practically addicted to pornography for years. Other reports described Swaggart, disguised in hats, sunglasses, or headbands, cruising the motel strip on Airline

Highway in New Orleans, where prostitutes and their johns met on street corners.

The Swaggart scandal delighted the media, and the critics of the Christian Right, who had become emboldened by the Bakker scandal, were eager to capitalize on Swaggart's disgrace. *Time* magazine ran a headline, next to a picture of Swaggart crying, which said: "Now It's Jimmy's Turn." *Time* also published a photo of the Travel Inn and a Tampa, Florida, police mug shot of Debra Murphree, prisoner number 297318. *People* magazine ran a full-page photo of Swaggart, tears streaming down his face, and an article that described the hypocrisy of Swaggart's predicament as "breathtaking."

Swaggart dropped from public view after his tearful plea for forgiveness. When I telephoned his headquarters, a worker in his public relations office said Swaggart was not scheduled to appear in public "for the foreseeable future." He was not available for interviews.

It was an astonishing toll. By the end of February 1988, nearly all the major TV preachers had been discredited. Oral Roberts had made a fool of himself with his fundraising; Swaggart and the Bakkers had been tarnished by their sexual scandals; Falwell had been tainted by his seeming desire to profit from the Bakkers' fall and take over PTL. Pat Robertson was the last crusader, still chasing the dream of Christian America.

In March, Robertson was in Texas, flitting from city to city, desperately trying to save his candidacy and, by extension, the Christian Right movement. I went there to watch him give a speech to the assembled students and faculty of the day school at First Baptist Church of Dallas. The huge, old mother church of Texas' conservative Southern Baptists, First Baptist was the most insulated bastion of born-again power in America. It was a place where Robertson would be sure to get a warm welcome.

I took a late-night flight from New York to Dallas, and the next morning, before I left the hotel, I called Rev. Paige Patterson, one of the pastors of First Baptist and a powerful figure in the Christian Right. Patterson said he was leaving town and wouldn't be at the church for Robertson's address.

"Does he have a chance in Texas?" Patterson asked rhetorically. "No."

I went to the church at about ten o'clock in the morning. There were TV vans parked outside and a cluster of reporters waited on the sidewalk. I joined them, and minutes later Robertson arrived and walked quickly up to a side door to the church, where he was cornered by the reporters.

"I'm here because I think I can win Texas," he began. But the reporters only wanted to know what Robertson thought about the Swaggart scandal. Was he suffering in the polls? Was he considering dropping out of the race?

"I'm not dropping out," Robertson said testily. He was obviously distressed by the Swaggart disaster. It couldn't have come at a worse time for him—days before the vote in those states where he really had a chance—and Robertson knew it could be a fatal blow to his hopes. Standing outside the church, he suggested that perhaps his political opponents were behind it all.

"It is kind of funny this came up two weeks before the most important primaries in the nation," he said angrily. "I think somebody had something to do with it. I'm afraid somebody else planned all these things."

Robertson pulled the door open and went inside the church, where he was greeted warmly by several of the pastors. I went up into the balcony of First Baptist to listen to the speech. The large sanctuary, with its high, bowed ceiling, was filled with several hundred school-children and just a handful of voters, all of them teachers. Again there was recorded music—Sousa marches this time—and again Robertson bored in on his main theme of "moral decay." But key parts of the stump speech had changed since I had last heard him speak. He was no longer touting himself as the candidate with Iowa momentum. He had become, instead, a David against the political Goliaths and the media. He described himself as the victim of dirty tricks—such as the Swaggart revelation—and the target of anti-conservative Christian bias.

In Dallas, Robertson again complained about the label "television evangelist." He insisted he was a viable political candidate and then asked the audience to back up the claim. "Give me the satisfaction," he said, pausing to grin, "of hearing Tom Brokaw say, 'Mr. Robertson, you won the South.' " Robertson went on to describe a rather vague platform of ideas that amounted to anti-government conservatism. "I don't want some government bureaucrat interfering with your lives," he told the students. "I want you to fulfill your destiny before God."

A few days later, Robertson finished a dismal third in his South Carolina "backyard." He didn't win in Texas or in any of the other eighteen Southern states that voted on Super Tuesday at the end of March. By April the Robertson campaign was barely limping on and political analysts wondered why he didn't drop out. He flew in and out of cities, appearing at small rallies and having less impact than a spring shower. Occasionally he would grab a headline with an outrageous statement. But for the most part, Robertson campaigned in a vacuum inhabited by his loyal entourage, his church-based audiences, and his determination. He crisscrossed the country until mid-May, trailing disappointment in his wake. Then, after a quiet meeting with the nominee apparent, George Bush, Robertson quit, promising to campaign for the Republicans in the fall. The general election would be a political campaign after all, not an evangelistic crusade.

With the demise of Robertson's campaign came the death of the Christian Right's political hopes. The born-again movement soon ceased to be a significant religious or social force as well. Each of the major ministers reported losses in the tens of millions of dollars. Each laid off hundreds of employees. Oral Roberts pulled his hour-long TV show from more than forty stations because he could no longer pay for the airtime. PTL's Heritage USA complex was sold to an Orthodox Jewish businessman from Canada who viewed it as a real estate investment. Meanwhile, the Swaggart and Bakker scandals continued to evolve, with new developments surfacing in the media every few weeks. It was revealed that Swaggart too had been involved in shady financial dealings, although not in a way that compared with the Bakkers'. He had put most of his family on the ministry payroll and had taken huge loans from the ministry, but there was little evidence of criminal misconduct. Jim Bakker, on the other hand, was eventually indicted on fraud charges. In July 1989, two of his key aides were convicted of tax evasion. They had apparently forgotten to pay taxes on $1.2 million in PTL money, which they had used to buy such personal luxuries as an apartment in Manhattan's swank Trump Tower and jewelry and designer clothes. Like Imelda Marcos, David and James Taggart apparently had a penchant for footwear. Among their purchases was nearly $100,000 worth of shoes.

The collapse of the Christian Right was noisily announced by the demise of the TV evangelists. After Robertson's presidential campaign sputtered and died, taking with it the born-again movement's political ambitions, the denunciations and infighting became so acute that the activities of the once-powerful TV preachers became comic fodder for every TV talk-show host in America. The dignity of the born-again crusade suffered even more as Jessica Hahn rose to a rather unseemly prominence. She was twice pictured nude in *Playboy* (once before plastic surgery, once after) and then took a job as a radio "personality." Finally, in a grotesque footnote to the whole evangelist phenomenon that had swept the country in the 1980s, a minor traveling preacher was convicted of dozens of incidents of child molesting, which had taken place in many locations over the course of several years. *The New York Times* displayed its highly detailed story about this malevolent born-again evangelist on its front page.

Despite the bizarre nature of the evangelists' downfalls, the failure of the Christian Right was caused less by the self-inflicted wounds of sexual scandal, political incompetence, and greed than by overarching historical trends, which born-again Christians had been powerless to affect. By the late 1980s it was clear that the success of the born-again movement had been tied to the particular wave of nostalgic politics embodied in Ronald Reagan's candidacy and his two terms in office. After all, the born-again movement could never have had the influence it enjoyed without Ronald Reagan's vociferous support. But it had not been an integral part of Reaganism, as the President's reluctance to move forward on the born-again agenda eventually proved. Despite the President's rhetoric, *Roe* v. *Wade* was not overturned, school prayer was not instituted, the Sandinistas were not dislodged from Nicaragua, and civil protections for homosexuals were not withdrawn. Indeed, by the end of President Reagan's two terms, the political figure whom this archconservative President seemed to respect the most was the Soviet leader Mikhail Gorbachev.

Without Reagan, the Christian crusaders were quickly disenfranchised. And in the presidential campaign of 1988, which was dominated by the Eastern establishment (the candidates were graduates of Yale and Swarthmore), they were pushed toward the political fringe. Even George Bush, who at first pandered to the conservative Christians by declaring himself a born-again Episcopalian, came to ignore them in the general campaign. With Bush's election, the country clearly opted for a more moderate conservative consensus, rejecting the reactionary, religiously colored agenda which the Christian Right had represented.

And just as domestic events seemed to conspire to exclude the born-again conservatives, world affairs unfolded in a way that stripped the movement of many of its most useful enemies. Under the liberalizing policies of *glasnost* and *perestroika*, the Soviet Union eased its human rights policies, pulled its army out of Afghanistan, experimented with capitalism, and joined in the process of nuclear arms reductions. At the same time, wars ended in the Persian Gulf, Namibia, Cambodia, and Nicaragua. The end of the Contra war in Nicaragua, soon after President Bush's inauguration, was particularly damaging to the Christian Right crusade. By accepting the reality of the Sandinista government, the U.S. government deflated the Christian Right's most frightening bogeyman and moved Nicaragua off the front pages. Taken together, the events of the late 1980s made the world seem somehow safer and more stable. With peace increasingly conceivable throughout the world, the rhetoric of Armageddon and the end times was bound to have a far narrower appeal than it had enjoyed during the period when the President of the United States inveighed against the Soviet Union as the "Evil Empire."

Similarly, the religious orthodoxy promoted by the Christian Right seemed to be difficult for great numbers of people to accept. Conversions to born-again faith leveled off in the middle of the decade, and, ironically, the dominant religious fad in 1989 was a highly unorthodox blend of philosophy and spiritualism loosely called the New Age. As the decidedly post-Christian New Age movement grew, millions of Americans began wearing crystals, which they believed had magical powers, and books by self-described spiritual guides became best-sellers. The rise of the New Age reflected many Americans' attempts to make peace with uncertainty and fashion a new way of thinking about the world as a single community. It also marked the end of the born-again revival, which for a few years had been the dominant trend in American religious life.

All this seemed to suggest that, despite the Christian Right's meteoric rise and undeniable success, the nation as a whole was continuing to become a more secular, less parochial society. The idea of America as a born-again promised land, a new Israel, had little relevance in an America that had been remade—culturally, politically, ethnically, and racially—since the turn of the century.

Indeed, at the end of the decade, Americans were affected more by environmental concerns—the Chernobyl nuclear disaster, the depletion of the atmosphere's ozone layer, the destruction of the Amazon rain forest—than by issues of personal morality. Internationalism, spurred by these global environmental issues and the easing of tensions between East and West, was beginning to color the general American outlook. By the late 1980s it was impossible to imagine that a jingoistic campaign to create a Christian America could capture the nation's attention. And the language of religious fundamentalism became so alien to most Americans that they could not comprehend the kind of religious impulse that led Muslim leaders to call for the murder of author Salman Rushdie because he had written a supposedly blasphemous book called *The Satanic Verses*.

In the end, defeated and exhausted, the Christian Right crusade of the 1980s could be seen as America's longing look backward at religious absolutism. It was, it seems, only a pause in the secularizing process that has been underway since the turn of the century. The failure of the Christian Right crusade demonstrated that the born-again construct of a Christian America is no longer possible.

In 1925, after the Scopes trial, H. L. Mencken wrote that conservative Christianity is a "fire still burning on a far-flung hill, and it may begin to roar again at any moment." That fire had roared in the 1980s. During the Christian Right crusade, television preachers and activists spent billions of dollars trying to turn born-again religion into a national identity. The TV audiences grew to the tens of millions, huge institutions were built, court battles were joined, and political pressure was applied. Then, very quickly, the fire receded, doused by scandal and failure. America had changed so much since Scopes that it would never again be just a Christian nation. After the great crusade of the 1980s, born-again faith returned to the place it had occupied before, warming the private lives of faithful believers, a minority creed in a diverse and secularized country.

Afterword

THE INCREDIBLE free-fall of the Christian Right movement continued well after Pat Robertson's defeat in the 1988 presidential campaign. Through 1989 the American public was entertained, and the faithful distressed, by the extended fraud trials of first, lower-level officials of the PTL ministry and then of Jim Bakker himself.

The ambiance of Bakker's trial was as garish as the lobby of the Heritage Grand Hotel and as melodramatic as a PTL Show broadcast. The street outside the federal courthouse in Charlotte, North Carolina was lined with TV trucks that hummed with the sound of electric generators. Each day the major networks would beam the story of Bakker's demise first to satellites in the heavens and then to the world. Over the course of two months, Bakker's reputation, built on television imagery, was destroyed by television imagery.

It was similarly ironic that the sidewalk sideshows captured much of the public's attention. The trial was conducted amid a carnival of protesters, gawkers and publicity parasites. Outside the courtroom were true-believing Christians with posters condemning the "false prophet" Jim Bakker. There were also Bakker-backers holding up signs that read "Forgiven". One PTL loyalist, a woman in her seventies, even suggested, to anyone who would listen, that Jessica Hahn had in fact raped Jim Bakker. Then there were the car rental agents who caused some excitement by appearing in life-like rubber masks of the boyish Jim and the gaudily-made-up Tammy Faye. After drawing a huge crowd, including TV camera crews, they took the masks off and explained to the reporters that they wanted to draw attention to their claim that PTL owed them thousands of dollars in unpaid rental fees.

Even more grotesque than the rubber-masked creditors was Bakker's fleeting brush with psychosis. According to his own lawyers, Bakker seemed to suffer a nervous breakdown, during which he collapsed in his attorney's office, curled into a fetal position, burrowed his head under a sofa, and refused to appear at his trial. When he was finally led weeping from his attorney's office, he crawled into the back seat of his lawyer's car and again curled into a ball. At court his attorney requested a delay for a psychiatric assessment of the defendant. A handcuffed Bakker was then taken to a nearby hospital.

The subsequent doctors' report described Bakker's ravings about "giant ants" who were outside the courthouse waiting to carry him away like a picnic crumb. But it also declared him competent to stand trial. It turned out that Bakker knew all along that those giant ants were only news reporters.

No delusion could have been more appropriate. Reporters *had* played key roles in the collapse of television evangelist Jim Bakker's huge PTL ministry, exposing both his seamy extra-marital sexual encounters and his criminal financial misdealings. But even if the members of the press were acting like scavengers – one disk jockey brought a sofa to the sidewalk outside the court house and tried to coax people into putting their heads under it – it was hard to work up much sympathy for their prey. Though some expressed it cruelly, public sentiment was obvious; Bakker was personally responsible for the scandals that had destroyed PTL and brought him to court.

Just how responsible he was became clear as the trial continued. The evidence presented showed that Bakker lived extravagantly – accepting $1 million bonuses, buying a string of luxury homes, misusing PTL's jet – while going on the air to beg for money and claim his ministry was near-bankrupt. Bakker wilfully ignored warnings about the fraudulent claims he made on TV and refused to deal with the basic mismanagement of his empire. He was described as a callous man, who described visitors to Heritage USA as "dumb" and complained about those who brought food onto the grounds rather than purchase it from vendors. Prosecutors painted a picture of an unseemly enterprise ostensibly raising millions for charity but instead funneling the money into the personal care of Jim and Tammy.

Perhaps the most glaring example of the charity flim-flam involved a facility for disabled children called "Kevin's House", after a severely handicapped, twenty-pound, seventeen-year-old named Kevin Whittum. Bakker presented Kevin, and other "handicapped" children who were actually healthy kids just posing in wheelchairs, in order to raise millions for this special residence to be built at Heritage USA. The TV preacher begged for donations, warning that Kevin might soon die, even though there was no medical reason to suppose this. In all, Rev. Bakker raised more than $4 million with these appeals and spent most of it on TV air time and other non-related projects, including man-made lakes and roads at Heritage USA. A huge, 13,000 square-foot home was eventually completed, but only Kevin and his family lived there. No other handicapped children ever benefited from the millions of dollars raised in their names.

The deception perpetrated in the names of crippled children was among Bakker's meanest acts. But the defrauding of PTL partners who had paid for time shares at the Heritage Towers Hotel turned out to be the scandal that caused him the most legal trouble. Testimony from witnesses inside and outside the PTL ministry proved that millions of dollars in extra sales were made by officials who knew they could never accommodate all those who, like the Clausens of Kutztown, paid thousands of dollars for the right to several days stay each year. It didn't help matters that, three years after its promised opening, Heritage Towers remained unfinished amid mountains of construction debris and unused materials.

In October 1989 Bakker was convicted of mail and wire fraud. Before Christmas he entered a medium security federal prison to serve a 45-year term, the harshest the judge could have imposed. Although Bakker would be eligible for parole in about ten years, for now the television pictures of him clad in white sneakers and blue prison garb, portrayed him as the felon he in fact was. Shortly after the trial, Tammy Bakker told the press that while a legal appeal was being pursued she would resurrect the PTL ministry from a new headquarters in Orlando, Florida. Pitifully, she was soon evicted from the shopping center storefront where she had established her ministry because she had failed to pay the rent.

Under different circumstances Jim Bakker's conviction and Tammy's eviction might have been considered the end of Christian America's long bad dream. But throughout 1989 other big-time evangelists were also dogged by image-wrecking problems. The one who suffered the most from his self-inflicted wounds was Oral Roberts. Roberts marked the Christmas season by closing City of Faith Hospital, laying off the staff, and sending the patients to other facilities. Medical school classes were continued, with students working at other hospitals, until the school was closed in May. The charade had lasted almost a decade but, in the end, the experts who had insisted that Tulsa didn't need another hospital were proven right. City of Faith Hospital closed with a $25 million deficit. Roberts said he would sell his home to help repay the debt.

Other famous ministers faced similar crises. Evangelist Marvin Gorman sued his fellow preacher Jimmy Swaggart for $90 million in damages because it was Swaggart who had brought the charges of adultery that had led to Gorman being defrocked by the Assemblies of God. The United States Supreme Court denied Swaggart's claim that the lawsuit unconstitutionally entangled the courts in church matters and sent the suit back to Louisiana for trial. Swaggart suffered another blow when California's Supreme Court upheld a state claim that Swaggart owed hundreds of thousands of dollars in back taxes on merchandise sold via his TV programs.

Finally, the end of 1989 found a total of thirty-four television ministers being investigated by more than a hundred agents of the Internal Revenue Services, the federal taxing agency. It seemed that the PTL scandal had inspired the federal tax agency to audit practically the entire televangelism industry, which claimed charity status and paid no taxes. IRS agents were looking carefully at sales of such items as record albums, cruises and books, and assessing the huge salaries paid many TV preachers. Among those being audited were Oral Roberts, Pat Robertson and Jerry Falwell. At the same time, all of the big-time evangelists were cutting their staffs, withdrawing from dozens of television markets and, for the first time in decades, reigning in their ambitions.

The scandals, defeats and convictions – and the attendant negative publicity – damaged the Christian Right in the same way that the Scopes trial and Mencken's reporting had damaged fundamentalism in the 1920s. Not since Scopes had the movement suffered such low credibility.

And, as if the travails of the televangelists were not enough, world events at the close of the decade – notably the collapse of communism – shattered the bedrock premise of the Christian Right world view. The Christian Right campaign of the 1980s was based, in large measure, on the conviction that a communist evil was threatening the survival of mankind. But with the sudden democratization movements in Eastern Europe and the humanizing of the Russian bogeyman, the leaders of the Christian Right lost the awesome enemy against whom they had rallied the faithful. The outbreak of peace and the unabated decline of the TV preachers suggested that the born-again crusade was being pushed into political and social oblivion.

In February 1990 I went to Washington to the annual convention of National Religious Broadcasters, the association of the Christian Right preachers, to assess the movement's condition. I arrived at the Washington Sheraton Hotel on the opening day of the convention, the day when, in the past, delegates swarmed around the many exhibits for companies that sold broadcasting equipment and services, literature and other of the industry's mainstays. I registered at the convention media center, where officials told me that, for the first time in a decade, there were fewer exhibitors and fewer delegates attending than in the previous year.

Downstairs, in the largest of the hotel's meeting rooms, I walked around the more than a hundred booths and displays for various companies and ministries. The best spot on the floor, right by the entrance, had been claimed by Lesea Broadcasting system, which sells air time to evangelists over networks of radio and TV stations. For the 1990 convention, Lesea had built a mock television studio with bright spot-lights, monitors showing pictures of satellites and a cozy sitting area with canvas directors' chairs, a glass-topped table and thick carpet. All of this was enclosed by a one-foot-wide, industrial-looking frame of shiny black plastic that defined the borders of a box the size of a very large sitting room.

Inside the box, the bright lights setting his wavy blond hair aglow, sat Craig Wallin. He looked depressed. Behind him two other salesmen – they preferred to be called "account executives" – stood chatting with each other. No one had come into the 'studio' to talk about buying broadcast time. In fact, there seemed to be hardly anyone on the convention floor, except other salesmen.

"It's dead," Wallin said when I sat down next to him and asked about the convention. "Here it is, the opening afternoon, and no one's here."

Wallin, a clean-cut, blue-eyed thirty-four-year-old, said the religious broadcasters were suffering the effects of a "shock wave" caused by the scandals of the past three years. "There is a lot of reassessing going on here this year," he continued. "A lot of people are hurting and they are thinking hard about what happened."

What had happened to Lesea, and to others in the field, was a sharp decline in revenues and a huge increase in bad debt. Wallin said that many of the preachers who had purchased time on Lesea's stations were not paying their bills. The problem was not the cost. In 1990 a half hour on Lesea's shortwave station – with worldwide coverage – cost just $90. The problem was that many people had lost faith in Christian evangelists and had stopped sending them money. Therefore, the evangelists couldn't pay their bills.

"It took a while for this to ripple from the big TV ministries, the Bakkers and others, to the smaller TV and radio guys and finally to us," said Wallin. "We're the ones who sell the broadcast service to the evangelists. When they aren't getting contributions, eventually they can't pay us. That's what's happening now."

The cash-flow crisis was all due to the televangelist scandals, Wallin said. "There were a few bad apples, like the Bakkers and Jimmy Swaggart, and now everyone is suspicious of everyone in Christian broadcasting. I have friends who aren't Christians and they are constantly teasing me, telling me I'm just like them. A lot of people feel that way, I think."

To make matters worse, there was strong evidence that many people had stopped watching the televangelists altogether. In their best years, Jim and Tammy Bakker could draw three or four percent of a local market's viewers to their PTL Show. "We could then go out and sell advertising on that hour, because those were ratings that would sell. Now," added Wallin, "the evangelists don't even show up in the ratings surveys." The pattern was repeated across the country. Pat Robertson's national audience, for example, had dropped from nearly half a million American households per day in 1986, to just over 200,000.

The low ratings had a direct impact on the finances of the hundreds of TV and radio stations that broadcast the born-again Christian programs. Lesea had been able to survive, ironically, by branching out into other, non-religious activities. Wallin said his organization rented studio time to anyone who wanted to make a commercial, or a program, Christian or not. And most importantly, he added with pride, "We became the flagship radio station for the South Bend (Indiana) White Sox." Wallin himself was the announcer for the minor league baseball team, and he said he had recently arranged for his station to carry games played by the Catholic Notre Dame University teams. It didn't matter to the born-again broadcasters that their salvation came from Roman Catholics, who, many thought, were unchristian idolaters. "Those deals help keep us afloat. And we're also much more careful about who we sell time to now. We do financial background checks and expect them to pay in advance at first," added Wallin. "That's how we'll survive."

Survival was on the minds of many of the delegates I met that afternoon. In past years the NRB convention had been a place for plotting the reformation of American society. This time the broadcasters seemed more concerned with recovering their credibility and returning to their original purposes: preaching and charity. Many of the exhibits on display advertised programs to feed the world's hungry or distribute Bible tracts. And many of the delegates noted, with some pride, that the major televangelists who had dominated their meetings for the last decade, were conspicuously absent.

That night, the only major TV evangelist scheduled to address the convention, Pat Robertson, made a speech that was much like the traditional "State of the Union Address" delivered by America's president at the start of each year. In his "State of Christian America" speech Robertson focused on the two big challenges confronting the Christian Right; the conundrum of peace in the world and the credibility crisis at home. First came his assessment of Christian America's domestic problems.

"In 1990 we find we have been weakened and in America we are in danger of becoming a persecuted minority," he warned. But Robertson never mentioned the scandals, and his own political blundering, which had brought about the crisis. Instead, he said, "We have been beaten by a tiny coalition of radical feminists, homosexuals and communists." He suggested that born-again Christians needed an anti-defamation league, of the kind founded by American Jews to fight anti-semitism, to protect themselves from rising anti-Christian bias.

In fact, Americans had taken to criticizing and lampooning TV evangelists, not born-again Christian believers. It was Robertson and Falwell, Swaggart and the Bakkers who appeared in political cartoons, not everyday church-going people. With this speech, filled with the familiar fear-mongering and exaggeration that he had used in his political campaign, Robertson showed he hadn't learned anything from his defeat. He ignored the message inherent in his declining viewership, overlooked the suffering of the believers who had been betrayed and assumed that his personal ambitions matched the hopes of the entire Christian Right movement.

After whining about the Christian Right's defeat in America, Robertson turned to world affairs. The year had seen shocking change in Eastern Europe as communist governments had fallen in Poland, Czechoslovakia and Rumania. In the Soviet Union, the Baltic states of Lithuania, Latvia and Estonia were hurtling toward secession and a democratization movement was about to end more than seventy years of one-party rule in Moscow. Finally, the Berlin Wall had come tumbling down and the reunification of the two Germanys, something that would have been unimaginable a year earlier, was a real and immediate possibility.

The sudden peace baffled born-again America. After all, the Christian Right's theological world view was dependent on a series of widely-held theories of Bible prophecy, which were loosely called Armageddon theology. These Armageddon or "end-times" theories suggested that the establishment of Israel in the 1940s presaged the end-of-the-world battle between good and evil which the Bible calls the battle of Armageddon. Armageddon theology required that the communist bloc (the "Evil Empire" as Ronald Reagan once called it) play the role of Satan's proxy. The scenario accepted by most American conservative Christians had the Soviets starting a war in the Middle East that would lead to nuclear annihilation and then, the 'Second Coming' of Christ.

The end-times ideas had provided a sense of urgency for the born-again movement of the 1980s and had strengthened the connection between the believers' religious convictions and their super-patriotism. So while the rest of the world joyously greeted the end of the Cold War, the prospect of a real peace threw the Christian crusaders into confusion.

Pat Robertson offered a predictable response. First he ignored the errors of the previous construct, which had described the Soviet Union as an unstoppable evil power. Then he called for the Christian Right to bombard the newly-opened communist world with his one real weapon: televangelism. Radio and television stations in Eastern Europe were willing to air paid evangelist programs. Glossing over the fact that the majority of Eastern Europeans already considered themselves

Christians, Robertson declared that he and his fellow TV preachers had "the greatest opportunity that has ever been presented to the church in our life time and very possibly in history" to bring the world to Christ. And he announced that he had been the first to establish a foothold in the Soviet Union. "Just before Christmas, on the communist television station in Leningrad, they began to air an animated series of cartoons that we had produced in Russian, teaching the people about the Bible," he said.

Robertson's ambition did not stop with Eastern Europe. In similarly Catholic Latin America, Robertson claimed, millions more awaited the power of televangelism. He suggested the televangelists could buy the same block of time, on every broadcast outlet in a country such as Nicaragua, every day for a week. "If anybody was going to watch any television program, they would have to watch our program!"

On the day after Robertson's speech I went back to the exhibition hall to visit with W. Ralph Mann, a lawyer-turned-evangelist who had erected a booth to display his new book, *Glasnost* and a videotape by the same title. Behind Mann, a young woman stood at a table, on which were piled many books and tapes, which she handed out to passersby. Above her was a banner, red letters on a white background, which asked, "Glasnost, For Good or Evil?"

The Glasnost booth was busy and Mann explained to those who stopped to talk that in the apparent decline of communism lurked an ominous threat. "At first, Gorbachev and what's happening over there are very confusing for a Christian," Mann told me. A tall, thin man with white hair, Mann wore a dark business suit and a steady smile. He allowed that the opening of the Soviet Union and Eastern Europe seemed, at least superficially, to be positive events. "But it could be a great deception," he said, waving a finger at me. "It could hide the development of an even greater evil." Mann argued that the current East Block peace offensive was a clever tactic that would lull the world into complacency and set the stage for the rise of a new evil.

"Some kind of doctrine that will be big enough to replace communism will appear and, with the exception of a small core of evangelical believers, it will dominate," said Mann. "I've been surprised by developments in the last year," he added. "It was easier to see the world in biblical terms when there was the evil empire of communism. But the evil is still there, threatening us. It's just harder to tell."

The replacement evil, said Mann, may be the New Age, that loosely defined movement that takes in everything from Eastern mysticism to 'channeled' spirits and healing crystals. New Age religion combined with "atheistic humanism" could sweep the world as an anti-Christ force, much in the way that communism was supposed to, under the old Armageddon notions. Pat Robertson had mentioned the New Age the night before, only he lumped it with "crack dealers and pornographers" as a threat to America's young.

Robertson and now Mann, were laying the groundwork for a new conservative Christian world view. The Christian Right's response to the spectre of peace on Earth would be the construction of a new enemy – New Agers and the like – and battling it with TV evangelism. This approach continued the tradition of conservative Christianity, which has always needed to define the outside world as evil and threatening and the community of faith as an island of goodness.

Of course there are problems with this new strategy. For one thing, the enemy described by Robertson and Mann is too vague. Secondly, the New Agers and their allies have no armies, no nuclear weapons, no organization, TV stations or hierarchy. They are a slippery target. Nevertheless in Mann's book, and Pat Robertson's speech, were the beginnings of a useful, albeit irrational, way to perpetuate the television evangelism business.

The Christian Right crusade failed, in part, because big-time TV preachers such as Robertson and activists such as W. Ralph Mann were unable to judge the political realities of the world or to recognize the needs of the great mass of born-again believers. That kind of myopia afflicted even the convict Jim Bakker who, after months in prison, refused to acknowledge that he had done anything wrong. In February 1990 he sent a letter from prison to thousands of his former donors. In it he described his suffering and insisted, once again, that he was innocent.

But while the leaders of the tattered crusade wilfully ignored their downfall, the people who had followed them were disillusioned and dispirited. A few days after the Religious Broadcasters Convention, I was a guest on a radio call-in program broadcast by a Christian radio station in Los Angeles. The station had advertised the hour-long program as a debate about the state of the Christian Right. But as the hour passed, it became clear that the station's born-again listeners agreed that the crusade to change America had failed. Their concern was focused on the damage that had been done to their local churches and to the reputation of born-again faith. Souls were being lost, they said, because the born-again religious message had been obscured. "I have to point out one thing," a young caller said on that program. "Everything that has happened could be driving people away from the Church. We ought to be trying to learn something from that."

If history is a guide, the great Christian Right crusade that swept America in the 1980s will soon be forgotten as other social trends and religious impulses capture America's attention. But the pain of the defeat will linger in the subculture of the born-again community. Some day, what happened in the 1980s may be re-cast into a parable about the wickedness of the world and the relative innocence of born-again believers. But until then, the failure of the 1980s crusade will reinforce the social and political isolation that its leaders had hoped to overcome.